T0215493

Game AI Uncovered

Game AI Uncovered: Volume One kicks off a brand-new series of books that focus on the development of artificial intelligence in video games. This volume brings together the collected wisdom, ideas, tricks, and cutting-edge techniques from 20 of the top game AI professionals and researchers from around the world.

The techniques discussed in these pages cover the underlying development of a wide array of published titles, including *Hood: Outlaws and Legends*, *The Escapists 2*, *Sackboy: A Big Adventure*, *Call of Duty: Strike Team*, *GTI+ Club*, *Split/Second*, *Sonic All Stars Racing Transformed*, *Luna Abyss*, *Medal of Honor Heroes I & II*, *Age of Empires IV*, *Watch Dogs*, *Battlefield 2042*, *Plants vs. Zombies: Battle for Neighborville*, *Dead Space*, and more.

Contained within this volume are overviews and insight covering a host of different areas within game AI, including situational awareness, pathfinding, tethering, squad behaviours, coordination, auto-generating navigation link data, fluid movement, combining behaviour and animation systems, pedal control for cars, tactical positioning, level of detail, infinite axis utility systems, hierarchical state machines, bots for testing, reactive behaviour trees, and more.

Beginners to the area of game AI, along with professional developers, will find a wealth of knowledge that will not only help in the development of your own games but will also spark ideas for new approaches.

This volume includes chapters written by Andy Brown, Dr Allan Bruce, Richard Bull, Laurent Couvidou, Steven Dalton, Michele Ermacora, Jonas Gillberg, Dale Green, Johan Holthausen, Dr Aitor Santamaría Ibirika, Dr Nic Melder, Sarat Rallabandi, Bruno Rebaque, John Reynolds, Paul Roberts, David Rogers, Andrea Schiel, Huw Talliss, Dr Tommy Thompson, and David Wooldridge.

Game AI Uncovered
Volume One

Edited by
Paul Roberts

Illustrations by
Nicholas Dent

CRC Press
Taylor & Francis Group
Boca Raton London New York

CRC Press is an imprint of the
Taylor & Francis Group, an **informa** business

Designed cover image: Sumo Digital

First edition published 2024
by CRC Press
2385 NW Executive Center Drive, Suite 320, Boca Raton, FL 33431

and by CRC Press
4 Park Square, Milton Park, Abingdon, Oxon, OX14 4RN

CRC Press is an imprint of Taylor & Francis Group, LLC

© 2024 selection and editorial matter, Paul Roberts; individual chapters, the contributors

ISBN: 978-1-032-34850-6 (hbk)
ISBN: 978-1-032-34323-5 (pbk)
ISBN: 978-1-003-32410-2 (ebk)

DOI: 10.1201/9781003324102

Typeset in Times
by codeMantra

Dedication

'For Kelvin Hilton.
A great mentor, a gifted colleague,
and above all - the best of friends.'

Contents

Preface

For me, game artificial intelligence is by far the most interesting part of game development. That is not to disparage the great work that is done in graphics, physics, tools, audio, and all the other vital components required to make a game, but there is something special about bringing an agent to life. It is not only about the end result though, but also about how you get there. The smoke and mirrors that are used for a player to buy into the illusion and keep them there. Whether it is finding a believable path across an environment, navigating a busy street, communication between agents, or building an architecture that handles everything the design department can throw at it. It is always a journey of discovery. You start with ideas, and these evolve as the game grows.

A starting point for me was the AI Wisdom books and later the *Game AI Pro* series. The amazing work that the authors of those books shared with the world has gone on to be incorporated in many games. I do not think I have met a game AI coder that has not got a copy of at least one of those books somewhere. And Kudos to CRC Press for allowing the books to be made available online for free, giving those ideas a wider reach.

Game AI Uncovered looks to follow in the footsteps of these earlier book series. In these pages will be shared the insights of extremely talented AI programmers from around the world, from many different studios with the aim of sharing knowledge and pushing our discipline forward. A huge thanks to all those studios who supported their staff and allowed for this information to be shared.

Paul Roberts

Acknowledgements

Game AI Uncovered: Volume One was quite an undertaking to bring together. Starting from scratch and reaching out to the game AI community to see if there was even any interest in such a project was a monumental undertaking. As it turned out, there was a great deal of interest. And a huge thanks to all those people (some of whom did not end up contributing a chapter themselves) who suggested colleagues or friends that would be interested in getting involved.

A special thanks to Allan Bruce, Rich Bull, and Steve Dalton who all not only wrote their own chapters, but also gave their time to give me their perspective and provide feedback wherever it was needed. And, thanks to Ryan 'Maverick' Buxton who read through the entire volume and gave invaluable feedback. And a final massive thank you to my wife, the amazing Emma Roberts who proofread the entire volume and pointed out a plethora of mistakes and issues.

The artwork throughout this volume was done by the super-talented Nicholas Dent. He took our programmer art and not only made them look professional but added a lot of character as well. Thanks Nick.

The amazing cover artwork for this volume was provided by Sumo Digital from the game *Hood: Outlaws and Legends*. Two chapters covering techniques from this game appear in this book: *Implementing an AI Framework in Unreal for Medium to Large Scale Numbers of Disparate AI in Hood: Outlaws and Legends* and *Predicting When and Where to Intercept Players in Hood: Outlaws and Legends*.

Thanks to the guys at CRC Press who have supported this project from the start. Especially to Will Bateman, who never doubted for a second that we would manage to garner enough interest to make this book a reality. And for being on hand to help with all the things you don't think of when you start a project like this.

Putting together a book of this kind takes a lot of time. Time spent at a desk writing, editing, drawing, rewriting, organising permissions, and much more. This time was taken through weekends and evenings over many months. So, a final huge thank you goes to all our families who have both supported us and allowed us to take the time to work on this project.

Editor

Paul Roberts is a Lead AI programmer at Sumo Digital. He has a Master's degree in Computer Science with Artificial Intelligence, where he focused on pathfinding and developed the DRS algorithm and ways to test the believability of generated paths. He has worked for a variety of studios in the UK from Team17, Traveller's Tales, Activision, and some smaller indie studios. Paul also managed the Games Programming department at Staffordshire University for several years where he oversaw the development of new degree programs that saw a close collaboration with the games industry. Paul has written a number of books – some fiction, others academic – the latest of which is *Artificial Intelligence in Games* published by CRC Press in 2022.

Contributors

Andy Brown began his career in 1997 at Gremlin Interactive where he worked on several sports titles, the last of which being a soccer game which was his first taste of AI programming in a commercial game. Following that, he spent 5 years at Eurocom, where he was part of the core gameplay team on *Spyro: A Hero's Tail* along with *Pirates of the Caribbean* where he focused on player mechanics as well as core AI systems. In 2008, he moved to Sumo Digital where amongst other things he helped develop AI systems for several of the studios driving titles, in particular *Sonic All Stars Racing Transformed*, as well as AI technology to support the development of *Crackdown 3*. His current role involves leading the gameplay team on an unannounced AAA title.

Dr Allan Bruce holds a PhD from the University of Aberdeen in the field of AI known as qualitative reasoning. He has a comprehensive background in the video games industry, beginning with Midway Games in 2006, moving to CCP Games in 2009, and joining Sumo Digital in 2018. Throughout this time, he has worked on AI and AI Systems for a number of games, including *Wheelman*, *EVE: Valkyrie*, *Hood: Outlaws and Legends*, and *Call of Duty: Vanguard*. He currently resides in County Durham, UK, with his wife, two sons, three cats and dog, Bowser.

Richard Bull has been a full-time professional programmer in the games industry since late 2000, following a short stint coding industrial software, after graduating a couple of years previously. He has specialised in architecting AI and gameplay systems, working as a lead AI programmer on *Empire: Total War* for The Creative Assembly, and on titles such as *Grand Theft Auto: Chinatown Wars* and *L.A. Noire* for Rockstar Games. Among his other previous employers, he counts Software Creations, Acclaim, Kuju, and Activision and is credited on numerous other titles including *Dungeons & Dragons: Tactics*, *Call of Duty: Strike Team*, *Nom Nom Galaxy*, and the *Lego Harry Potter* remasters. Since 2014, he has been working on various original and co-developed projects through his own company Gentlemen of Science, with co-founder and fellow veteran games industry programmer Ash Henstock. They are currently assisting development on an unannounced cross-platform title with Ice Beam Games, for Secret Mode.

Laurent Couvidou is a professional game developer who has worked at Ubisoft, Arkane, and others. Notable credits include titles such as *Rayman: Origins*, *Dishonored 2*, and *Deathloop*. He recently joined Build a Rocket Boy as a Principal AI Programmer. You can sometimes find him at game development conferences or maybe riding somewhere in the French countryside.

Steven Dalton has spent the last 13 years at various UK-based studios including several years as Team17's AI specialist, a stint as a freelance AI programmer, and presently leads the AI team at a relatively new studio, Steel City Interactive working on their inaugural project *Undisputed*, a competitive boxing game. After developing an interest in videogame AI in the final year of a Computer Game Programming degree at Teesside University, Steven undertook a variety of different programming roles in industry before landing at Team17 and pursuing a definitive AI role. He hasn't looked back since!

Nicholas Dent is an experienced Game Designer with over 30 years of games industry experience in various creative roles from Artist and Animator to Producer through to his current role for over 18 years as a Game Designer (Senior, Lead, and Creative Director). He has worked with some of the biggest names in the entertainment industry: Disney, EA, Bandai Namco, Konami, SEGA and Square Enix as well as developing many original Sports IP's.

Michele Ermacora is a senior AI programmer at Smilegate Barcelona. He has worked for the past 10 years in the game industry on games such as *Red Dead Redemption 2*, where his main focus was on the cover systems and AI cover behaviours, and *Tom Clancy's The Division* as a networking programmer. Previously, he also contributed to the development of the AISandbox at AIGameDev and was one of the conference speakers at the Game/AI Conference.

Jonas Gillberg is a Principal AI Engineer at EA helping game and research teams push game testing further using game AI & machine learning. He presented early results of this work at the GDC AI Summit in 2019 (AI for Testing: The Development of Bots That Play *Battlefield V*). Before joining EA, he worked at Ubisoft for many years and was fortunate enough to work on the Snowdrop engine from a very early stage. He shipped *Tom Clancy's The Division* as the Technical Lead AI Programmer and gave a talk on some of it at the GDC AI Summit 2016 (*Tom Clancy's The Division*: AI Behavior Editing and Debugging). He is also the creator of Magic CardSpotter, an open-source Chrome Extension that detects cards on live streams of *Magic: The Gathering*, perhaps more notably forked by VirtualEDH which became SpellTable (Wizards of the Coast).

Dale Green is a software engineer who has worked in a range of disciplines, settling within AAA video games. Dale has worked on multiple AAA titles for both PC and console, focussing mainly on AI systems. He has self-published a PC title, authored a book on *Procedural Content Generation for C++ Game Development*, and is working on a game library for x64 assembly. Dale currently works for Red Kite Games.

Johan Holthausen is an AI programmer with 4+ years of experience in the game industry with a specialisation in AI systems. He has worked on and shipped a range of titles with his most notable work being on Frontier's *Planet Zoo*.

Dr Aitor Santamaría Ibirika has been working in the games industry as an AI engineer since 2015. He has worked on the AI for several games, such as *Hitman*, *Hitman 2, Suicide Squad: Kill the Justice League, New World*, and *God of War:*

Ragnarok. He received his PhD in Procedural Content Generation for games in 2014 from the University of Deusto, Basque Country, Spain. He is currently working at Sony Santa Monica Studio as a Senior AI Programmer.

Dr Nic Melder has over 15 years' experience developing vehicle AI systems. Previously he was the Lead Vehicle AI Programmer on *Watch Dogs: Legion* where he was responsible for developing the traffic AI and the felony (chase) systems as well as maintaining and enhancing the level design and build tools for creating the road network. He also worked on the Vehicle AI systems for *Watch Dogs 2* and *Far Cry 6*. Prior to that, he worked at Codemasters on the *Dirt*, *Grid*, and *F1* series of racing games, where he released ten titles. In a previous life, he spent 5 years working in academia and attained a PhD in Multi-Finger Haptics.

Sarat Rallabandi currently works at Rebellion North as an Experienced Programmer focussing primarily on AI. He previously worked at Sumo Digital on a couple of unannounced titles as an AI programmer. Sarat got his start in the games industry in 2019 at EA Sports Tiburon where he worked on the *Madden* franchise, after he graduated university with a master's degree.

Bruno Rebaque is a Senior AI programmer at Hexworks (CI Game Mediterranean). He has worked in the games industry for about 7 years; before that, he was just another boring programmer (no games involved). He started working as a Gameplay/AI programmer on *Sackboy: A Big Adventure* (Sumo Digital), then worked as an AI programmer in *The Ascent* (Neon Giant), and right now is working as Senior AI programmer on *Lords of the Fallen 2*.

John Reynolds has worked in the games industry for over 25 years and has held senior AI positions at studios such as Ubisoft and Activision. He has contributed to several books on Game AI and was a columnist in the UK games industry magazine, *Develop*. He is currently Lead programmer at Bonsai Collective and founder of Tall Studios.

Paul Roberts is a Lead AI programmer at Sumo Digital. He has a Master's degree in Computer Science with Artificial Intelligence, where he focused on pathfinding and developed the DRS algorithm and ways to test the believability of generated paths. He has worked for a variety of studios in the UK from Team17, Traveller's Tales, Activision, and some smaller indie studios. Paul also managed the Games Programming department at Staffordshire University for several years where he oversaw the development of new degree programs that saw a close collaboration with the games industry. Paul has written a number of books – some fiction, others academic – the latest of which is *Artificial Intelligence in Games* published by CRC Press in 2022.

David Rogers is a senior AI programmer who is currently working for PlayStation London Studios, after having worked at various other studios including Ubisoft Reflections, Bossa Studios, and Team17. It was at Team17 where they developed their skills in all aspects of game development, finding a particular passion towards game AI. There they would work on many of the titles in *The Escapists* franchise, as well as others. David holds a Master's degree in Computer Science with Artificial Intelligence from the University of York, UK, having explored the application of MCTS in social deduction games.

Andrea Schiel is currently an AI technical lead for the *Assassin's Creed* franchise at Ubisoft. Formerly a principal AI architect at Worlds Edge (Microsoft, *Age of Empires*), she's been working in game AI for over 25 years. She's worked on a wide variety of titles including *EA Sports FIFA*, *Medal of Honor*, and *Mass Effect*. Her academic work includes Genetics, Archaeology, and partial order planners in the field of AI. She has a vague dream of somehow combining all three fields someday.

Huw Talliss is a Senior Programmer at Sumo Digital and previously worked on the AI for *Sackboy: A Big Adventure*. He grew up in Birmingham and then studied at the University of York during which time he briefly worked at Boss Alien as part of a Summer Internship, before graduating with a Master's Degree in Computer Science. He joined Sumo Digital as a Graduate and has been working there since.

Dr Tommy Thompson is the director of AI and Games Ltd., a company that provides consultancy and solutions for artificial intelligence technologies in the video games industry. The company is largely known for its YouTube series of the same name that has achieved millions of views worldwide educating viewers on how AI works in games. As of 2021, Tommy is an adviser to the GDC AI Summit in an effort to support developers in promoting their contributions to the game development community. Prior to working in the games industry, Tommy was a senior lecturer in computer science and researcher in artificial intelligence applications for video games, publishing over 40 academic publications in areas such as artificial general intelligence, machine learning for non-player characters, and procedural content generation.

David Wooldridge is a 17-year veteran of the games industry, starting out at Rebellion where he worked on AI for games such as *Harry Potter*, *Call of Duty*, *Sniper Elite*, and *Zombie Army*. Over this time, David has continued to study academically holding a BSc in Information Systems and an MSc in Computer Science, and is currently studying for a PhD in Artificial Intelligence. David currently works at Sony Firesprite as a senior game programmer.

1 The Changing Landscape of AI for Game Development

Dr Tommy Thompson

1.1 INTRODUCTION

If you have a passing interest in all things technology, it is hard to go a single day without news about the latest innovation in artificial intelligence (AI). Computer systems are now learning to tackle challenges in a variety of problem spaces that seemed impossible even a decade ago. This ranges from art and image generation tools to voice synthesis to replicate human voices, deep fakes that digitally augment faces in videos, and improved language models that can write large swathes of text when given a prompt. But what about in the world of video games? As this rise of AI proliferation continues throughout so many facets of technology, what impact is it having on game development?

Perhaps you have seen news of great successes of AI for video games over the past couple of years, as new autonomous players defeat the very best of human competitors in popular titles. The year 2017 saw the release of 'OpenAI Five', capable of defeating professional players in *Dota 2* (Berner et al., 2019), while Google DeepMind's 'AlphaStar' attained grandmaster status for *StarCraft 2* in 2019 (Vinyals et al., 2019). More recently, Sony AI's GT Sophy defeated professional players of *Gran Turismo Sport* in 2021 (Wurman et al., 2022). While these are all highly impressive technical feats, the work being conducted here is, in its current form, often of little use to the video game industry.

This is less a criticism of their function, but rather a reality check. These AI players are built specifically to learn the intricacies of a game such that they can perform at the highest levels of skill. This means that for anyone who is not in the top 1% of the player base for these games, these AI players are virtually undefeatable and, critically, uninteresting to play against. The methods of how they operate are not amenable to the needs of a game developer: they cannot be customised or controlled such that they can easily adapt to different difficulty settings or specific scenarios within a particular project. Perhaps critically for competitive online titles, none of these systems can adapt to changes brought on by patches that influence the in-game 'meta'. Plus, there is the cost of training them on large-scale computing infrastructures – often to the tune of millions of dollars – so they can achieve these superhuman feats. This alone makes them unattainable for around 99% of all games in production.

This chapter serves as an introduction to how AI has historically been used in games, followed by the new horizons that are emerging in the sector. For those new to the field, or still learning much of its intricacies, ideally this will help familiarise

DOI: 10.1201/9781003324102-1

you with many of the ideas you will see in later chapters. But also, it will hopefully build your enthusiasm to explore many of these emerging application areas where AI is only now beginning to provide interesting and practical results.

1.2 A PRIMER: FOUNDATIONS OF AI

Before we proceed any further, let us take a moment to discuss some foundations of AI. This is useful for two purposes; critically we need to distinguish the application of AI in video games compared to its more typical usage, but perhaps more importantly, this book, like any other, has the potential to be someone's first in the field. So, let us start on the right footing.

The consensus surrounding the operation of artificially intelligent systems, commonly referred to as *agents*, is any software system that makes an informed decision based upon the information available to it. Critically, they always adhere to two distinct properties: they are *autonomous*, and they are *rational*. The former implies that they act without any external input from a human or other system, and the latter indicates that they always act based on the knowledge they have accumulated (Russell & Norvig, 2020).

How the agent executes is another matter entirely. You may establish a search space within which to identify and discover solutions, or you may try to train a model based on existing data, such that it can reproduce desired behaviour in key situations. The former is an approach known as *symbolic* AI, whereby we identify the initial situation or state of the problem, followed by the available actions and a desired goal state. From this, a myriad of possible approaches can be taken to select actions in such a way that the goal state can be achieved. Typically, the idea is that the system will search within this defined space of states using the actions available, to make a series of intelligent decisions that yield a positive outcome. Image 1.1 depicts this search for a goal state (the state that achieves a win condition) with the classic game *Tic-Tac-Toe*.

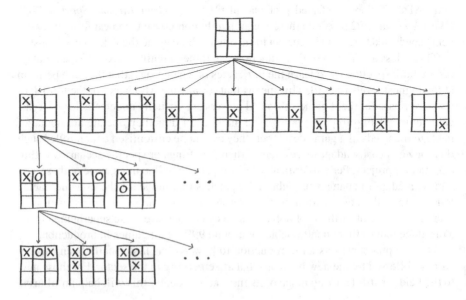

IMAGE 1.1   *Tic-Tac-Toe* search space.

　　Conversely, an increasingly popular approach is *machine learning*, a branch of AI whereby we *train* a system to make intelligent decisions for a given task. As shown in Image 1.2, it is provided with a set of existing data, and from this an algorithm adapts or tweaks the system such that it becomes better at solving the task. Over time, the performance of the system should improve, thus giving the perception that the system 'learns' to solve the problem over time. Quite often, machine learning is ideal for more complicated situations whereby the problem itself is difficult to encapsulate more directly, and there are a lot of data available from which the system could seek to adapt and learn.

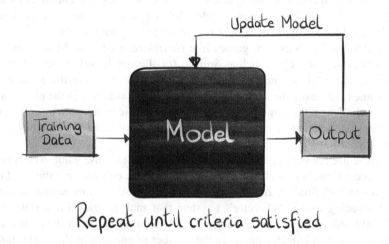

IMAGE 1.2　Machine learning model.

　　In either case, we are seeking an optimal solution to a complicated problem, with the designer either identifying the range of possible actions and information that could comprise a given state or providing the dataset from which to learn from. In either case, we are providing information to the system that should ultimately lead to a series of intelligent actions that can yield the desired outcome. The real difference lies in how these types of systems identify the problem and seek to establish the solution.

1.3　GAME AI EXPLAINED

When we apply AI to games, while the general idea is the same as before, with rational and autonomous agents making decisions to service a particular need or goal, the big change is in its purpose and function. The notion that an AI should generate an optimal solution is no longer sacrosanct. AI for games is often designed and implemented specifically for the purpose of creating *entertainment*. This leads to systems calculating solutions that, in some cases, are optimal in the context of the problem, while in others a more sub-optimal solution may be selected given it will prove more *interesting* or *fun* for a player to experience. This led to the formation of what is typically referred to as *Game AI*: a set of tools, techniques, and methodologies that handle the application of AI specifically in the context of games. Many of these ideas originate from outside of games but are used for specific games purposes. For example, navigating characters in a game world through use of pathfinding algorithms and navigation meshes is a common practice in modern engines such as Unity and Unreal but is derived from academic research in robotics from the 1980s. These techniques are then used for a myriad of purposes. The most common is the creation of non-player characters (NPCs), be it to create adversaries in the likes of *DOOM* (id Software, 1993), allies who support the player like in *Half-Life 2* (Valve, 2004) and *BioShock: Infinite* (Irrational Games, 2013), or characters with routines and agendas of their own as seen in *The Sims* (Maxis, 2000) and *Cities: Skylines* (Colossal Order, 2015). In addition, we can expect game AI to be used in strategic controllers that manage opposing actions even without a physical avatar, such as card games like *Hearthstone* (Blizzard Entertainment, 2014) or real-time strategies such as *StarCraft* (Blizzard Entertainment, 1998). In either case, these AI systems make decisions that make sense in the game world, and in some cases using the same suite of tools that are available to the player, all to provide a challenge, thereby forcing you to change strategy, adapt to circumstance, and learn to counteract or compliment the decisions of other systems effectively as you play.

But these are not the only ways in which a designer may use game AI to control or influence a player's experience. The post-apocalyptic co-operative shooter *Left 4 Dead* (Turtle Rock Studios, 2008) introduced the use of AI as a mechanism to control gameplay pacing with its 'Director': a system that analyses the current state of the game world and acts upon it in a manner akin to a dungeon master in tabletop role-playing games. The Director manages the number of enemies in the world, targets specific players, and even dictates the ambient noises and music that play as players fight their way through hordes of the undead. Director systems are now a common game AI implementation in many open-world games such as *Far Cry 6* (Ubisoft Toronto, 2021), given the need to not only put the lens of the experience on the player, but also to manage the overall performance of the game: disabling NPCs that are too far away from active players, and ensuring that all CPU resources are being used where they are needed the most.

In addition, one approach that has seen much resurgence in recent years is procedural content generation (PCG), a technique for the automated creation of in-game content. While the field originated courtesy of level generation for the likes of *Elite* (Braben & Bell, 1984) and *Rogue* (Toy et al., 1980), the idea has continued to be used in modern games like *Spelunky* (Mossmouth, 2008) and *No Man's Sky* (Hello Games, 2016), and has been expanded beyond this remit to crafting weapons in *Borderlands* (Gearbox Software, 2009) or entire characters with backstories and lives in *Watch Dogs: Legion* (Ubisoft Toronto, 2020). Regardless of their intent, they all operate under the same core concept: crafting content against a set of design rules that impose hard and soft constraints, while using pseudorandom number generation to add some variety between each individually crafted item.

1.4 THE STATE OF GAME AI

Now that we have covered the basics, it is time we got to grips with some of the approaches taken in game AI. Many of the techniques discussed in the following pages will appear in subsequent chapters in this book, as my fellow authors highlight specific implementation challenges, lessons learned from applying them in specific game contexts, and alternatives developed in academia. Despite this, even that which we discuss throughout this book is far from exhaustive, as game AI continues to be a collection of varied algorithms and design patterns that cover a wide range of different possible gameplay scenarios (Millington, 2019).

1.4.1 PATHFINDING ALGORITHMS

As the name implies, pathfinding algorithms enable an in-game character to traverse an environment in a game world. This area may be discretised into a grid structure of equal unit size, or a collection of more fragmented and disjointed shapes that is typically achieved using a navigation mesh. Provided there is a sense of connectivity between them, this provides a graph framework from within which we can search for the optimal solution, as shown in Image 1.3.

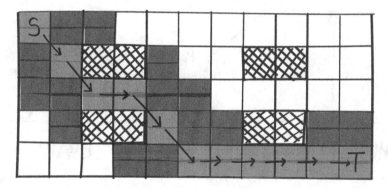

IMAGE 1.3 Pathfinding through an environment.

Uninformed algorithms such as depth-first and breadth-first search are often adequate in trivial pathfinding situations but fail to scale up as more complicated environments arise. The A* algorithm is often a starting point for pathfinding approaches in games (Russell & Norvig, 2020) but can then be built into more hierarchical or optimised frameworks such as D* or D* Lite to service specific game design challenges (Millington, 2019).

1.4.2 Finite State Machines

With regard to the decision-making process of characters, the two most common techniques are Finite State Machines (FSM) and Behaviour Trees (BT). As shown in Image 1.4, state machines operate from a 'bottom-up' approach to behavioural design by identifying individual behaviours (states) and the events that would trigger transitions between them. This gives designers a lot of freedom to identify unique contexts or scenarios the NPC may exist within and how they may transition between them as they interact with the player and other gameplay systems. While these have been used in some form dating all the way back to *DOOM* and *Pac-Man* (Namco, 1980), the more contemporary implementations lean on that popularised by *Half-Life* (Valve, 1998). Meanwhile, *Halo 2* (Bungie, 2004) popularised the idea of the behaviour tree shown in Image 1.5.

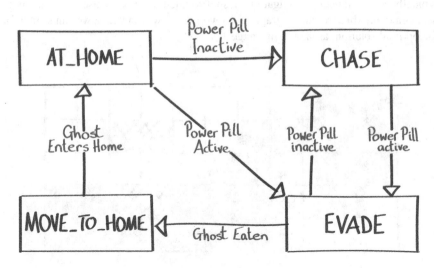

IMAGE 1.4   Finite state machine example (*Pac-Man*).

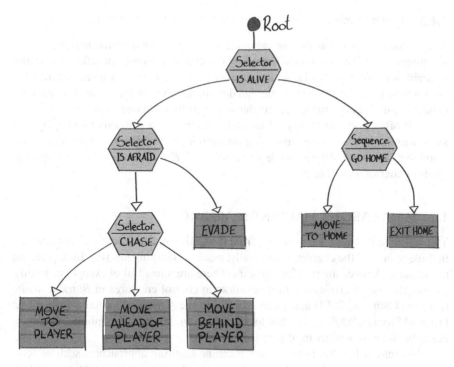

IMAGE 1.5   Behaviour tree example (*Pac-Man*).

1.4.3   BEHAVIOUR TREES

BT are focused on the 'top-down' approach to design: identifying the conditions that would lead to a specific set of one or more actions to be executed based on the current game state. BT are in many regards the standard of the AAA gaming industry and are the default AI tool provided in many contemporary game engines such as Unreal and CryEngine.

1.4.4   AUTOMATED PLANNING

A less pervasive mechanism that is nonetheless effective is planning, an idea that originates once again from existing AI research in robotics but did not appear in games until *F.E.A.R.* (Monolith Productions, 2005). In this instance, we are interested in identifying, at a high level, the sequence of actions that will enable us to achieve our goals. However, a planning system imposes constraints on action execution and allows for designers to exert greater control on the resulting behaviour by defining the pre-conditions that dictate whether an action is applicable for a given state. The resulting approach in *F.E.A.R.* denoted Goal-Oriented Action Planning (GOAP) finds plans of actions to satisfy goals, with the execution of those actions controlled by a small yet highly parameterised finite state machine. Much like BT, planning actions can also be structured in a hierarchical fashion, creating 'macros' of desirable behaviour in the eyes of designers. Hierarchical Task Network (HTN) planning has become more popular in recent years, with titles such as *Dying Light* (Techland, 2015) and *Horizon Zero Dawn* (Guerrilla Games, 2017) adopting this technique.

1.4.5 UTILITY SYSTEMS

A less common, but nonetheless valuable, mechanism for decision making is utility systems. This approach is achieved by creating equations that reflect the utility or desirability of a particular action or item in the context of a game. By reading information from the game state, we can determine whether the need for a character to heal themselves or attack a particular target shifts from one moment to the next. You will often find that Utility AI is used in conjunction with other gameplay systems, with notable examples including action selection in *Dragon Age: Inquisition* (BioWare, 2014), identifying goals to satisfy in *F.E.A.R.*, and addressing specific needs of characters in *The Sims*.

1.5 WHAT ABOUT MACHINE LEARNING?

You will note that we have refrained from discussing machine learning applications in this segment of the chapter. Historically, machine learning has seen little practical use in game AI over the past 20–30 years. There are a handful of exceptions to this, such as the use of artificial neural networks to control creatures in *Black & White* (Lionhead Studios, 2001) and more recently in the 'Drivatar' system of the *Forza* (Turn 10 Studios, 2005) series. But for the most part, traditional symbolic AI continues to be the most readily used approach.

A big reason for this is that many machine learning approaches, such as reinforcement learning, and neural networks rob the designer of oversight and control. A designer may wish for specific behaviours to be tweaked or refined for particular circumstances, and with many of the techniques described in this chapter, this can be achieved. A state transition can be adjusted, or a behaviour tree condition can be amended. But with a trained machine learning model, making these smaller incremental changes can be difficult to achieve, or expensive to realise given the system needs to 're-learn' the problem it is solving.

We are seeing significant gains in this space, more recently in titles such as *Halo Infinite* (343 Industries, 2021) and *Age of Empires IV* (Relic Entertainment, 2021) highlighting how machine learning techniques can be applied in game AI. But in truth, the real value of machine learning is not in game AI, but rather in other areas of game production.

1.6 THE EVOLUTION OF AI FOR GAMES

As described throughout this chapter, the tools and practices of game AI are largely built upon the foundations provided by symbolic AI techniques. While recent innovations in machine learning and deep learning have led to this subset of AI becoming increasingly more practical for a lot of game AI applications, we are seeing more traction in these techniques being used in other areas of the game production pipeline.

A big reason for this is that machine learning models, when trained effectively, are very good at identifying specific patterns within large portions of data. Hence, it is used in areas of *player modelling* as seen in the *Forza* series: given it can successfully identify how players are behaving on average in specific gameplay contexts.

In fact, this has often led to machine learning being a more useful technique in areas such as game analytics: processing information about players in each gameplay environment to better understand how they interact with it and how that information can be used to positively affect the production itself. This is an idea that dates to the earliest of Massive Multiplayer Online Role-Playing Games (MMORPGs) (El-Nasr et al., 2021). This same benefit can then be applied in other contexts, which could ultimately speed up game production as a result.

One of the most notable examples in recent years is in animation controllers and blends. An ever-pressing challenge for games with 3D characters is the blending of animations: identifying the points in a walk and jog animation where a character can transition between them. This is a difficult and time-consuming process that requires a great deal of manual labour by animators. Many games ranging from *Hitman* (IO Interactive, 2016) to *For Honor* (Ubisoft Montreal, 2017) and *FIFA* 22 (EA Vancouver, 2021) have embraced a technique called 'motion matching' in which machine learning is used to identify the most likely animation frames that would yield a smooth transition. In addition, this approach also enables for animation blends to be identified and implemented much faster than before.

Perhaps the most exciting innovation in recent years is one that most game players will never see in action. As games become increasingly more complex, the number of bugs and other issues that manifest can increase exponentially and trying to curtail their growth and prevent the re-emergence of previously resolved issues is a big challenge. The use of automated testing much like in traditional software engineering is proving increasingly popular with large-scale productions (Masella, 2019). However, more recently we are seeing the use of AI as part of this process to identify bugs deep in navigation systems and core mechanics (Gordillo et al., 2021), or whether a change will prevent a mission being completable or is causing performance overheads on different platforms (Paredes & Jones, 2019).

Meanwhile, another area that suffers from finding the problems nested deep within is in-game toxicity, an issue that can suffocate online games lest it is cut off at the root. Toxicity can appear in a myriad of forms, be it hostile text or speech communications, activities in-game that go against the rules of play, to the use of cheat systems and other programmes that can circumvent the typical operation of a given game. But how do you identify a toxic player? The amount of data being processed in a live gaming ecosystem is vast and simply too much even for the best of content moderation teams to flag in real time. Hence, the likes of *CS:GO*'s Overwatch system (McDonald, 2018) that uses machine learning to identify issues in real time and then report those issues to human moderators, who ultimately have the final say on whether a player is simply being weird, or proving a detriment to the overall experience.

Plus, more recently we are seeing machine learning being used as part of real-time graphics rendering, all to support consumers' hardware specifications and enable high-resolution gaming without significant cost overheads. The most notable example is NVIDIA's Deep Learning Super Sampling (DLSS) technology: a process that trains deep learning AI to upscale the output of a graphics card to higher resolutions. Enabling players to enjoy games at 4K resolutions, while the GPU only renders the game at half, if not a quarter, of the target output.

This is far from an exhaustive list and is merely indicative of how machine learning is proving of use to game development in ways not previously envisaged. In many of these examples, the use of machine learning, notably in animation, quality assurance, and in-game toxicity, is to speed up time-consuming and difficult work that has historically taken up significant time and energy from a production team for a given game. While the issue of worker rights in the context of ongoing automation courtesy of AI is going to be a complicated one, it is already providing gains in areas of production previously thought impossible.

1.7 CONCLUSION

Game AI is a vast and complicated subject matter, as many a bespoke methodology is crafted to service the complex and nuanced challenges of game development. With this chapter, the aim was to introduce the field as a whole and give some background for many of the tools and techniques you will see throughout this book series. AI for games is in an exciting period of transition as the deep learning revolution that has dominated other technology sectors is now being used in several areas within the game production pipeline; finding practical and meaningful applications for a technology that has long been considered irrelevant given its inability to play nice with others. It has often been this author's belief that AI makes for better games, while games make for better AI, and we are finally beginning to see the fruits of that labour.

REFERENCES

343 Industries. (2021) *Halo Infinite*. Xbox Game Studios.
Berner, C., Brockman, G., Chan, B., Cheung, V., Dębiak, P., Dennison, C., Farhi, D., Fischer, Q., Hashme, S., Hesse, C., and Józefowicz, R. (2019) *Dota 2 with large scale deep reinforcement learning*. arXiv preprint arXiv:1912.06680.
BioWare. (2014) *Dragon Age: Inquisition*. Electronic Arts.
Blizzard Entertainment. (1998) *StarCraft*. Blizzard Entertainment.
Blizzard Entertainment. (2014) *Hearthstone*. Blizzard Entertainment.
Braben, D., and Bell, I. (1984) *Elite*. Acornsoft.
Bungie. (2004) *Halo 2*. Microsoft Game Studios.
Colossal Order. (2015) *Cities:* Skylines. Paradox Interactive.
EA Vancouver. (2021) *FIFA 22*. Electronic Arts.
El-Nasr, M., Nguyen, T.-H., Canossa, A., and Drachen, A. (2021) Game Data Science. Oxford University Press.
Gearbox Software. (2009) *Borderlands*. 2K Games.
Gordillo, C., Bergdahl, J., Tollmar, K., and Gisslen, L. (2021) *Improving Playtesting Coverage via Curiosity Driven Reinforcement Learning Agents. IEEE Conference on Games.*
Guerrilla Games. (2017) *Horizon Zero Dawn. Sony Interactive Entertainment.*
Hello Games. (2016) *No Man's Sky*. Hello Games.
id Software. (1993) *DOOM*. id Software.
IO Interactive. (2016) *Hitman*. Square Enix.
Irrational Games. (2013) *BioShock Infinite*. 2K Games.
Lionhead Studios. (2001) *Black & White*. Electronic Arts.

Masella, R. (2019) *Automated Testing of Game Play Features in Sea of Thieves.* Retrieved from GDC Vault: https://www.gdcvault.com/play/1026366/Automated-Testing-of-Gameplay-Features.

Maxis. (2000). *The Sims.* Electronic Arts.

McDonald, J. (2018) *Robocalypse Now: Using Deep Learning to Combat Cheating in 'Counter-Strike: Global Offensive'.* Retrieved from GDC Vault: https://www.gdcvault.com/play/1024994/Robocalypse-Now-Using-Deep-Learning.

Millington, I. (2019) *Artificial Intelligence for Games* (3rd ed.). CRC Press.

Monolith Productions. (2005) F.E.A.R. Vivendi Universal Games.

Mossmouth. (2008) *Spelunky.*

Namco. (1980) *Pac-Man.* Namco.

Paredes, J., and Jones, P. (2019) *Automated Testing: Using AI Controlled Players to Test 'The Division'.* Retrieved from GDC Vault: https://www.gdcvault.com/play/1026382/Automated-Testing-Using-AI-Controlled.

Relic Entertainment. (2021) *Age of Empires IV.* Xbox Game Studios.

Russell, S., and Norvig, P. (2020) *Artificial Intelligence: A Modern Approach* (4th ed.). Prentice Hall.

Techland. (2015) *Dying Light.* Warner Bros, Interactive Entertainment.

Toy, M., Wichman, G., Arnold, K., and Lane, J. (1980) *Rogue.*

Turn 10 Studios. (2005) *Forza Motorsport.* Microsoft Game Studios.

Turtle Rock Studios. (2008) *Left 4 Dead.* Valve.

Ubisoft Montreal. (2017) *For Honor.* Ubisoft.

Ubisoft Toronto. (2020) *Watch Dogs: Legion.* Ubisoft.

Ubisoft Toronto. (2021) *Far Cry 6.* Ubisoft.

Valve. (1998) *Half-Life.* Sierra On-Line.

Valve. (2004) *Half-Life 2.* Valve.

Vinyals, O., Babuschkin, I., Czarnecki, W.M., Mathieu, M., Dudzik, A., Chung, J., Choi, D.H., Powell, R., Ewalds, T., Georgiev, P., and Oh, J. (2019) Grandmaster level in StarCraft II using multi-agent reinforcement learning. *Nature*, 575(7782), pp. 350–354.

Wurman, P.R., Barrett, S., Kawamoto, K., MacGlashan, J., Subramanian, K., Walsh, T.J., Capobianco, R., Devlic, A., Eckert, F., Fuchs, F., and Gilpin, L. (2022) Outracing champion Gran Turismo drivers with deep reinforcement learning. *Nature*, 602(7896), pp. 223–228.

2 Implementing an AI Framework in Unreal for Medium- to Large-Scale Numbers of Disparate AI in *Hood: Outlaws and Legends*

Dr Allan Bruce

2.1 INTRODUCTION

Hood: Outlaws and Legends is a third-person, multiplayer action game based in mediaeval England. The primary game mode is a heist style mode with up to eight players split across two teams that try to steal treasure from an AI-controlled army. The AI army is led by the tyrannous Sheriff and consists of melee and ranged guards, with more than one hundred characters spread across the map. The large numbers of disparate AI characters, and the fact that players could be individually spread across the map, meant that the AI framework had to be robust and efficient to ensure that the game was as immersive as possible. Furthermore, the servers running *Hood* were chosen to be as cost effective as possible, which meant that the amount of memory and processor power available were very limited. *Hood* was developed in Unreal Engine 4 (UE4) and shipped on all major platforms at the time; however, all the AI logic would be run on low-cost AWS (Amazon Web Services) server instances. This chapter will cover some of the design choices and limitations that were overcome to deliver the desired player experience. Whilst these techniques were applied specifically to get the AI running efficiently in *Hood*, some of them should be applicable to other areas of gameplay development too.

2.2 SERVER LIMITATIONS

When playing online multiplayer heist matches, the servers are responsible for executing all of the AI characters. The maps in *Hood* were large and would have around 100–200 AI characters, which all had to be executed on the server. To keep costs to a minimum, the target server architecture was chosen to be as low as possible. The server hardware architecture contained several virtual CPUs running on a single

DOI: 10.1201/9781003324102-2

physical CPU. *Hood* ran a server per virtual CPU, so it could be running at the full CPU capacity of the hardware. This meant that there was very little room for running extra CPU intensive threads, which could stall on one server and have an impact on the other servers running at the same time. As such, it was imperative to ensure that a single server instance had minimal thread usage that could stall. *Hood* set out with a single-core budget of 5 ms per frame for all AI execution (not including pathfinding), resulting in some large architectural choices being made to allow for the best experience within such a low budget. This chapter will discuss the methods chosen and how they were implemented to achieve our aims.

It is worth briefly mentioning that disk I/O on these server instances was extremely slow, with the worst impact occurring when writing to disk. This slow I/O was a big bottleneck throughout development. When running servers for day-to-day playtests and internal stress testing, we wanted to enable as much useful logging as possible to aid with bug fixing. One incredibly useful tool that Unreal offers is the Visual Logger, especially for server debugging, including debugging AI. We made heavy use of the Visual Logger but found that the slow I/O was causing large stalls and therefore a network lag. To get around this, we had to make an improvement to the Visual Logger which forced it to flush frequently and to do it on a separate I/O thread. This thread required very little CPU usage and did not impact any of the other running instances. Once this was implemented, all the I/O overhead of using Visual Logger was alleviated and was successful enough that it proved possible to continue to use the Visual Logger in the released game environment.

2.3   NAV-MESH AND PATHFINDING IMPROVEMENTS

In the dynamic world of *Hood*, there are doors and portcullises that open and close throughout a match. Except for the Sheriff, the AI were not allowed to open and close these and therefore had to pathfind around them if closed, or pathfind through them if open. Unreal has run-time nav-mesh generation functionality which allows for these doors to affect the navigation. Unfortunately, even at its least CPU intensive setting, this caused large CPU spikes when doors or portcullises would open or close. These CPU spikes would often cause a few seconds of network lag afterwards due to the network code not getting updated quickly enough. These spikes would cause strange behaviours visible to players who would see their characters, and others, move erratically. To overcome these spikes, it was found that run-time nav-mesh generation could be disabled to instead allow use of Nav Modifier Volumes. These can be enabled and disabled at run-time without requiring any nav-mesh to be rebuilt. It just merely affects the cost of the paths when calculating them.

One further CPU spike we kept observing was when an AI was trying to pathfind between two points, but all possible routes were blocked by having all the doors and portcullises closed. In this scenario, the algorithm for finding the path was exhausting every possible combination before ultimately failing to find a path. To combat this, the design decision was made to guarantee a path between any two points in the world. In other words, a path would always be found. This was achieved by ensuring that there were crawl spaces or ladders throughout the level that would always guarantee a valid route. With these choices, the nav-mesh and pathfinder performed well and could be used to generate all paths for the AI.

2.4 AI STUBS

Having fully animated characters in any game can be CPU intensive and the Unreal Engine is no exception in this regard. Because of this, it made sense to try to have the minimum number of animated AI characters being updated per frame as possible. If an animated character was not required, they still had to move around and execute their behaviours. To do this, the simplest form of an Unreal Actor was implemented to meet this requirement, which was named an AI stub. These AI stubs would only exist on the server and therefore required no network replication. They were the owner of all the AI components required for them to behave and move around the world. To keep the performance as efficient as possible, the AI stubs would be moved around the world with no physics. They would, instead, move blindly along nav-mesh generated paths and not follow the landscape or level geometry exactly. These AI stubs had no rendered geometry and were therefore invisible until their animated character was required, at which point this would be spawned.

2.5 OVERCOMING POOR CACHE COHERENCY

One problem that many have observed (Holmes, 2019; Rätzer, 2020) is the way that actors and components are ticked in Unreal, causing very poor cache coherency. The main issue is that actors and components are ticked in order of how they are stored, regardless of the class type. This can cause the instruction cache and/or data cache to stall when differing class types get ticked. To overcome this, an approach similar to how an Entity Component System functions (Ford, 2017) was taken. For all in-house implemented AI components and actors, the built-in Unreal ticking was disabled and controlled manually. This was achieved by having an AI Manager that was ticked manually. Within this AI Manager's tick, groups of AI stubs would be gathered to be ticked (more on this later). The components from these stubs would then be gathered and then grouped by type. For each group of component type, the tick function would be called on them manually. This was the same technique used in a previous project which saw a speed-up of almost an order of magnitude. There is an extra cost associated with this approach since you need to gather the objects to tick; however, the advantage of not stalling the instruction and data caches far outweighs this small amount of extra work.

2.6 AI STUB TICKING

In a game world with as many as 200 AI stubs ideally requiring a call to their tick function each frame, a budget of 5 ms is challenging. The ECS-style tick aggregation allows better utilisation of the CPU, but not enough that you can tick every AI stub in a single frame. To maintain this tight budget, groups of 20 AI stubs could be added to the AI Manager's tick process at any one time. This could be repeated to tick batches of 20 AI stubs at a time until the budget was hit.

These groups of AI stubs were chosen in two ways. Firstly, any stubs that have a full animated character were ticked every frame, since any faults in their behaviour would be noticeable to players. Secondly, a circular buffer of the remaining AI stubs was used. This allowed us to continue to add groups of 20 AI stubs from this circular buffer until either the budget was met, or all the AI stubs were ticked. If any of the AI stubs were not ticked in the current frame, these would be the first to be grouped from the circular buffer to receive their tick on the next frame. To track which AI stubs had been ticked, each one had to maintain a manual record of the last time they were ticked and the current time to ensure that the delta time was correct.

It is worth noting that under normal circumstances, all the AI could be ticked within the 5 ms budget. It was only when several of the AI stubs were running more complex behaviours that it was not possible to tick all of them in one frame. In the final release of the game, with optimised behaviours, the AI stubs would never go more than two frames without being ticked. This was mostly due to the cache coherency being addressed as described above, and the custom behaviour tree implementations discussed in the next section.

2.7 BEHAVIOUR TREES

After some initial testing using the built-in Unreal behaviour tree implementation, it was decided that *Hood* would require its own implementation of a behaviour tree. The reasoning for this was that the Unreal event-driven behaviour trees were cumbersome to get working for the complexity of AI behaviours desired. Almost none of the built-in behaviours or decorators had the desired features so these had to be written from scratch too. Writing your own behaviour tree implementation allows you to get the desired level of complexity whilst making the trees simpler to author and more efficient to execute. The resulting architecture was an amalgamation of a decision tree (Magee, 2014) and a behaviour tree. The flow of deciding which branch to execute was taken from the ideas in a decision tree, but the execution order of the behaviours within a branch was taken from behaviour trees. That is, behaviours were run in sequence until a behaviour failed, or selected by running until a behaviour succeeded. One addition made to the tree was the ability to run any number of branches at the same time. This would allow, for example, a simple 'Move' behaviour to run following a moving target, whilst also running a behaviour to 'Aim' at a target, which could be the same as or different from the one it was moving toward. At the same time, it could also be running a 'Bark' behaviour which selects an appropriate line to shout out, something like "I'm coming to get you Loxley". This approach allowed the leaf behaviours to be relatively simple, but also to have different 'Move' behaviours. Sometimes it was desirable to have the AI agent move directly towards the target, but at other times they would need them to move whilst maintaining cover, or perhaps move whilst remaining in the open form. Having a single decision node above the type of 'Move' meant that the type of movement could be changed without affecting the other running behaviours.

Each game mode phase during a heist match in *Hood* had varying elements of gameplay. For example, the initial stage was where players would move around the world stealthily trying to find the treasure and the AI would largely be in an idle state which would mostly be patrolling or standing guard, with the occasional interaction between two guards if they walked past each other. The last phase involved the players carrying the treasure to an extraction point and using the extraction device to extract the treasure. Once the AI were aware of this, they would no longer be idle and would instead be in combat or setting up blockades to confront oncoming players. Because of these distinct changes in types of behaviour the behaviour trees could be changed at any time using distinct behaviour trees, each catering for a different game mode stage. These could be swapped in and out as required. This meant that the behaviour trees could be kept as simple as possible, knowing that they only had a smaller subset of behaviours to run for the given circumstance. This in turn meant that the behaviour trees would execute very efficiently.

2.8   PLAYER MOVEMENT PREDICTION

One of the biggest performance improvements made throughout the development of *Hood* was to ensure that, wherever possible, a fully animated AI character was not rendered. However, it was essential that players never saw AI characters pop in or out on screen. To achieve this, the player's location in the immediate future needed to be predicted. Some complex models using Euler's method and higher order Runge-Kutta were tried, but found that a much simpler approach yielded the best results. This was to simply store the previous x seconds of a player's location and direction, and then to use the following steps:

1. $\text{dir}_{\text{delta}} = \text{dir}_t - \text{dir}_{t-x}$
2. $\text{dir}_{\text{predicted}} = \text{dir}_t + \text{dir}_{\text{delta}}$
3. $\text{loc}_{\text{delta}} = \text{loc}_t - \text{loc}_{t-x}$
4. $\text{loc}_{\text{inter}} = \text{loc}_t + \text{loc}_{\text{delta}}$
5. $\text{loc}_{\text{predicted}} = \text{loc}_{\text{inter}} + \text{dir}_{\text{predicted}} * |\text{loc}_{\text{inter}}|$

Setting x to a value of 1 second worked well for predicting the player's movement.

2.9   DETECTING THE NEED FOR FULLY ANIMATED CHARACTERS

As mentioned previously, having fully rendered and animated characters is CPU intensive. The goal in *Hood* was to have the minimum number of animated characters possible, yet still appear to the player that they were never in any other state. The method implemented to achieve this was as follows.

For every AI stub that had no animated character spawned, the following check against each of the eight players was done:

1. If the player is very far away (further than the network replication distance) then we do not need a full character.
2. Otherwise, if the player is in combat with the AI, then we want a full character.
3. Otherwise, if the player's current position or their predicted position is very close (approximately 5 metres) then we want a full character.

4. Otherwise, if the player's current position or their predicted position is relatively close (approximately 15 metres) and the AI stub's location is within the player's view frustum, then we want a full character.
5. Otherwise for the player's current position and their predicted position, check to see if the AI stub is within the view frustum and within a long distance (approximately 100 metres). If it is, then perform some Line-of-Sight checks.

The line-of-sight checks would perform a ray cast from the player's current location and predicted location, to one of the AI stub's pre-defined bone locations. These bone locations were defined to approximate where the AI character's main body parts would be if rendered, for example: each foot, each hand, torso, and head. These would be chosen sequentially each frame and if the ray cast did not hit anything then the full character would be desired.

Once a character was desired, it was placed in a queue to be spawned. Spawning characters is relatively CPU intensive as they are built up of several actors, all of which need to be spawned. Because of this expensive operation, the number of full AI characters to be spawned in a single frame was limited to be just one. If there was more than one full character to be spawned in a single frame, then the one that would have the most impact on gameplay was prioritised. Each desired character was scored by distance (closer distance means a higher score) and by angle from the centre of the player's view (the closest to the centre results in a higher score). The AI stub with the highest combination of these scores would be the one chosen to be spawned into a full character.

We continually checked to see if a full character could be de-spawned, therefore, keeping the number of full characters in-game at the same time to a minimum. These checks were the same as those described above, but instead, if they all failed then the de-spawn process was started. This process would trigger a de-spawn timer. If the checks continued to fail for several seconds, then the full character would de-spawn and revert back to the basic AI stub. However, if one of the checks passed before the timer reached the limit, the timer would be reset. This would continue until the full character was de-spawned or the character was killed. After testing different time durations, a 2-second de-spawn timer was deemed sufficient.

When spawning full characters, it was of utmost importance to ensure that they spawned in the same visible state as when they last de-spawned – if they had previously been spawned. The potential visual differences could be blood decals or arrows stuck in the character's helmet, amongst other things. This meant that when de-spawning a character, every attached visual artefact and where it was on the body was recorded. And when a character was re-spawned, it was simply a matter of reapplying the visual artefacts.

2.10 FADING CHARACTERS

In the unlikelihood of a character being spawned or de-spawned in sight of a player, the characters would be faded in when spawning and faded out when de-spawning. This was also used when any full characters (both player-controlled, and

AI-controlled) were far away. If a character got closer than x metres from the camera, they would be faded in, and if they went further than $x+y$ metres they would be faded out. For *Hood* it was found that setting x to be 140 metres and y to be 5 metres achieved the desired effect.

2.11 CONCLUSION

This chapter has discussed several techniques that were used to allow large numbers of disparate AI characters to populate the game world in *Hood: Outlaws and Legends*. All these techniques worked well and allowed the game to be released with no performance issues and, more importantly, no perception of the fact that the AI characters were not always present in their fully rendered, animated form.

REFERENCES

Ford, T. (2017) *Overwatch Gameplay Architecture and Netcode. YouTube* [online]. Available from: https://www.youtube.com/watch?v=zrIY0eIyqmI&ab_channel=UnofficialGDC Archive (accessed November 2nd, 2022).

Holmes, J. (2019) *Aggregating Ticks to Manage Scale in Sea of Thieves | Unreal Fest Europe 2019 | Unreal Engine*. YouTube [online]. Available from: https://www.youtube.com/watch?v=CBP5bpwkO54&ab_channel=UnrealEngine (accessed November 2nd, 2022).

Magee, J.F. (2014) *Decision Trees for Decision Making*. Harvard Business Review [online]. Available from: https://hbr.org/1964/07/decision-trees-for-decision-making (accessed November 3rd, 2022).

Rätzer, D. (2020) *Speeding up Game Logic in Unreal Engine | Unreal Fest Online 2020*. YouTube [online]. Available from: https://www.youtube.com/watch?v=QlKXPBFh5BM&ab_channel=UnrealEngine (accessed November 2nd, 2022).

3 Predicting When and Where to Intercept Players in *Hood*: *Outlaws and Legends*

Dr Allan Bruce

3.1 INTRODUCTION

Hood: Outlaws and Legends is a third-person, multiplayer action game based in mediaeval England. Two teams, each of four players, compete against each other to try and steal as much treasure from the AI-controlled, tyrannous Sheriff and his army of guards, known as *The State*. The initial phase of a match sees each team of players trying to steal a key from the Sheriff and then locating a locked vault that houses a treasure chest. If players are spotted by the Sheriff or his guards during this phase, *The State* will be pushed into high alert. This results in the guards being poised for battle, making them more difficult to overcome. On top of this, the guards can communicate between themselves to warn of incoming attacks from players and bring in reinforcements. It is in the best interests of the players to move around stealthily and pick off guards one-by-one, thus reducing the number of guards and not alerting *The State.* To promote stealth, the players have the ability to take-down guards using stealthy melee attacks. When executed perfectly, these takedowns would make no noise, and would not be visible to any of the other guards. After a lot of testing, it was discovered that this preferred method of combat could be circumvented quite easily by running through the level, alerting all the guards but avoiding any form of combat. This chapter discusses the approach taken by the AI to predict when players were exhibiting such behaviour. The AI also punished these players in the hope of persuading them to play the game utilising the stealth mechanics as originally intended.

3.2 COMMANDER

In *Hood*, there is a Commander which is responsible for issuing commands to the guards. The Commander continually monitors the state of the guards and reacts by issuing commands such as: "Attack My Target" in response to a guard getting shot or "Form Formation Around Me" in response to the Sheriff detecting players' presence, in a bid to stop the key from being stolen. All the commands had a priority assigned to them. If a guard was issued a command, they would only follow that command if they were idle or following a lower priority command. One thing to note is that if a

DOI: 10.1201/9781003324102-3

guard was engaged in combat, they would not respond to any commands. A guard was considered to be engaged in combat as soon as they were fully aware of a player. The awareness system is beyond the scope of this chapter but, in its simplest form, to be aware of a player, a guard would have to see the player for an amount of time. If a player was seen for less than this time threshold, the AI would be suspicious and search for the player, but they would not be fully aware of them.

This Commander system was used to issue commands to make guards intercept players when they were deemed to be circumventing the combat system as discussed below.

3.3   PREDICTING A PLAYER'S GOAL

The main phases of the game have distinct target locations that form a player's goal. In the initial phase of the game, the players search around the map to try and find, and steal, a key attached to the Sheriff; therefore his location is the players' likely goal. In the remaining phases of the game, the treasure chest is the player's likely goal. The treasure chest could be found in one of three locations: located inside the locked vault; being transported around the map by another player; or being extracted at an extraction point. The approach taken was to take the player's current location and the current predicted goal location, then to perform a path find between the two points. One caveat to this is that there are doors and portcullises that can be opened and closed, not only by the players, but also by the Sheriff as well. When performing the path find from the player to the goal, it was performed on a simplified nav-mesh which had all doors and portcullises open.

3.4   CHOOSING WHEN TO REACT

With a predicted goal for the player and the likely path they would take, it was up to the Commander to choose if and when to react to players attempting to circumvent the desired play style for *Hood*. There were three checks that a player must pass before the Commander would intervene. The intention was to merely discourage players from continually moving around the map and avoiding combat.

3.4.1   CHECK 1: MOVEMENT SPEED

Players running around the map are more likely to be disregarding the stealthy play style of *Hood* than those moving at a slower pace. So, any player moving faster than their walking speed was deemed as a potential for AI intervention and would pass this check.

3.4.2   CHECK 2: PLAYER'S ROUTE

Another check was to assess whether a player was progressing along the predicted path towards the goal. This was achieved by taking the player's velocity direction and finding the angle between that and the current predicted path segment direction. If this was within a certain tolerance, say 20°, then it was assumed the player was moving towards the goal and they would pass this check. Players not following the path were likely engaged in the battle and not navigating towards the goal and would therefore fail this check.

3.4.3 CHECK 3: AWARENESS

What if players had played stealthily and taken out all the guards in the area? Or, if there were guards around but they were not aware of the player, then how would they be able to alert *The State*? A final check was introduced to add an element of fairness, as it would be viewed as unfair, or worse, as AI cheating, to punish the players in these scenarios. Therefore, a player only passed this check if any guard, or the Sheriff, was *fully* aware of their location.

3.5 DECIDING WHERE TO INTERCEPT

A mechanism was put in place to try and thwart the players' progress when trying to circumvent the combat system by constructing blockades at certain pre-placed points throughout the level. The best locations for such blockades were choke-points such as doorways, bridges, steps, or if all else failed, at the vault and extraction point. These blockade locations were pre-determined by level designers to get the best experience. For the blockade to be effective, multiple AI-controlled guards needed to be at the blockade, ready to try to intercept the player.

After determining a player was circumventing the combat system, a blockade location needed to be chosen. As mentioned above, the AI already has a predicted path calculated for the player's route to the goal location. Using this path, all the blockade locations along this route were set and for each, the time it would take for the player to reach it was calculated. For simplicity, it was assumed the player would continue to run at maximum speed. For each blockade location, and the predicted time for the player to arrive at it, all guards in the area that could reach the blockade before the player were issued a command to intercept. The guards would have to be able to respond to this command as discussed in Section 3.2. If the blockade would attract at least n guards, then that blockade location would be added to a list of potential candidates. Otherwise, this blockade was discarded. With this done for each blockade, the AI would choose the location that would take the player the least amount of time to arrive at. It was found that having n set to three guards resulted in the best chances of the blockade slowing down the player and engaging in combat.

With a blockade location selected, the Commander then commanded all the guards to move towards the location as quickly as possible. They would then stand in formation ready, waiting to intercept the abusing player.

3.6 WHEN TO STOP WAITING TO INTERCEPT

If the player continued along the predicted path, the blockade did its job; however sometimes the player would not follow the predicted path. This meant that the guards were out of position and waiting to intercept a player who would never arrive. To overcome this, when the blockade command is issued to the guards, a timer is also started. This timer gets reset every frame that the player is detected to be still following the predicted path. If the timer runs out, the guards will go back to their pre-blockade locations.

Guards could also be interrupted from intercepting if a higher priority command was issued to them.

3.7 CONCLUSION

This chapter described how the AI handled an exploit in the intended way players would navigate around the level in *Hood*. By taking advantage of the game mode, it was possible to predict where a player was heading, and if they were behaving in the undesired manner. A command was issued to the guards in the area to intercept and block the players path in the hope of slowing them down and forcing them to enter combat. The methods used to choose a suitable location for this blockade and how it was decided which guards should get involved were discussed. The approach taken that allowed guards to abandon these blockades was also discussed.

With these methods developed and added to the game, it was found that players would initially still run around but would confront the blockades as intended. When confronting one of the blockades, players would then be slowed down and would be forced to engage in combat as intended. In this regard, the method was successful, however, more could have been done to signal the reason for the blockade and make this more obvious to the player.

4 Getting Caught Off Guard
Situational Awareness *in* The Escapists 2

David Rogers

4.1 INTRODUCTION

This chapter will present how situational awareness was handled for the non-player characters (NPC) in *The Escapists 2*. 'Situational awareness' builds upon the foundations of NPC perception systems (Puig, 2008), focusing on the detection of the actions of both NPCs and players. This includes the perception of actions that occurred in the past and present, as well as those which can be inferred; perception of an action can either be from the direct observation of a character, or the observation their actions have had on the environment. The complexity of solving situational awareness is that many actions we want to detect are not instantaneous events; they often persist over many frames and can vary from a few seconds to entire play sessions. As *The Escapists 2* is a highly systemic game, situational awareness provides the majority of information the NPCs use for their behaviour selection and context.

4.2 GAMEPLAY OVERVIEW

The Escapists 2 is a cooperative multiplayer game that tasks up to four players to plan and execute a prison breakout under the watchful eye of the NPC guards and the prison facility. The prison is a multi-layered, tile-based sandbox with a top-down view, where the vast majority of tiles can be removed, modified, or replaced, given the correct item. Items are critical to enabling our inmate players to access previously inaccessible areas to further their escape plans. For any given map, the players must procure certain items (via the map-specific quests, jobs, and looting), plan a route through the prison to the outside, and enact this plan without raising suspicion from the guards. Failure, where the guards have sufficient evidence against you of an escape attempt, results in the devastating reset of progress. A reset can include removing player items, repairing any found damage to the prison, and for the player to take a short visit to solitary. Anything that may cause suspicion in this prison setting leads our NPCs to need situational awareness.

DOI: 10.1201/9781003324102-4

4.3   SITUATIONAL AWARENESS

Situational awareness can be split into three categories of observable suspicious actions, *Direct*, *Indirect*, and *Inferred*. Directly suspicious actions squarely attribute an action to a player, such as observing a player unscrewing a vent cover. Indirectly suspicious actions are anything that indicates something that happened in the past, such as spotting a missing vent cover. Inferable actions require some context to know whether something should be suspicious. An example would be spotting an inmate in the corridor, which would be suspicious if they were scheduled to be in the gym, but perhaps not if they were disguised as a guard. It would also be suspicious if one inmate never turned up to the morning roll call.

The game mechanics also reflect the type of suspicious action being observed. Direct actions are those directly attributable to a player and when the guards detect such an action, a complete reset of their progress is expected. Indirect actions, which do not attribute themselves to any particular player, will increase the overall prison difficulty via the 'security level'. Finally, inferred actions, indicating a player is suspicious but not actively escaping, should result in heightened per-player difficulty via increased player 'heat'.

4.4   GAMEPLAY EVENT SYSTEMS

When a player or an NPC performs an action we want to be detected by another NPC, a framework is needed that can package and disseminate the desired information about the action to the relevant NPCs. The approach used in *The Escapists 2* was to use a system of 'Signals', which will be described in more detail later in the chapter; however, a practical and common strategy in gameplay programming is to achieve this using an event system (Orkin, 2002a; Millington & Funge, 2009a). An exploration of the usage of gameplay events within the context of *The Escapists 2* follows as a point of comparison.

Gameplay events allow us to communicate and propagate information between different gameplay systems using event messages. In this model, you generate a message containing information about the event when a specific action occurs. You then pass this message to an intermediary object, where this intermediary object maintains a list of other systems that have previously subscribed to it. With this list, the intermediary object can then show each subscribed system the message about the action that has happened, allowing them to react. This design pattern is useful because it is simple to implement and decouples the producer and consumer of the event information, as they need to only know about the intermediary object.

Let us look at how we might apply gameplay events to the problem of situation awareness. When either the player or an NPC starts an action that we want an NPC to detect, we generate a *SuspiciousActionEvent*. This event could contain information about who triggered the event, what type of action it was, where it occurred, and any other relevant details. When we initialise an NPC wanting to detect suspicious actions, they subscribe as a listener to the intermediary object that handles the event type. When the *SuspiciousActionEvent* is generated and posted to the intermediary object, every subscribed NPC will then be shown the *SuspiciousActionEvent* message (often implemented via a callback). At this point, each NPC needs to decide what they should do with this information, and more critically, should they have been aware of it? For example: they would need to check if the event was nearby, whether they had line-of-sight (LOS), if required, and test any other constraints imposed on detection. Therefore, every NPC needs to filter out every event that is irrelevant to them. Once an NPC learns about an event, other internal systems to that NPC can react to this information, such as changing behaviour or triggering a context-sensitive bark.

4.4.1 TEMPORAL ACTIONS

An issue that quickly arises when using events is handling actions that happen for some extended duration rather than as a one-off, instantaneous action (a common trait to many of the detectable actions in *The Escapists 2*). For this reason, a single event might not be an appropriate solution. What happens if an NPC misses the start of the action? How might they detect the action mid-way through?

There are several strategies that could be used to solve this problem with events. One possibility is to have a mechanism that can re-emit them whilst the action is active, effectively pulsing at some frequency. Another option may be to allow all NPCs to remember all ongoing events that have yet to be detected. With this strategy, a given NPC can keep re-testing for detection over this list. This will then require another mechanism to remove events when they have ended. This can be achieved by either having an additional event that flags when it has ended or a method to ask the event owner about its current validity.

4.5 SIGNALS

The Escapists 2 took a different perspective on the problem of detecting actions, in the hope of avoiding some of these added complexities. Rather than have all NPCs listen for events of ongoing actions and then have them all tested for detection, each NPC would directly detect all nearby entities with ongoing actions. This method then puts the onus on the NPC to pull information rather than the entities to push (and then filter), as is the case with events.

To define some terminology, 'Signal' refers to the information we can detect, 'Signal Producers' are entities with information to share, and 'Signal Observers' are those interested in this information. Conceptually, every entity that could have interesting information for the NPCs has a set of signals that it can turn on/off depending on whether it has anything to share; this signal is then observable to those who look.

4.5.1 SPATIALLY AWARE SIGNALS

In *The Escapists 2*, for any given frame we would expect hundreds of moving Signal Observers (usually NPCs) and a few dozen Signal Producers, many of which would be static (usually damage in the world). In addition, almost every signal used in the game has a spatial element, requiring that there is LOS between the Signal Observer and the Signal Producer. With so many potential tests between every observer and every producer, it makes sense to filter out the most redundant tests using spatial partitioning structures against a maximum detection distance. Signal Producers manage their position within this structure and this allows the Signal Observers to query for any nearby Signal Producers.

Using these structures requires an understanding of how large and often they will need to be updated, in combination with how many unnecessary detection tests may be run. As with everything we do, profiling is the only accurate metric.

4.5.2   SIGNALS – ADVANTAGES

There are some advantages to consider when using Signals. By giving the Signal Producers the responsibility to manage their position within a shared spatial partitioning structure, this allows them to update based on a local context. For example: Signal Producers on characters will move frequently, so they should continually update. Conversely, holes never move, so they do not need to update. Desks never move unless a character picks them up, so they only need to update in those situations. We can also give the Signal Producers the responsibility of adding/removing themselves from the structure, depending on whether they have any active information to share. For *The Escapists 2*, only a few Signal Producers would have anything to share at any given time, especially given that most inmates are well behaved and player damage to the prison is done sparingly.

For a spatial partitioning structure, a simple grid of large tiles for each floor proved to be sufficient. Signal Producers are assigned to a given tile, and Signal Observers can check all tiles which overlap a given view cone during detection. However, it is possible to build levels with large vertical openings and for players to dig holes in the floor that was otherwise another floor's ceiling. To handle this, the Signal Producers may also be assigned to multiple tiles on different floors based on expected visibility.

Another advantage of using signals is that they allow the Signal Observers to decide when they want to query for information; this decouples the handling of the event from its creation. This is beneficial when using aggressive time-slicing on NPCs, who may not need to run detection as frequently as the events being created. This allows the detection tests to be performed by the scheduling of the NPCs, and not by the scheduling of the event.

4.5.3   SIGNALS – DISADVANTAGES

A disadvantage to using signals as opposed to events is that there is still the potential to miss an action occurring if you do not update frequently enough, which could occur as the effect of aggressive time-slicing. Most actions in the game stay active for a reasonably long time, so they are often noticed. Pushed gameplay events do not suffer from this problem, as they may directly update the NPC at the time of the event or retain the information in a buffer for later retrieval. It could be possible to mitigate these effects if the Signal Producers remained visible for an extended period, with some additional tests between when the observer last checked and when the signal was dropped. The only instance this showed as an issue was with the 'Punch' action, which had a short animation that was played when one NPC hits another. The simple solution taken was to keep the signal alive for a slightly longer duration than the animation requested – long enough to be detected by the worst-case detection rate. A side effect of this solution was that detecting punches was not frame perfect, but for players this was generally imperceivable.

4.6   SIGNALS – IMPLEMENTATION

4.6.1   SIGNAL PRODUCERS

Every detectable entity contains a Signal Producer. The Signal Producer provides all the currently active signals to be detected and the entities with Signal Producers are responsible for managing their list of currently active signals. Different gameplay components on the entity will inform Signal Producers when a given signal has become active and when it has been deactivated. This differs depending on whether the action is *Direct*, *Indirect*, or *Inferred*. To put this into context, an example for each type of action is described below.

> **Direct Action:** When a player uses an item to dig a hole, the item manages the visibility of the 'IsDigging' signal on the operating character. Therefore, the entity owning the Signal Producer represents the instigator of the action.
>
> **Indirect Action:** When the player has finished digging the hole, the dug tile is given a Signal Producer with a visible 'HasHole' signal. The player is not stored as an instigator of the hole, as the guards who later detect it should have no reason to attribute it directly to anyone.
>
> **Inferred Actions:** Rather than have guards attempt to understand if a character is acting suspiciously, we can have the characters *snitch on themselves*, telling the guards that they are doing something they should not be doing. For example, each inmate tracks whether they have yet gone to their designated routine. If, after an initial grace period at the start of a routine they have still not arrived, they enable the 'IsLateForRoutine' signal on themselves. This allows passing NPC guards to detect this signal and shout at them for being late.

The alternative implementation, where the guards would need to work out whether an inmate was late for a routine, would very quickly add complexity to the detection logic. For every inmate they could see, they would need to check where they should be, how much grace period they have been allotted, and whether they had attended. All this logic would need to be performed by our guard, and this is only one of many inferable actions. This slight swap in perspective is what enables *The Escapists 2* to handle a lot of complex, contextual situational awareness. With this method, you can implement social stealth simply by having the inmate not announce that they are in the guards' quarters when wearing a guard's uniform. You can implement 'contraband detectors' that can detect items in the inventory without needing the contraband detector to know what an item is. You can have the cell bed snitch when the player is not present at night, unless a 'bed dummy' is placed in the bed, without the guards needing to know what a bed or a bed dummy is.

4.6.2 SIGNAL OBSERVERS

Signal Observers, in the context of *The Escapists 2*, are either NPCs that react to other NPCs and the environment or in-world gameplay elements that respond to nearby NPCs such as cameras and contraband detectors. Each Signal Observer will have a detection test to check whether it can 'see' a given Signal Producer and which specific subset of signals it can detect. Often the detection test is against a vision cone with a LOS test, but in the case of a contraband detector, it is just the presence inside a trigger volume. When a detection test has passed, the Signal Observer can decide what to do with the information. In *The Escapists 2*, the outcome of detection was always to generate a signal memory.

4.7 SIGNAL MEMORIES

A signal memory is a data structure that stores details about an event that occurred (Buckland, 2005). This could include a reference to the Signal Producer who generated the signal, the type of signal detected, the last time the Signal Producer entity was seen, and its last known position. These memories are then stored and maintained by a memory system on each Signal Observer.

The memory system is then responsible for cycling through the memories and updating them. Depending on the signal type, it checks whether it has LOS to the producer of each memory, updating the Time Last Seen (TLS) and the Last Known Position (LKP). Most memories are forgotten when the TLS gets beyond a defined threshold, all of which were configurable based on the signal type. This was an intentional design choice; it was decided that the NPCs should be forgetful about a player's actions when they are not in view, eventually allowing a chased player to lose the guards. This feature also naturally allows players to hide inside lockers and have the guards lose sight of them. Implemented directly, this would mean that a player who jumps into a locker in front of a guard would cause them to forget about the player instantly. A useful technique was to add a small grace period after the TLS, where although the NPC might not have LOS, they pretend they do. This slight grace period gives a short-lived omniscience and allows NPCs to detect players who have just jumped into lockers. The omniscience also has the benefit of updating the LKP just past the point where they were last seen. In a chase scenario, this causes the NPC to intelligently track players around corners and at sharp turns behind a door.

4.7.1 SIGNAL MEMORY AND BEHAVIOUR SELECTION

The NPC behaviours were implemented with a top-level priority selector, with each sub-behaviour defined as a Behaviour Tree (BT). The priority selector selects the highest priority memory based on the signal type. This memory is then set as the active memory, and the appropriate sub-behaviour BT is executed, using the active memory as context for the behaviour's actions. Interestingly, there were some cases where the behaviours would be responsible for forgetting the memory after appropriately dealing with it, rather than when the signal itself became invalid. In these cases, we wanted to avoid the NPCs looking omniscient and reacting to a change in the world they could not have seen.

A good example of this behaviour can be seen with the Maintenance NPCs tasked with fixing damage to the prison. If they were to turn around just as the player patches up a hole in the wall on their way to repair some damage, it would either look broken or, worse, look like the AI is cheating. Therefore, it is much more desirable for the NPC to walk up to the hole, react with a confused bark, and then turn around. In practice, the implementation looks as follows: when the guards report damage to the prison computer, a manager is tasked with directly injecting the memory of the damage to the nearest Maintenance NPC. This triggers the 'FixPrisonDamage' behaviour on the Maintenance NPC, who walks over to the damage to fix it. However, on arrival, we can test if the signal has been disabled, maybe because a player has covered up the hole with a poster, and instead of using the 'FixPrisonDamage' behaviour, a confused bark is triggered instead.

4.8   SIGNAL SERIALISATION

As *The Escapists 2* is a networked title, it needed to handle the serialisation and deserialisation of the world state as well as host migration. The network architecture defines one player as the host, responsible for the entire game simulation. When the host disconnects, either intentionally or unexpectedly, the game needs to be able to migrate to a new client, with all the NPCs continuing their active behaviours. This is trivial to achieve using signal memories. With the serialisation of each NPC's memories, a restart of the behaviour system (and given the complete set of memories) will return to the same previous sub-behaviour with the right memory as context. Memory serialisation is simple, as you only need to deal with a set of floats for the LKP and TLS, and a reference to the Signal Producer, which can always be converted to unique IDs or tile coordinates.

The BTs that implement each sub-behaviour, specifically those with multiple steps, then need to be written in a format that allows them to be interrupted and resumed without requiring additional state or serialisation.

For example, if we have a multi-stage laundry job, the steps might be:

1. Take dirty laundry from the dirty laundry basket.
2. Take held dirty laundry and place it in the washing machine.
3. Take any washed laundry from the washing machine.
4. Place the clean washed laundry in the clean laundry basket.

If our NPC is interrupted, perhaps due to host migration, or the NPC got distracted by combat, we would want them to continue where they left off. The strategy to do so, without any additional state data, is to attempt each step in reverse. So, if they are holding clean laundry, put it away. If there is washed laundry to take, take it. If they are holding dirty laundry, put it in the machine. Otherwise, pick up new dirty laundry. This structure is what BTs are most suited to, where behaviours are ordered in terms of priority. This way, NPCs can resume their behaviours without the need to network any additional data to do with their progress.

4.9 SIGNAL TOKENS

One aspect not yet touched on is when a signal should be removed from a Signal Producer once an NPC has detected the signal. Not doing so would lead to an impractical situation where every passing NPC will react. For example: when the player starts a fight in the canteen, every inmate in the room would bark about it, and every guard would come barrelling down on the player. Inversely, if we do remove the signal when it is detected, only one NPC will ever be able to react to the player's actions. This and other examples of an over or under-reaction from the NPCs lead to an inability for the team to balance the game and its levels.

Tokens provide a neat solution to this problem and, with some slight extensions, can be quite a powerful balancing tool. A Signal Producer can define a specific number of tokens per signal type it owns, with separate token pools based on the Signal Observer type. For example: Medics (tasked with carrying KO'd characters to the infirmary) have their own pool, so they do not need to compete with other NPCs over the same 'IsKnockedOut' tokens. A set of cooldowns is employed for each token, allowing a grace period to be set after a token is returned before it can be retaken. Finally, as Signal Producers are directly aware of what tokens have and have not been taken from them, they can remove themselves from the set of entities to be detected when no tokens are available. Through the use of tokens, you can control the intensity and frequency of the NPC responses. As *The Escapists 2* is a systemic game, a decentralised approach was taken.

4.9.1 DECENTRALISED TOKENS

Tokens are a helpful tool to coordinate the behaviour of multiple NPCs. An NPC who obtains a token is granted permission to perform a behaviour based on the kind of token they have. In the Centralised approach, tokens are given to NPCs in a top-down fashion, typically via a gameplay manager (Miles, 2014). In the decentralised approach, an NPC can independently decide to take one of the tokens from a limited pool (Millington & Funge, 2009b). By limiting the tokens that can be handed out, you can control and balance the responses of a group of NPCs. For example: a commonly used token is an 'attack token'; the number of attack tokens available sets the maximum number of simultaneous attacks a player can receive (Loudy & Campbell, 2018). This places a ceiling on the amount of damage per frame a player could take relative to the number of attackers. In a similar manner, tokens can also be used to limit the number of NPCs simultaneously searching for the player, where it would be unfair if every NPC went hunting for them.

4.9.2 DRAWBACKS

Decentralised tokens have some drawbacks, specifically in cases where there is contention over which NPC should be granted the token. In these situations, the desirable solution is to award it to the 'best' NPC (perhaps the closest). This is tricky in decentralised environments but is solvable. It requires some mechanism for cooperation between NPCs to decide who should be the one to take the token, but this adds complexity. Although this situation does arise in *The Escapists 2*, the additional complexity was avoided by using the simple non-cooperative first-come-first-serve approach, which worked well enough. This was a product of the top-down view of the game, which makes the choice of 'best' NPC a little more lenient from the players' viewpoint as they can see everything that is occurring.

4.10 CONCLUSION

Signals provide a different perspective on the problem of situational awareness than that of gameplay events; it frames the problem as "what observable actions can I see" rather than "from this action I am presented, could I have seen it". This structure also swaps the responsibility of detection from a pushed architecture to a pulled one – only updating when the NPC is ticked rather than when the event is created. It also lends well to spatial partitioning over Signal Producers which seldom move vs spatial partitioning over Signal Observers who usually do. The extension of the Signal Producers to be aware of tokens to implement decentralised agent coordination allowed the balancing of NPC responses to a given object's situation without explicit coordination logic. By placing context specific logic for detecting actions onto the Signal Producers the complexities of such a task were reduced – having an NPC tell the guard they are late is much more straightforward than having the guard look up where that NPC should be and whether they had already been.

The mindset of putting responsibility into the world, rather than into the AI systems, is a common one; Jeff Orkin gives the advice to "Put the Smarts in the World, Not in the AI" in their chapter entitled "12 Tips from the Trenches" in *AI Game Programming Wisdom* (Orkin, 2002b). We can also see this with the use of 'smart objects', such as in *The Sims* (Doornbos, 2001) and *Final Fantasy XV* (Skubch, 2015). This perspective was used extensively for the AI in *The Escapists 2* and was not limited to situational awareness. When an NPC walks into a room, the room tells them what actions are available, and for a job room, it even tells them how to perform that job. When an NPC uses an item or an interactable object, it is that object that implements the behaviour. Hiding the world's complexities from our AI systems meant that we could be confident in adding new signal types, tokens, behaviours, interactions, and some systemic features without the risk of breaking what came before.

REFERENCES

Buckland, M. (2005) Raven - *An Overview, Programming Game AI by Example*. United Kingdom: Wordware Pub.

Doornbos, J. (2001) *Those Darned Sims: What Makes Them Tick*, Games Developer Conference 2001.

Loudy, K., and Campbell, J. (2018) *Embracing Push Forward Combat in DOOM*, Games Developer Conference 2018.

Miles, B. (2014) *How to Catch a Ninja NPC Awareness in a 2D Stealth Platformer*. Game AI Pro, CRC Press.

Millington, I., and Funge, J. (2009a) *Event Managers, Artificial Intelligence for Games* (2nd ed.). Boca Raton, FL: CRC Press, pp. 748–755.

Millington, I., and Funge, J. (2009b) *Emergent Cooperation, Artificial Intelligence for Games* (2nd ed.). Boca Raton, FL: CRC Press, pp. 565–568.

Orkin, J. (2002a) A general-purpose trigger system, *AI Game Programming Wisdom*, edited by Steve Rabin. Hingham, MA: Charles River Media, pp. 46–54.

Orkin, J. (2002b) 12 Tips from the trenches: 5. Put the smarts in the world, not in the AI, *AI Game Programming Wisdom*, edited by Steve Rabin. Hingham, MA: Charles River Media, pp. 29–35.

Puig, P. F. (2008) Generic perception system, *AI Game Programming Wisdom 4*, edited by Steve Rabin. Hingham, MA: Charles River Media, pp. 285–294.

Skubch, H. (2015) *Not Just Planning: STRIPs for Ambient NPC Interactions in Final Fantasy XV*, nucl.ai Conference 2015.

5 Stitching It Together
The Enemies of Sackboy: A Big Adventure

Huw Talliss

5.1 INTRODUCTION

Sackboy: A Big Adventure is a 3D cooperative platformer initially released on PlayStation 4 and as a PlayStation 5 launch title. When making a direct sequel to a game or franchise, you usually have a solid design foundation laid by the prior games to build on. However, when creating a spin-off game – especially one that is intentionally exploring a different direction – you do not have that same clear design framework to use. For a long time during the development of *Sackboy: A Big Adventure*, it was not clear exactly what role enemies would play in the game experience, and as such it also was not clear how complex they needed to be.

5.2 ENEMIES

On one end of the complexity scale, there are extremely simplistic early Goomba-style enemies that simply move towards the player and damage them on contact. On the other end, there are enemies like you might find in an action game: enemies that have specific telegraphed attacks, counterplay, and the like. We did not know where we wanted or needed our enemies to fall on that spectrum, and as such we made early prototypes at several points along it. As development progressed and the desired role of enemies became clearer, we pulled back from some of our most complex prototypes (some of which involved parries, counters, and enemy group attacks), ending up with a set of moderately complex and varied enemies that dealt damage through specific telegraphed attacks, generally had their own method of movement, could celebrate dealing damage, patrol around, and had their own enemy-type specific behaviours.

A guiding principle that was followed during the development of the enemies was that they should not break the illusion that they are living, decision-making creatures. Enemies should always be aware of, and reactive to their surroundings, in any situation. Enemies staring directly at walls, constantly bumping into, or getting stuck on each other, and not reacting to the player when their friend right next to them did, are a few of the illusion-breaking situations that needed to be addressed. This principle was just a lower bar for apparent intelligence; it was OK for enemies to charge off cliffs if the player dodged them, accidently hit each other while trying to attack the player, or make mistakes in other slapstick ways as long as their actions appeared to have intent behind them.

DOI: 10.1201/9781003324102-5

Sackboy: A Big Adventure ended up with two different classifications of enemies, developed by two different teams: Complex enemies (developed by the AI team), and Simple enemies (developed by the Gameplay Objects team). The line between what a Complex enemy was versus a Simple enemy was extremely blurry, but a loose definition was that simple enemies were things like static turrets, spline-following enemies, and so on, essentially enemies that cannot freely path around. This chapter will focus on the complex enemies and some of the systems behind them. First let us introduce two of the enemies we will talk about: The Sniper and The Rammer.

The Sniper is a four-armed enemy that can throw damaging projectiles (one from each arm) before it needs to reload. It will approach the player if they are out of range, and run away if the player gets too close, cowering in-place if it has nowhere to run. There are two variants of the Sniper that are used in later levels: the Undersea Sniper which has fish projectiles that home towards the player, and the Space Sniper which flies into the air before throwing fast-moving rockets at the player.

The other enemy of interest is the Rammer, a four-legged box-shaped enemy that attacks by charging at the player, dealing damage if it collides with them.

5.3   DETECTION

One of the first things you need for your enemies to do anything other than just wander around aimlessly is a method for detecting the player, to allow them to look at, move towards, and attack the player. Two common requirements for whether an enemy should detect a player are *distance* and *line-of-sight*. You usually do not want enemies to detect a player from across the entire level, or from behind a solid wall. These two checks alone are often sufficient, but *Sackboy: A Big Adventure* ended up with a slightly more complicated detection system.

So, how might you handle detection for a generic set of enemies? A somewhat naïve approach would be for each enemy, every frame, to independently gather a list of all the players and then perform the necessary *distance* and *line-of-sight* checks to determine whether they can detect that player. However, this approach is not ideal for performance, since each additional enemy added to a level results in an extra set of detection calculations performed every single frame. While you can limit performing the more expensive *line-of-sight* ray cast only if the cheaper distance check has passed, you are still ending up with a system whose performance cost increases with every enemy added into the level. This can also lead to unpredictable performance spikes. For example, if the player walks in range of many enemies, each enemy will pass their distance check, and then immediately do the more expensive ray cast, triggering their actual behaviour logic straight after. A better solution is to instead manage detection separately from the individual enemies, which lets us group up enemies for detection, and control how often their detection is updated.

On *Sackboy: A Big Adventure*, the detection of one enemy in each enemy group was updated per frame. An enemy group contained all the active enemies of a given type of enemy. So, there was one group for all the active Rammers and another for the Snipers. Only one Rammer and one Sniper from each group would update their detection each frame. A different enemy from each group would be updated each frame, ensuring all enemies received their detection update over time. This approach gave a knowable upper bound for the number of enemies that can have their detection updated on a given frame (equal to the number of enemy groups), irrespective of any other factors.

The downside to this setup is clear: the detection update frequency for each enemy is reduced, and as the number of active enemies in a group increases, the detection update frequency for a given enemy decreases. This is an obvious trade-off, but since the game was targeting 60 frames per second, unless our enemy groups had 60 or more active enemies per group, which even early on seemed unlikely, each enemy would be getting at least one detection update per second, and usually much more frequently than that. Given the style of game, animation durations, as well as the alert propagation system (described below), this was acceptable and did not look at all strange.

Each type of enemy used a slightly different method for selecting their target, which depended upon their specific needs. However, they all used a shared concept for their base detection: vision cones. It is a simple concept and very much a standard for detection in games. You specify a cone in front of the enemy that potential targets must be inside of to be detected. This provides both a distance limit for detection and prevents the enemy from detecting things that are behind them (i.e., outside of the cone). As the top-down example in Image 5.1 shows, vision cones on *Sackboy: A Big Adventure* were more like wedges, since the total angle of the cone was usually more than 180°. Initially these wedges were purely 2D, but later height limits were included so enemies could easily ignore targets that were too far above or below them. In addition to the wedge check the enemies also had a simple *line-of-sight* check using a ray cast from between the enemy's eyes and the target's eyes to make sure there was not a wall or other obstruction in the way. If a potential target passed these checks, then they would be added to the list of detected targets. Several of the enemy types then sorted their detected targets by distance, and by the angle between their facing direction and the direction from them to the target, preferring the target closest to and most in front of the enemy. After the list of detected targets had been gathered through the initial cone check, most enemies would also do further specific processing as part of their behaviour logic to filter and select the best target.

IMAGE 5.1   Top-down example of a vision cone with the enemy at the centre.

As mentioned, enemies performed a *line-of-sight* check between them and the target, but the Sniper was an interesting special case in that it did not use this check. The Sniper was allowed to attack players that were hiding behind an obstacle by throwing projectiles over it. So, instead of a simple line trace to target, the Sniper calculated the trajectory its projectile would travel if thrown at the target and traced along that trajectory. If the trace successfully reached the target, then that target would be detected. A special case on top of a special case was the space variant of the Sniper, which flies up to hover above the ground before firing its projectile. The additional height was taken into account for the projectile trajectory trace too, which resulted in situations where the Space Sniper looked very intelligent as it flew up into the air to fire down at a player hiding behind an obstacle.

5.4   ALERT

A system that works in tandem with detection is the Alert System. Enemies have two high-level behaviour states: Idle and Fight, which the Alert System manages. Idle is the default state of an enemy and the state they return to automatically after a short duration when not detecting a target. In the Idle state, enemies either stand on the spot, patrol along a hand-placed spline, or patrol randomly inside of a placed volume. When an enemy detects a target, it immediately stops what it is doing and enters the Fight state, which contains the bulk of the behaviour flow for the enemy. When an enemy enters the Fight state it plays a "Notice" animation to indicate it has detected a player, and then begins the rest of its behaviour.

We have already established that for a target to be detected by an enemy it must be within the enemy's detection/vision wedge. This led to a problem when there were several enemies grouped close to each other. As the player approached the group, the closest enemy to the player would detect them first and react. For the other enemies the player would still be outside of their detection range and so they would not react at all. This caused the enemies that did not detect the player to look quite oblivious as they idled around as their comrade charged off into battle alone. To address this problem *alert propagation* was introduced, meaning when an enemy detected a target and its alert state changed to Fight, it would propagate out the Fight state to all other enemies within range of itself, which set them to their Fight state as well. A speed was added to the propagation to make it act like an expanding wave instead of instantly affecting all enemies within the area, and with that, we had a simple system that made our enemies appear much more intelligent. Instead of the initial enemy just charging off on their own, their nearby comrades would react too. The wave propagation, as well as vocalisation sound effects that enemies played during the notice animation, made it appear that each enemy was informing their neighbours about the foe, and helped contextualise this propagation nicely.

In the Idle state, enemies used the limited-angle detection wedges as described earlier. However, in the Fight state they instead used full circles with a much larger range (up to double the range). This not only meant that once an enemy detected a target and entered Fight state it would not immediately lose that target again if they moved slightly away, but it also meant that enemies that were put into Fight state via alert propagation would often immediately detect the target that caused the initial propagation through the normal detection system.

A final element of the Detection and Alert systems not yet discussed is something called a *sixth sense range*. This was a very short-range 360° detection area that each enemy had around them in addition to their main detection wedge. An issue that had been observed was that the player could walk up to an enemy from behind (in their normal wedge's blind spot) and even touch the enemy without it reacting. Simply adding this very short-range detection area around each enemy prevented this situation without feeling unfair to the player. If they had snuck up behind the enemy, there would always be ample time to attack before the enemy could respond. Image 5.2 shows an example of the final detection regions for an enemy in the Idle and Fight states, including the sixth sense range visible in the Idle state.

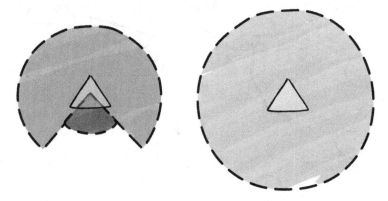

IMAGE 5.2 Example detection regions for an enemy in Idle state (left) and Fight state (right).

Overall, the Detection and Alert systems were quite successful in making the enemies appear reasonably intelligent in most situations. Additionally, due to limited target caching during the attack logic, players could briefly break line of sight or run around corners without enemies instantly losing or forgetting about them.

5.5   HOOK POINTS

To attack a player, enemies generally need to move towards them by either walking, jumping, spinning, or charging. A problem they encountered was that since they are all converging on a single point (the player), they would pack tightly together and get into each other's way, not only blocking each other but hitting and knocking back other enemies with attacks meant for the player. For example: the Rammer would charge through the other enemies, knocking them away, and the Sniper's projectiles would hit enemies instead of the player. This meant that enemies would appear bumbling and would constantly interfere with each other, which made these situations a bit of an unreadable mess. A solution to this problem is to get the enemies to spread out more around the player, which would decrease how often they would interfere with each other. The Hook Point System was designed to handle this.

Eight points were defined in an even circle around the player, independent of the player's rotation. Enemies could register with the Hook Point System and would be assigned the "best" Hook Point that was not currently in use, or "occupied". The heuristic for the "best" Hook Point was the Hook Point for which the angle between the direction from the enemy to the player, and the direction from the enemy to the Hook Point was smallest. In Image 5.3, Hook Point A is the best for this enemy since θA is smaller than θB.

IMAGE 5.3   Hook Point A is "better" than Hook Point B as θA is smaller than θB.

With an enemy registered to a Hook Point, when it wanted to move towards the player, the enemy would instead move towards their assigned Hook Point. This spread the enemies out compared to when they were all moving directly towards the player. Hook points were not a fixed distance from the player; instead, the distance of the Hook Point would change based on the enemy assigned to it, with ranged enemies using larger distances. This meant that ranged enemies would naturally stay further away from the player, which was ideal behaviour. Even for enemies like the Rammer that did not use its assigned Hook Point directly for movement – it would always charge directly at the player, having the Rammer still assigned to a Hook Point encouraged other enemies to stay out of its way, since they would be moving towards their own Hook Points. For the same reason, this spreading out of enemies also reduced incidences of the Sniper hitting comrades with its projectile.

To further aid separation a Weighting system was added so adjacent Hook Points would not be assigned when possible. This meant that the first four enemies would not get adjacent Hook Points, instead being assigned Hook Points spread around the player. Only from the fifth registered enemy onwards would the remaining four Hook Points be filled. Compare the two simple examples in Image 5.4, one using the Hook Point System and the other not. Without Hook Points, all the enemies converge together while moving to the same target and get into each other's way. Using Hook Points and the Weighting system they instead spread out, reducing enemy-enemy interference, and making them look much more intelligent.

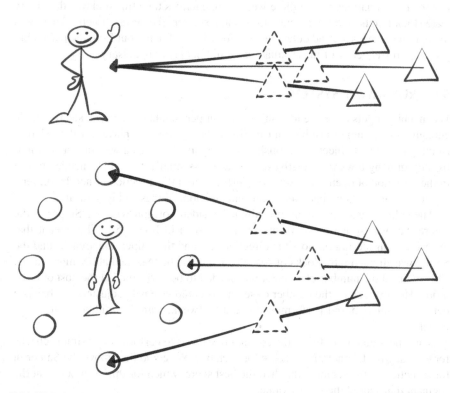

IMAGE 5.4 Examples of enemies moving towards a player, without using Hook Points the enemies converge together whereas with Hook Points they spread out.

An issue with the described system is that as the player and the enemies move, the optimal Hook Point for each enemy changes, meaning that if you do not regularly update which Hook Point each enemy is assigned to, you would end up with the enemies all trying to cross over each other's path. The solution was to let an enemy swap to an unoccupied Hook Point if it was better than their current one – with a cooldown between swaps. However, as the Hook Points fill up this does not help too much since there are less free Hook Points to be swapped to, and they are often not better than their current Hook Point. To alleviate this, a random enemy with a registered Hook Point was selected each frame to see if swapping its Hook Point with any other registered enemy would be beneficial (i.e., if the swap is strictly better for both enemies, or the swap would reduce the total angular distance between the enemies and their Hook Points). Since there were only ever up to eight registered enemies, this would quickly resolve multiple enemies getting stuck with bad Hook Points.

On the whole this system worked quite well and did not require much tuning. Enemies looked more intelligent in their movements without looking unnatural and were not getting hit by each other anywhere near as much as before. Eight Hook Points was a good trade-off in terms of angular separation and the number of enemies supported (most combat encounters had fewer than eight enemies per player). For the rare situations where there were more enemies targeting a player than there were Hook Points, additional enemies would just target the player directly. There was the option to have a second outer shell of Hook Points further out from the player, but given the infrequency of those situations, it did not prove necessary.

5.6   RUN-AWAY SYSTEM

When a player gets too close to a Sniper, the Sniper should run away. It seems simple enough, but we cannot just have it run directly away from the player for the risk of it running directly at objects, or foolishly trapping itself against a wall instead of intelligently moving towards a nearby open space. Essentially, the Sniper needed to run in the direction of open space that was furthest from the direction of nearby players, and to do this in a way that was performant and looked reasonably natural.

The solution was to use an axis-aligned n-sided polygon with the Sniper at the centre that was split into segments as can be seen in Image 5.5. This meant that instead of considering all possible directions around the Sniper, the area around the Sniper was divided into blocks of space which could be reasoned about more easily. This reduced the number of calculations needed to be performed at the cost of resolution. However, since the number of segments could be easily adjusted, the balance between resolution and performance could be tweaked until a middle-ground was found.

With the segments defined, the core approach was to perform some simple checks for each segment, generating a score for each one. We could then move the Sniper in the direction of the segment that had the best score, which for this system meant the segment that scored the lowest value.

For each segment the first check was to see if there was a player inside it, and if there was, then the segment would be marked as occupied and the segment's score would be incremented by the player's distance to the Sniper.

Next, a check was performed using the navigation mesh to look for obstacles. A ray cast from the Sniper was projected for a set distance along the centre of each segment, and if the ray cast found an obstacle (i.e., an edge/gap in the navigation mesh) then the segment would be marked as blocked and would not be considered further. This prevented the Sniper from running too close to walls or other obstacles.

After those checks, the scores for the unoccupied segments were calculated. This involved checking both of each segments' neighbouring segments. For each occupied neighbouring segment, that neighbour's score would be added to the segment in question's score. Essentially what this did was make unoccupied segments next to player-occupied segments be less attractive to the Sniper.

With all the scoring done, the lowest scoring segment was selected. An unoccupied segment would always be selected over an occupied segment if two or more segments scored the same.

The exact details of the scoring system are perhaps somewhat irrelevant as there are several methods that could have led to the same outcomes. What is more important is the resulting behaviour we got from this method. Due to the navigation mesh check, the Sniper would never move too close to obstructions. Segments containing players are scored based on the distance to the player, meaning the Sniper is less likely to move towards players that are closer to it, and if the Sniper must move towards a player, it will move towards the player that is furthest away. Unoccupied segments between or next to player-occupied segments are scored worse, which further discourages the sniper from running in the direction of players when it does not need to. When choosing between running towards an occupied segment and an unoccupied segment, it will always choose the latter. An additional step at the end was that if there were multiple segments with a perfect score of zero, then the largest group of such segments would be selected instead of a single segment.

Once the "best" segment, or group of segments, had been decided, the Sniper then needed to choose where it would actually move to. When a group of segments was selected, the Sniper would run in the direction of the centre of that group. However, for the case of a single best segment, if the Sniper was to always run along the centre of that segment, then especially with lower numbers of segments it could make the Sniper's movements look robotic and unnatural. This was made less noticeable by letting the Sniper run along the left or right edges of the segment as well as the centre, as long as the neighbour that shared that edge was unoccupied. This effectively doubled the possible directions the Sniper could run, which along with some simple interpolation when changing direction, resulted in much more natural motion.

To visualise how this worked, take a look at Image 5.5 where the Sniper is depicted at the centre of the segments. There are two players, each in different segments around the Sniper. The colour of the segment indicates its score, with a darker colour indicating a higher (worse) score. The Sniper chooses to move in the direction of the centre of the best-scoring group of segments.

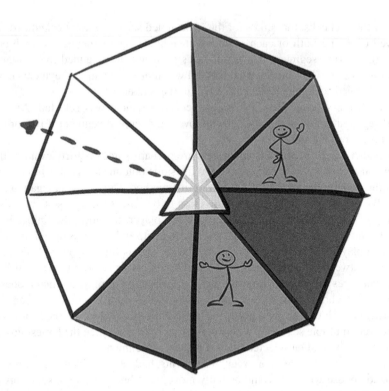

IMAGE 5.5   The Run-Away System with the Sniper at the centre and two players positioned nearby.

This system resulted in natural-looking movement that made the Sniper appear moderately intelligent in how it ran away. The limited-range navigation checks made the Sniper follow boundaries like walls or corners nicely which made it quite fun to chase after. The system is very performant (mostly simple vector maths and just one navigation ray cast per segment when calculating the scores) and given the density of objects in the levels as well as the Sniper's movement speed, only eight segments were needed and were re-scored once per second to get good results. The fidelity of the system could easily be improved by increasing the number of segments, and the frequency in which the scores were updated.

5.7   CONCLUSION

Maybe one of the most interesting things concerning game AI is how you can achieve seemingly complex behaviours by the combination of simple systems. Hopefully, a small glimpse of that can be seen through the systems described here; each one was built up from a few simple calculations and checks which were added to and refined over time as weaknesses and undesired behaviours were observed. As always in games, it is a case of smoke and mirrors to build up a cohesive whole, and perhaps it can be said that if no one comments on the AI and it fades into the background of the main gameplay experience, then you have done a good job.

6 Squad Behaviour Using a Task Stack Approach for *Call of Duty: Strike Team*

Richard Bull

6.1 INTRODUCTION

Call of Duty: Strike Team was a mobile-first. It was a completely original single-player title set within the *Call of Duty* universe. On the development team, several of the coders had previously enjoyed a lot of success utilising the MARPO methodology (Laming, 2008) when developing the AI on previous projects, such as *Grand Theft Auto: Chinatown Wars*. This chapter covers the architecture that underpins everything the AI can do in *Call of Duty: Strike Team*, how it evolved from the MARPO methodology and the benefits of this approach.

6.2 THE MARPO METHODOLOGY

In the high-level interpretation of these methodologies, every non-player character (NPC) has a task hub. This hub contains several task stacks, ranked by priority, and the task at the head of the highest-ranking stack is the one that is currently executing, providing the NPC with their current behaviour. These tasks can be as simple, or as complex, as the developer requires, and are often finite state machines (FSM) or hierarchical finite state machines (HFSM) in their own right.

The pushing of new tasks can occur at any time, from any gameplay system. This leads to a surprisingly powerful and adaptive behavioural framework for such a simple concept, although maintaining game system abstraction externally from the task hub and tasks themselves can be challenging.

Ambient pedestrian behaviour in a sandbox game such as *Grand Theft Auto* lends itself beautifully to this framework and will be used as an example as the approach is described in very basic terms.

DOI: 10.1201/9781003324102-6

Image 6.1 depicts an example snapshot of a NPC's task hub, beginning with a 'Daily routine' task on the 'Planning' (lowest priority) task stack. 'Daily routine' pushes the 'Office worker' task onto the 'Action' task stack, the next priority up, which automatically makes 'Office worker' the new executing behaviour task. Next, the 'Office Worker' task spawns the 'Commute to work' task, which in turn spawns the 'Drive' task. This is simple goal-oriented action planning at work. Lower density tasks to achieve the current objective could be spawned if required. Each stacked task pauses the one beneath it in the stack, and once the current task is finished (or fails), it will unwind back down the stack again to see if each underlying task in turn has more to do before it, too, self-terminates. Finally, just to make this example even more interesting, this NPC is hit with something whilst executing the 'Drive car' task, and a reactive task (the highest priority) is applied to deal with a 'Recoil' task. This will apply any reactive behaviour required to deal with having been hit, pausing the 'Drive car' task, before completing and re-awakening the 'Drive car' task again. At this point, the NPC can decide if they still feel like driving to work after all!

IMAGE 6.1   Ambient pedestrian behaviour.

6.3   THE FRAMEWORK

A single task can be described as an interface or an abstract/pure virtual class, with a few methods to fill in. See Code Listing 6.1.

The Update method returns the current state of the task, so that the calling code knows whether the task is still active or has finished with success or failure. This is achieved using a simple enum, which has been supplied in Code Listing 6.2.

Code Listing 6.1: iTask Interface

```
public interface iTask
{
        public string    GetDebugName();
        public TaskState Update(float deltaTime);

        public void      OnSleep();
        public void      OnAwake();
}
```

Code Listing 6.2: Task State Enum

```
public enum TaskState
{
    Active,
    Failed,
    Succeeded
}
```

The task stack is a wrapper around a stack of tasks, surprisingly enough, with a few simple utility functions. Code Listing 6.3 supplies all the functionality for this wrapper.

Code Listing 6.3: The Task Stack Class

```
public class TaskStack
{
    public Stack<iTask> Tasks { get; private set; }
    public TaskStack()
    {
        Tasks = new Stack<iTask>();
    }
    public void AddTask(iTask task)
    {
        Tasks.Push(task);
    }
    public void PopTask()
    {
        if (Tasks.Count > 0)
        {
            Tasks.Pop();
        }
        else
        {
            LogError("Stack has no tasks to pop!");
        }
    }
    public iTask GetActiveTask()
    {
        if (Tasks.Count > 0)
        {
```

```
                return Tasks.Peek();
        }
        else
        {
                return null;
        }
    }
    public iTask[] GetTasks()
    {
            return Tasks.ToArray();
    }
    public bool HasTasks()
    {
            return Tasks.Count > 0;
    }
}
```

Finally, the task hub holds our three prioritised stacks, and manages the runtime logic of determining the currently active task, pausing any previously active task if it has changed, updating it, and checking if it is still running after doing so. If it has stopped, it is popped from its stack, and the next active task is unpaused. The functionality for the task hub is provided in Code Listing 6.4.

6.4   TASK GENERATION FROM PERCEPTION

The previous section defined what our task system looks like but does not specify any details about how tasks are generated and applied, and from where. One of the main reasons for this is that we remain open to tasks being generated from anywhere in our gameplay codebase. This may sound somewhat unmanaged and chaotic, but it is surprisingly powerful and can lead to some very effective, natural, and reactive behaviour.

Consider the example described earlier, with the 'Recoil' task on the reactive stack. In our gameplay logic which resolves a gunshot, for example, you might choose to implement something similar to the code supplied in Code Listing 6.5.

This means that no matter what behaviour the NPC was currently executing, a reactive task has now taken priority. It means that firstly, we do not have to add custom handling into every task for how we should respond if we have just been hit by something, or killed, and secondly, for something like a blocking 'Dead' task, it means that, if the NPC happens to get resurrected at some point in the future, it could theoretically unwind right back into the behaviour it was doing before it died. The NPC essentially has a historical behaviour it can pick up.

With such an open architecture, there is inevitably going to be some risk of different systems or tasks attempting to force a reactive task onto a stack when the current task does not want it to. For example: imagine that some task chooses to respond to events from the perception system, maybe the NPC has just perceived an enemy. The task it is

Code Listing 6.4: The Task Hub Class

```
public class TaskHub

{
    public TaskStack Planning { get { return m_Planning; } }
    private TaskStack m_Planning = new TaskStack();

    public TaskStack Action { get { return m_Action; } }
    private TaskStack m_Action = new TaskStack();

    public TaskStack Reactive { get { return m_Reactive; } }
    private TaskStack m_Reactive = new TaskStack();

    private iTask m_PreviousTask;

    public void Update()
    {
        var activeStack = GetActiveStack();

        iTask activeTask = null;
        if (activeStack != null)
        {
            activeTask = activeStack.GetActiveTask();
        }

        if (activeTask != null)
        {
            if ((m_PreviousTask != null) &&
                (m_PreviousTask != activeTask))
            {
                m_PreviousTask.OnSleep();
            }

            var state = activeTask.Update(deltaTime);
            m_PreviousTask = activeTask;

            if ((state == TaskState.Succeeded) ||
                (state == TaskState.Failed))
            {
                activeStack.PopTask();

                var wakingTaskStack = GetActiveStack();
                if (wakingTaskStack != null)
                {
                    var wakingTask = wakingTaskStack.GetActiveTask();
                    wakingTask.OnAwake();
                    // In case we're put back to sleep again
                    // between now and the next update.
                    m_PreviousTask = wakingTask;
                }
            }
        }
    }

    private TaskStack GetActiveStack()
    {
        if (Reactive.HasTasks())
```

```
            {
                return Reactive;
            }
            else if (Action.HasTasks())
            {
                return Action;
            }
            else if (Planning.HasTasks())
            {
                return Planning;
            }

            return null;
        }
    }
```

Code Listing 6.5: Recoil Function Example

```
if (damage > 0)
{
    target.HitPoints -= damage;
    if (target.HitPoints <= 0)
    {
        targetTaskHub.Reactive.AddTask(new TaskDead(target));
    }
    else
    {
        targetTaskHub.Reactive.AddTask(new TaskRecoil(target));
    }
}
```

currently processing may want to handle (or choose to ignore) this internally. It could be running a custom animation task, which wants to blend to a custom 'alerted' animation state appropriate to itself, rather than allowing a reactive task to be pushed and coping with potentially unnecessary additional checking for the same result when re-awakening. There is no right or wrong answer to the approach here, simply whichever produces the least amount of code is likely to provide the most amount of elegance!

6.5   SOLDIER BEHAVIOUR

With the behavioural framework defined, and an example of how it could be applied to a pedestrian in an open-world sandbox, what about managing the behaviour of a soldier in combat? Particularly one that might be part of a unit team, which is itself part of an army that might be receiving high-level orders from above.

A classic high-level approach to this kind of wargame behaviour management is to tier the logic into hierarchical order management, as seen in Image 6.2.

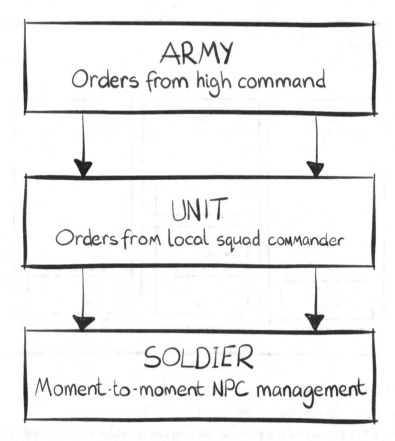

IMAGE 6.2 Classic high-level approach to war game behaviour management.

Our task system structure fits neatly into the Soldier level of this hierarchy – self management of reactive behaviour, whilst maintaining a historical knowledge base of retained decisions. In fact, all that is needed is a 'Planning' task, something analogous to the 'Daily routine' in the pedestrian example, where the soldier can distribute himself Action tasks based on perception, history, and knowledge. To develop a fully autonomous soldier like the task hub snapshot shown in Image 6.3 our soldier simply needs to ask:

- Do I perceive an enemy?
- Do I remember encountering an enemy recently, and if so where might they be now?
- What intrinsic knowledge do I have of my current world that I can use to make decisions about what to do next?

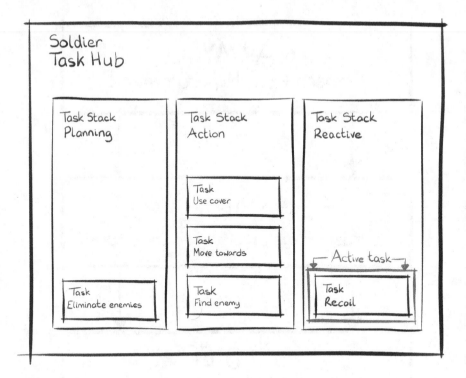

IMAGE 6.3   Soldier task hub snapshot of behaviour stacks.

Although this is fine and is a great default template or fallback behavioural system to drop an NPC into a world with, it has one major flaw. This soldier is not a team player, and without further artificially tethering them, it could potentially wander off autonomously around the world of its own volition, hunting for enemies. This ultimately leaves them incapable of acting in a fully coordinated manner (the *Unit* tier of order management), and their high command management (the *Army* tier) is also going to be a problem to solve.

6.6   THE UNIT COMMANDER

To maintain the planning task methodology and allow the soldier to continue to act with a certain degree of autonomy as supplied by the task system, a new planning task was developed that could allow for self-generation of actions but was from a source which had a constant knowledge base of the team in which the soldier existed. This resulted in the 'Commandeered' task being pushed onto the stack. Literally all this task does, is to request orders from the virtual commander, as can be seen in Code Listing 6.6.

Code Listing 6.6: Commandeered Task

```
public TaskState Update(float deltaTime)
{
        return m_Commander.RequestOrders(m_Owner, m_ActionTaskStack);
}
```

As for the virtual commander itself, there is no reason why this could not be distributed from another soldier running another bespoke task for this very purpose, for added simulated realism. If you follow this to its logical conclusion, there is no reason why another soldier could not poke tasks directly on to a team members' action task stacks and bypass the 'Commandeered' task altogether. But, by having the 'Commandeered' task be responsible for asking our commander for orders, it allows for a certain degree of additional autonomy to be engineered into an individual soldier's behaviour.

Whichever approach you choose, the commander logic can ultimately distribute an order to the member of its team requesting such, based on the 'bigger picture' knowledge it has at its dispersal. For example: suppose our updated review of our team positions and our known enemy positions generates us a series of outflank positions, which could then be used to coordinate a team flanking manoeuvre. When an individual team member then asks for their next order, the commander could pick the best position for them, with the knowledge of where his teammates are, without each of the individual soldiers needing to perform any coordinated analysis and prediction of their own. The commander can then subsequently manage holding them in position and timing a coordinated attack.

By executing the behaviour in this manner, the 'Commandeered' task can run as long as the commander is active or willing and able to distribute orders, and if this should expire for any reason, this planning task can be popped from the soldier's planning task stack, and they can revert to their default autonomous behaviour.

6.7 BESPOKE BEHAVIOURAL MANAGEMENT

The system described thus far provides the fundamentals for a framework to handle intelligent and cooperative squad-based behaviour for our NPCs, but there is one component missing. What if our game requires more scripted behaviour. For example: enemies sitting at a table playing cards, or a patrolling enemy walking the perimeter of a building, or an enemy who, even though he has sensed danger, is compelled for gameplay reasons to stay put at all costs and engage only from their spawn position. Each of these scenarios can be handled as a task on their respective stacks. And even if some or all these scenarios eventually result in the NPC cancelling their scripted rigid behaviour and joining in with the 'Commandeered' task, they all add to the greater game world immersion. Each of these tasks will sit on the planning stack, on top of the default combat behaviours that we would therefore unwind to.

6.7.1 THE ANIMATION TASK

Despite its simplicity, the animation task is very powerful in terms of general usefulness, and if it is created with enough abstraction, will become a staple of creating interesting default set-piece behaviours for NPCs to exhibit before they fall back into the self-managed combat behaviours.

Every placed NPC the player may come across in the game world could potentially be running this task on their action stack as part of their initialisation, and this could result in anything from them casually leaning against a wall, smoking a cigarette or even as part of a larger multi-NPC group animation, such as the example given of a group of soldiers playing cards at a table.

A paired animation sequence requiring at least two interacting NPCs is something a little more complex in terms of requirements, and this will be covered next. This task is merely for a single NPC with no other NPC dependencies.

The animation task will be popped either by perception events or through re-awakening from a completed reactive task such as a hit reaction. In the latter case, the NPC may not be able to effectively resume its previous task even if it wanted to. For example: a hit recoil probably does not want to behaviourally switch straight back to lighting up another cigarette!

6.7.2 THE PAIRED ANIMATION TASK

Call of Duty: Strike Team required set pieces where two NPCs could be interacting in some way, perhaps having a conversation, or shaking hands. To achieve this, both NPCs running their own individual tasks need to be linked in some way. This is so that if one of the NPCs happens to break out or suppress their animation task, by being startled or shot, the other one immediately knows to self-terminate their own running task, preventing them from continuing and looking ridiculous. For this, the 'Paired' task was developed and runs on both NPCs, which reference back to each other. The implementation of this is very simple. The first NPC running the 'Paired' task needs to play their animation and keep a record of the frame number, and a reference to the second NPC's 'Paired' task for monitoring purposes. The second NPC running the 'Paired' task needs to take a reference to the paired task of the first so that they can monitor the frame number, and synchronise their own playback to match, much like a server-client architecture in networking. If either task is put to sleep or terminated, the link is broken, and the paired NPC should immediately cease their 'Paired' task as well. This task relationship architecture is quite powerful in its simplicity and usefulness and can be used in many different scenarios.

6.7.3 THE PATROL TASK

The patrol task gives both life to a spawned NPC and scripted movement to facilitate stealth gameplay. All that is required here is a referenceable data object containing a list of sequential and/or randomised world position markers, and for the 'Patrol' task itself to manage pathfinding to a current marker, reaching it within some acceptable tolerance, and moving onto the next. On occasion, having some scripted animation playback on reaching a marker also adds quite a bit to the perception of intelligence. For example: having the NPC pause and look around or stopping to light up a cigarette.

Unlike the 'Animation' or 'Paired' tasks, it is possibly more likely that the NPC may desire to return to the 'Patrol' task if it is paused due to being alerted by perception. For example: if the NPC hears the player make a noise, out of line-of-sight. If it is not already in an alert state, which would be the case if they were running their base high-level 'Eliminate enemies' or 'Commandeered' tasks, then this event may directly push an 'Alerted' task, which puts the 'Patrol' task to sleep. The 'Alerted' task could then make use of a 'Flush out enemy' action task, initialised with data from the perception event. If these tasks were then to unwind without an engagement task causing the NPC to ever become fully alerted, and the 'Patrol' task is resumed, it may be intelligent to simply pick up from the nearest patrol marker and continue. This is a great example of how the task stacks can quickly become relatively complex in terms of iterating towards a goal, and then naturally unwind to a base historical state.

6.7.4 THE SENTRY TASK

There will be occasions where you do not want an enemy NPC to engage with the player, but simply to spawn in a specific location and remain just there. This might be for the purposes of a sniping spot, or it might just be that you want to guarantee that when the player goes around a specific corner, they will come face-to-face with this NPC. This is only possible if you know the NPC in question will not have taken it upon themselves to go off investigating a curious noise in the meantime.

The 'Animation' task could potentially be used for this purpose, but the intention is that, when finished, that task will wind back into a default and fully featured 'Eliminate enemies' or 'Commandeered' planning task. Therefore, the 'Sentry' task would either sit on top of those on the planning stack and potentially never complete, complete in extreme circumstances (the player runs past the NPC without engaging them, and they need to give chase), or replace those original core planning tasks altogether. It would then, whilst in operation, simply dish out 'Shoot', or, at best, 'Alerted look-at' tasks as targets come into range or view.

6.8 CONCLUSION

In this chapter, was outlined the core technical framework used with success in *Call of Duty: Strike Team*. The toy box of tasks used to implement these behaviours has been presented, and the relationship between the tasks themselves explained, along with the underlying gameplay engine. This approach allowed for agents to be both tightly scripted and intelligently procedural.

REFERENCE

Laming, B. (2008) *The MARPO Methodology: Planning and Orders, AI Game Programming Wisdom 4*, edited by Steve Rabin. Charles River Media, pp. 239–255.

7 Reactive Behaviour Trees

Sarat Rallabandi and Paul Roberts

7.1 INTRODUCTION

While working on a yet to be announced title, the AI team hit a snag. Behaviour trees were the decision-making architecture of choice, but they are not reactive. And for a tree to respond to an event, the response, and the conditions leading up to it, must be part of the tree. Reactive Behaviour Trees (RBT) were designed to solve this problem, but before delving too deeply into the problem this architecture aims to solve and why you would choose to implement this approach, we need to take a brief look at traditional behaviour trees.

7.2 BEHAVIOUR TREES

Behaviour trees have been around for a while. They were originally developed by Damian Isla as an improvement on Finite State Machines (FSM) in the development of *Halo 2* (Isla, 2005). Since then, they have been used in a wide range of games and had numerous articles and had research papers written about them. Behaviour trees are now the preferred approach for AI behaviours across the industry. Epic's Unreal Engine even has them built into the engine.

Traditionally, behaviour trees are graphs with a bunch of composite nodes that dictate the type of execution (branch nodes, in normal tree terminology), and behaviour/task nodes (leaf nodes), that execute some kind of logic, or more colloquially 'do things'. They are almost always associated with a blackboard, which is essentially a common data store for trees to share data amongst one another. A blackboard has a one-to-many relationship with behaviour trees, meaning that a single blackboard can be associated to multiple behaviour trees but each behaviour tree can only ever be associated with the one blackboard. This greatly adds to the flexibility of the system because data can be set in one agent's behaviour tree and then be used by another agent in a completely different behaviour tree.

On each update, the tree evaluates which task node is the best one to execute and goes through all the nodes in order, usually from top to bottom and left to right, until a particular task node returns true. The most commonly used composite nodes and a brief description of their purpose are as follows:

- Sequence – These composite nodes execute each of their child nodes from left to right until all of them return success.
- Selector/Fallback – These composite nodes execute each of their child nodes in any order until at least one of them returns success.

DOI: 10.1201/9781003324102-7

- Parallel – These composite nodes execute the child nodes at the same time. These composite nodes return success when some number m of n number of child nodes succeed and returns false when all n child nodes fail. The term 'parallel' is used but the process is not usually true parallelism. It is more akin to a coroutine. For example: on each tick, each child class will individually tick in sequence from left to right and be suspended until the next tick.

In addition to the blackboard, there are decorator nodes that usually modify a child node with a unique policy, for example, using the Loop/Repeat decorator at the root of a subtree to repeat a certain subtree or using the Invert decorator to flip success to failure and vice-versa. There are others, but this is plenty to get the point across.

Combining all the nodes mentioned above, one can create a great looking AI agent quickly. So, let us do just that.

7.2.1 Patrolling Example with Traditional Behaviour Trees

Imagine you are developing a strategy game and have set up a group of units to patrol around the perimeter of your base camp. The group of units will, ideally, have a 'leader' who will be running a behaviour tree, with all other agents following their lead. The first thing we need to do is to set up the blackboard. In this case, our blackboard will have a couple of items – the current patrol location and a list of all patrol locations.

From the root of the tree, we add a selector, and its first leaf node could be a task node called 'UpdatePatrolList' that checks to see if the list of patrol points is empty, which on the very first iteration would be. This list will be populated with data from the world using some form of query system.

From the second iteration onwards the patrol list does not need updating, so a branch that allows our agent to enact the patrol is needed. Next, a sequence node can be added to the selector whose child nodes will be a task node to set the current patrol location. A task node named 'MoveTo' can then be added that will move the agent to the designated patrol location and a task node named 'Wait' that will have the agent wait at the location for a set time. A depiction of the resulting behaviour tree can be seen in Image 7.1.

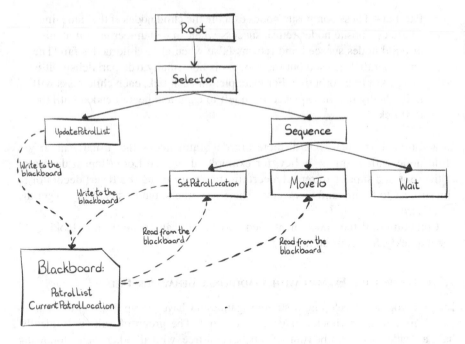

IMAGE 7.1   Basic patrolling behaviour tree.

The blackboard in the bottom left of Image 7.1 is there only as a visual aid to show how the blackboard acts as a data store for the entire tree. In the later examples, the blackboard will not be visualised, but if any task is referring to a value, then it is most likely getting/setting it from/in the blackboard.

A good addition to this basic patrolling behaviour would be to have a behaviour to attack any enemy units that are close by. The perception systems will take care of setting a target in the blackboard, so all this behaviour needs to do is to move to said target and attack if a target is available. Image 7.2 depicts how the behaviour tree now looks.

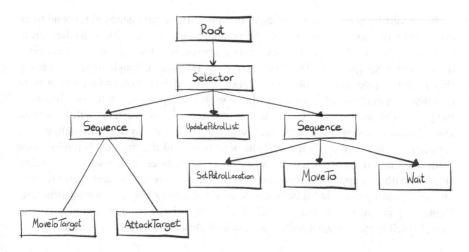

IMAGE 7.2 Patrolling tree with attack logic.

The reason the new attack sequence has been added before the rest of the nodes is because that is the order in which a behaviour tree executes. Remember, the tree executes from top to bottom and left to right. The agent should attack the enemy if the target is set. Only if the target is not set should it continue its patrol. So far so good. All of this seems like sound system design. So, what is the problem?

Well, this is a very simple example. In a more tactical game, there will be a lot more things to consider. For example:

- Are there items in the environment that can be used to the agent's advantage (Oil drums, crates of explosives, and the like)?
- Is this the right time to call in reinforcements (Air support, backup, etc.)?
- Should they retreat?
- Should long-ranged units fire at the oncoming target or pull back and let the melee units defend them?

Depending upon the game, the problem only gets worse when using behaviour trees for the AI. Consider a first person or third person shooter where we need to consider the following:

- Is the player in cover?
- Do they have allies?
- Is there a way to flank the player?
- Does the agent have enough grenades to blast the player out of cover?
- Is the player in an armoured vehicle?
- Can the AI do anything against armoured vehicles?
- The list goes on.

To be fair, you may not want all the above, but you can see where this is going. Things can get very complicated very quickly, and this is not even considering the different archetypes of enemies you may have in your game.

Behaviour trees are also not reactive in nature. If the tree needs to respond to an event that can happen in the world, the response, and the conditions leading up to it, must be part of the tree. This exhaustive approach is the reason why behaviour trees in big AAA games end up looking like a giant mass of spaghetti and as a result they become large, unreadable, and cumbersome to debug. You end up with a giant tree that is pruning or executing very large subtrees depending on the conditions of the game. The worst-case scenario is that the execution of decisions will be slowed down because traversing the tree itself will start to tax the system. Sometimes, the subtrees are authored as their own behaviour trees and the 'master' behaviour tree is the one that runs those behaviour trees via a 'RunSubtree' task node or something similar. With this approach, the subtrees become more readable, and it ensures you are not repeating code, but it does not do much else to resolve the overall structure. Debugging is still a pain and traversal, if the tree is large enough, and may still be slow. Which is exactly what led to the development of the RBT architecture.

7.3   REACTIVE BEHAVIOUR TREES

Reactive behaviour trees take inspiration from the MARPO methodology (Lamming, 2008), an architecture that combines tasks (usually individual states) and academic goal-based reasoning to produce believable AI. MARPO is an acronym which stands for Movement, Avoidance, Routing, Planning, and Orders. The core of the 'PO' part of the methodology is self-contained tasks, with limited input and limited output that are arranged in multiple queues or stacks (whichever works for the game). The limited input is the current game state, and the limited output is the action the agent needs to perform. The queues or stacks add an element of 'memory' to the AI as the AI knows what it needs to do next or what it was doing in the past.

Reactive behaviour trees take advantage of MARPO's multiple queue/stack approach, but for small, manageable behaviour trees. In the MARPO approach, a total of three stacks are used. One stack is tagged as the long-term stack, which is basically the agent's end goal. A second stack, called the reactive stack, deals with the agent's response to any world events, and the third is called the immediate stack, which allows the agent to handle the most pressing of concerns. Tasks are pushed onto these stacks by an external monitor, which interrupts the execution of the current active task and pushes a task onto one of the stacks. The immediate stack suppresses the execution of the reactive stack, which in turn suppresses the execution of the long-term stack.

Reactive behaviour trees use only a long-term stack and a reactive stack. More stacks will facilitate different types of reactions but will mean more processing. By having a second stack, you can flush the entire stack if the need arises and drop back to processing the long-term stack. The stacks in this architecture will consist of small, self-contained behaviour trees, rather than individual states as in MARPO.

The execution flow of the Reactive Behaviour Tree architecture is as follows:

- The AI System goes through each agent's update cycle.
- Each agent consists of a Behaviour Tree Component and a Monitor Component

- The behaviour tree component is responsible for the execution of the stacks. Handling the updates of the topmost behaviour tree, backtracking, data storage from the blackboard, handling push and pop calls from the monitor, etc.
- The monitor component is responsible for handling events from various game systems to push or pop behaviour trees to or from the stacks.

The overall system architecture is depicted in Image 7.3.

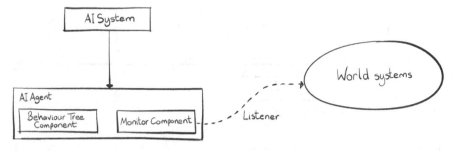

IMAGE 7.3   Overall system architecture.

7.3.1   REACTIVE BEHAVIOUR TREE COMPONENTS

The principle of self-containment is simple to adhere to in RBTs by having behaviour trees that take care of one thing and only one thing. Consider the following: Does the 'Patrolling' behaviour tree need to know if an enemy is visible or not and how to attack them? The answer is no. The behaviour defined in that tree is patrolling, so why not only have that tree handle the logic for patrolling and define a separate tree for how to go about attacking the target(s)?

The long-term stack is the main stack which houses any behaviour trees that the agent would have by default. In the patrolling/attacking examples described earlier, using RBTs we could assign a default patrolling behaviour to the long-term stack to get the simple behaviour shown in Image 7.1. It does not need any of the additional logic that was added in Image 7.2. The RBT would look something like that shown in Image 7.4.

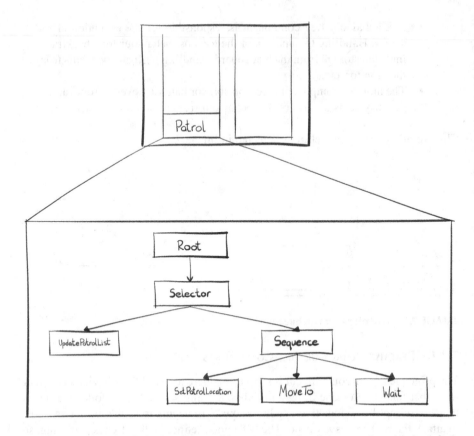

IMAGE 7.4   Reactive Behaviour Tree architecture – showing the two stacks, with the default patrol BT pointing to a version of the simplified BT it consists of.

It is important to note that if an agent had a different purpose they should have a different default behaviour. For example: a sniper has no need to patrol. They will maintain a position and wait for targets, or a more complicated approach could have them hold position for a period of time before seeking out a more advantageous position. Either way, the sniper does not need a default patrolling behaviour. They require something bespoke to them.

The behaviour tree at the top of either stack pushes any additional subtrees it wants to execute onto the current stack. The topmost behaviour tree on the stack would then get the update and the previous behaviour tree goes dormant. Once the execution of the topmost tree is complete it can pop itself off the stack and the execution returns to the previous tree which carries on with its logic. As is clearly demonstrated by the way the execution returns to the parent tree, the element of memory that is evident in the MARPO methodology is maintained.

There is one key element missing – the monitor. The monitor controls the external pushing of behaviour trees onto a relevant stack should an event take place that our specific agent is capable of handling. It is a system that receives notifications from the perception system and/or other world systems of the game and responds only if our specific agent is interested. This means that a monitor is archetype specific. The benefit of this approach is that it allows for different agent types to react differently to world events. For example: a patrolling guard may be interested in the discovery of a dead body, but a sniper may not.

Each behaviour tree has access to the monitor, allowing them to fire events to the monitor themselves, which will then allow the monitor to determine how this particular agent should respond.

7.3.2 PATROLLING EXAMPLE WITH STACK-BASED BEHAVIOUR TREES

Using the same patrolling example as before, while the agent is patrolling, it spots some disturbance and/or noise in the bushes or the tree line nearby. The monitor pushes an 'Investigate' behaviour tree onto the reactive stack, which now receives the update. The 'Patrol' behaviour tree now falls dormant. Image 7.5 depicts the current state of the architecture.

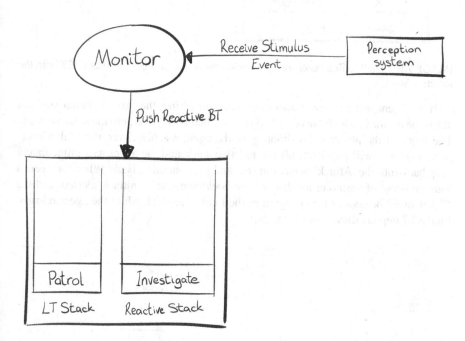

IMAGE 7.5 The Monitor receives a perception event and pushes the 'Investigate' BT onto the Reactive Stack.

The agent goes to the location and scouts to see what the disturbance could have been. If the player makes a sound or becomes visible while the agent is investigating, the 'Investigate' behaviour alerts the monitor of this event, which reacts by pushing an 'Attack' behaviour tree onto the reactive stack. As can be seen in Image 7.6, the current top of the reactive stack pauses execution, and the 'Attack' behaviour begins.

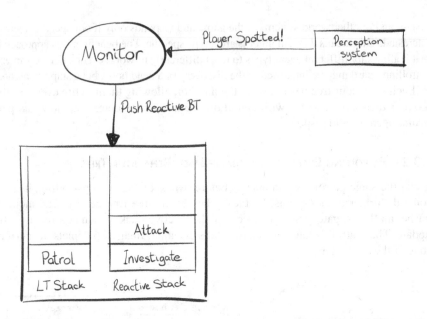

IMAGE 7.6 The Monitor receives a perception event and pushes the 'Attack' BT onto the Reactive Stack.

If the agent starts to come under fire while attacking, the 'Attack' behaviour tree alerts the monitor, which pushes a 'TakeCover' behaviour tree onto the reactive stack. The moment the player stops shooting or the agent reaches cover, the 'TakeCover' behaviour tree will pop itself off the reactive stack and the agent will immediately drop back into the 'Attack' behaviour tree and start shooting back. When the agent's weapon is out of ammo or an ability is on cooldown, the monitor is alerted, and the 'TakeCover' behaviour tree is again pushed onto the stack while the agent reloads. Image 7.7 depicts these two scenarios.

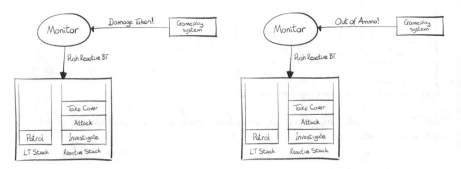

IMAGE 7.7 The Monitor receives the damage/reload event and pushes the 'TakeCover' BT to the Reactive Stack.

While the agent is in cover and reloading, the player cleverly uses stealth to duck away from the battle. Once our agent has finished reloading the 'TakeCover' behaviour tree is popped off the stack, but there is no target to attack, so the 'Attack' behaviour tree pops itself off the stack too. Now the agent drops back into the 'Investigate' behaviour tree. The player stealthily slinks away from the area at this point and the agent fails to find them. At this stage the 'Investigate' behaviour tree pops itself off the reactive stack and the agent goes back to the top of the long-term stack, which was its default, the 'Patrol' behaviour tree.

In the entire scenario, which is depicted in Image 7.8, everything happened without behaviours having any knowledge of how other behaviour tree's function. A behaviour tree such as 'Attack' described above only needs to know that it is taking heavy damage and can send out an alert to the monitor that will prompt the 'TakeCover' behaviour tree being added.

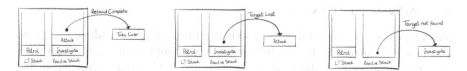

IMAGE 7.8   First the 'TakeCover' BT pops off the stack, then the 'Attack' BT pops off as the target was lost, and then the 'Investigate' BT gets popped off because no new target was found.

7.4   CONSIDERATIONS

One of the huge benefits of this architecture is that it allows the team to create small, manageable behaviour trees that are reusable. However, if you do not hold the line on this, people will continue to develop behaviour trees that are large and unwieldy. This not only defeats the point but makes debugging more difficult than just sticking with the traditional behaviour tree approach.

Before adding a behaviour tree to a stack, it is important to check to see if this behaviour tree is already on a stack somewhere. If that is the case, then do not add it again, instead, remove trees from the stack until you get to the required behaviour.

7.5   CONCLUSION

In traditional behaviour trees, each and every behaviour would need to account for what happens when the agent spots a disturbance, when to get into combat, and all the logic required to handle the fallout. Bringing us right back to the finite state machine like linkage between tasks that behaviour trees were created to avoid. Using the Reactive Behaviour Tree approach, the trees were short and to the point, tree traversal was snappy and debugging compartmentalised and the creation of new behaviour trees was easy.

REFERENCES

Isla, D. (2005) *Handling Complexity in the Halo 2 AI.* GDC Proceedings 2005. Available online: https://www.gamedeveloper.com/programming/gdc-2005-proceeding-handling-complexity-in-the-i-halo-2-i-ai (accessed September 4th, 2022).
Lamming, B. (2008) *The MARPO Methodology: Planning and Orders, AI Game Programming Wisdom 4,* edited by Steve Rabin. Charles River Media, pp. 239–255.

8 Tailoring Racing AI to the Genre

Andy Brown

8.1 INTRODUCTION

Racing games were once the bread and butter of many game studios, and Sumo Digital was no different; in fact, its reputation was built upon the excellent work the studio had done on the game *Outrun: Coast 2 Coast*, a conversion of the much-acclaimed arcade original. Around the beginning of 2008 Sumo was about to go driving game crazy as they began working on a multitude of different driving titles that covered almost every style of racing game. This chapter will explain at a high level the process of developing the AI for each game, what was learned on each title, their similarities, and most importantly their differences and the impact this made.

8.2 ARCADE-STYLE RACING

The first of these titles was *GTI Club+* for the PS3. The task was quite simple – to remaster the original arcade title with modern versions of the original's cars but sticking with the original circuit layout. With the arcade title for reference, the team set about trying to work out how to approach the AI.

First and foremost was laying out the track data for the AI to follow and by association also track where each of the cars were relative to each other. The data itself is relatively simple and was constructed using a left and right vector to mark the edges of the track. By repeating this process at regular intervals, you create track segments that allow you to do some simple maths to work out which segment a car is currently in and how far through that segment it is. This is depicted in Image 8.1.

DOI: 10.1201/9781003324102-8

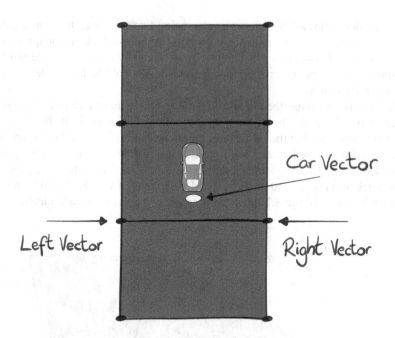

IMAGE 8.1 Track segmentation and car positioning.

Using this approach, you can now work out where human controlled cars are relative to each other and thus interpret their positions on the track. If you assume that one of the segments is the start-finish line, which is a safe assumption to make; you can also track the number of laps each car has completed.

At this stage there is almost a game! But it is still lacking one crucial element. Whilst human players can race each other, the AI has no idea what to do. For an AI controlled car to navigate the track, it needs a point to follow. Ideally this will be the optimal line, otherwise known as the racing line. The track data already contains the left and right edges of the track, so it was possible to extend this to add an additional point for the racing line.

The placement of these points could be placed by hand, given that there was only one track to worry about and these values would not change, but automating the process is so much better. Detailing this is beyond the scope of this chapter, but there are a few algorithms available that do this, one of which is described in great detail by John Manslow in his chapter entitled 'Fast and Efficient Approximation of Racing Lines' (Manslow, 2004).

At this point it is important to note that the handling model for the AI cars was to be the exact same as the human controlled cars. There would be no AI cheating. So, the AI cars would need to point their wheels using the steering wheel much like a human player would as well as applying the accelerator and brake. Working out where to point the wheels is just a case of working out where on the track the vehicle is and looking ahead on the racing line. Whilst doing this and applying a little bit of acceleration the AI could follow the track, but there were a few issues.

Firstly, depending on how far down the racing line you look, different problems arise. The handling model can begin to fishtail if you do not look far enough in front, or it could veer off track if you look too far away. Secondly, at this stage, the cars have absolutely no concept of cornering speeds and will shoot off the track unless they are moving really slowly.

To solve the first issue, the look ahead point should be adjusted based on the speed the car is travelling at. This reduces the fishtailing. The point itself should also be clipped/clamped, so that the car is never told to drive off the track. And by applying some smoothing to the line it can be treated as a spline. To solve the cornering issue, the track data need some additional data. This should include identifying a segment of the track as a *corner* and an ideal speed with which a vehicle should be moving at for each corner. Image 8.2 shows an example of a section of track identified as a *corner*.

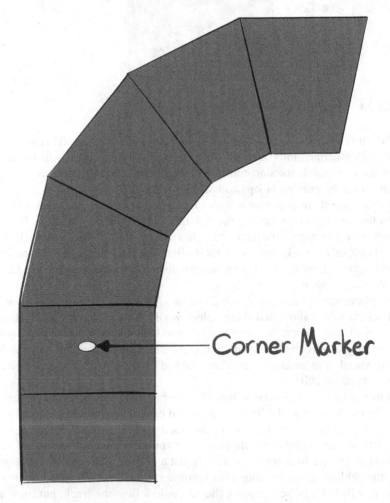

IMAGE 8.2   Additional data required for *corner* segments of track.

To determine the desired cornering speeds, you need to have some human play testers. Whilst the play testers race around the track, you need to record their speeds at each corner. These values can then be used to set appropriate corner speeds in the track data. With this speed data, you can scale them to make the AI vehicle cars easier to race. By working out the distance it will take the AI to reach a certain speed if the brake was applied, the AI can predict when to apply the brake and take the corner on the absolute limit. In reality, this was not quite the case. Any AI coder will tell you that a considerable amount of time is spent tweaking values and this, the development of the AI for *GTI Club+*, was no different. Corner data was moved, speeds were tweaked, even the racing line was modified if it was felt that it was impacting the AI's competitiveness.

The final piece of the puzzle is avoidance. *GTI Club+* is based on rally cars, which means that hand brake turns and cars rubbing up against each other was perfectly acceptable, but the AI should still try to avoid slower moving cars or obstacles. There are a few approaches that can be used here but the solution chosen for *GTI Club+* was to split the track into sections as depicted in Image 8.3. The idea being that the AI would favour the section with the racing line in it but it would also consider other vehicles in close proximity and their relative speeds to give each section of the track a rating. The section of track with the higher rating would be the one it would pick to follow. This produced surprisingly good results; it was crude in places but good enough for this type of game.

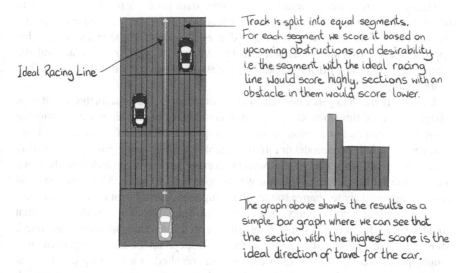

Ideal Racing Line

Track is split into equal segments. For each segment we score it based on upcoming obstructions and desirability. i.e. the segment with the ideal racing line would score highly, sections with an obstacle in them would score lower.

The graph above shows the results as a simple bar graph where we can see that the section with the highest score is the ideal direction of travel for the car.

IMAGE 8.3 Track data split into sections.

8.3   SIMULATION TIME

The next driving title offered a different challenge to that of *GTI Club+*. Codemasters' *F1 2009* had multiple cars, all with different settings that could be tweaked at run-time, and multiple tracks. Despite this, one thing that was needed was the concept of splitting the track into segments with a racing line and corner data, and in fact, it has proven to be suited to more or less all driving games.

All the cars in an F1 game have subtle differences which impact straight line speed and how they approach corners. This presented the team with a bit of a dilemma; the cornering data was generally based around one handling model. Now there were 20 cars on track that could all have different handling characteristics. Did we need corner data for each car? Since the game fell into the simulation category there was also the extra complication of the handling of cars being adjusted at runtime. Whilst wanting to remain true to the goal of making the AI drive in the exact same way as a human would, with so many variables in play a simplified approach was going to be needed.

Since F1 cars by their very nature all have a similar look, it was decided that the handling model would remain consistent no matter which vehicle the AI was controlling. This solved the immediate headache of reducing the corner data down for each track, but *F1 2009* had 17 different circuits. This would be a vast amount of data to create by hand for each track segment designated as a corner. With the handling model evolving constantly and the tracks being worked on daily it became apparent that generating the corner data for each track would need to be automated. Codemasters were using a learning algorithm to send cars around the tracks to work out the optimal speed at each section of the track. Using this approach, no corner data was set, and the AI was allowed to drive around the circuit. If the car flew off the track, the process was repeated until there was some usable data.

Ultimately the data generated reasonably competitive AI but unfortunately it took a huge amount of time to reach this point. It could take hours, even when running the game simulation as fast as possible on a high spec PC. Factor in 17 circuits and any changes to the handling model or circuits meant that the learning process was having to run overnight. To speed up the process, corner markers were added to the track data, so the AI was aware of when it was approaching a corner. This was a manual process, but unlikely to change too much throughout development as the tracks were all based on real world circuits. A modified learning algorithm was then used that could assume that if it was out of range of a corner, maximum speed was assumed, allowing it to concentrate on just the corners. To speed up the learning time further, rough speeds were added for each corner. This resulted in a learning process that could run in a few minutes, which made the data much easier to keep in sync with any handling changes.

The next challenge was avoidance. It was clear that the method used for an arcade racer would not be appropriate for an F1 game. To mimic an F1 driver there were rules that needed to be followed and the AI behaviours needed to be far more complex, which relied on track data that was broken down into more sections.

Navigating these sections required adherence to a few extra rules. Firstly, when driving competitively the AI vehicles could not just go for any gap on the track. If there was a corner coming up and they were behind a slower car they needed to match the other car's speed until a more appropriate time to overtake presented itself – on a straight perhaps. This was of paramount importance on the opening lap of a race where all the cars are hurtling to the same corner, most off the ideal racing line. Without additional work you get complete carnage on the opening lap at the first corner. This does happen from time to time in the real world of course but for a video game it is better if it was avoided. Street circuits also create unique problems. Narrow roads track segments with walls, all with high-speed corners leaving little room for error. To handle these issues, it requires a vast amount of tweaking to values and in some extreme cases labelling some corners as simply not appropriate to try an overtake unless there was a stationary car.

Once the avoidance was in and the AI was competitive, variance to their movement was added. F1 can be a procession at times but subtle differences to racing line offsets on a straight can create a more believable experience. The remainder of the work was driver behaviour and adding in some degree of chance for mistakes, such as braking too early or driving off-line, can give the illusion that the AI is almost human-like.

8.4 AN ARCADE RACER WITH A DIFFERENCE

The next racing title we developed was *Split/Second* on the PSP which was a conversion of the PS3/XBox360 title that was nearing completion. From the offset we decided to only use the upcoming game as the reference rather than trying to cram the code from much more powerful machines onto the PSP. This allowed for a fair degree of freedom with the AI and it borrowed many ideas from the previous titles discussed. The core track data was more than suitable for this genre of game so getting the AI going round a track was straightforward. Again, the handling model for the AI cars was kept consistent to allow for corner speeds so a basic prototype was up and running within a few weeks. Where this title differed from the previous titles discussed was in the layout of the tracks themselves. Each track was made up of a series of short sections of track with some sections being blocked or opening up as the race progressed. This meant the track data itself had to be expanded to cope with alternate routes.

To handle this, the track was chopped up into individual sections. Take a look at Image 8.4. Think of this as a simple A to B section of track, where at the end of each section there is a list of track sections that could be connected. These are then either marked as open or closed depending on the state of the race. It is a simple concept but worked brilliantly in allowing us to define the various course layouts. This simple concept allowed us to create extra track layouts that were not in the original game.

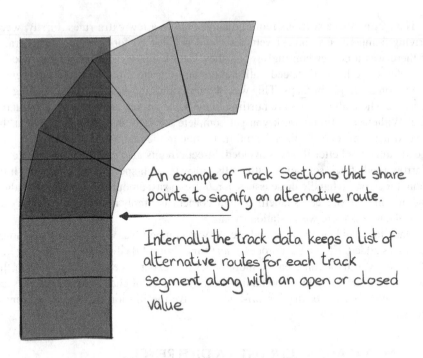

An example of Track Sections that share points to signify an alternative route.

Internally the track data keeps a list of alternative routes for each track segment along with an open or closed value

IMAGE 8.4   Segments of tracks linked to a list of other track segments.

Corner data was hand authored in *Split/Second*. Whilst the learning process from *F1 2009* had proved successful, the many variations of circuit layouts in this title and its dynamic nature meant that it was often quicker to just do it manually.

The avoidance could also be scaled back a little compared to the previous titles discussed. Cars crashing into each other was not ideal, but close racing and cars touching was all part of the game and this reduction in complexity gives you back some precious CPU cycles, which meant that *Split/Second* maintained its desired frame rate.

AI difficulty benefited from the lessons learned from both *GTI Club+* and *F1 2009*. On lower difficulty settings, some cars run slower than they were able to on the straights and corners, but on the higher difficulty settings they would run faster than usual, and on occasion even have additional grip on corners.

Split/Second's unique selling point was in its powerplays and track events which the AI would also be able to trigger. It also had track hazards, parts of the track that blew up, short cuts that opened, and more. This added an extra dimension to the AI difficulty not available in the other titles. With all this chaos, the easy AI would take the longest route possible whilst the harder difficulties would take the shortest. Easy AI would also be less effective in triggering powerplays whereas the harder AI would aim to take you down with expert timing.

Despite what was going on under the hood it never appeared as though the AI was cheating. Catch-up logic was present but ensuring that no AI assists were carried out if human players were around hid it well. Generally, the best place to optimise driving AI performance is to make it as effective as possible with the track's layout, be that the racing line or cornering speeds.

8.5 THE KART RACER

The last racing game of the quartet was the Sega title: *Sonic All Stars Racing Transformed*. This is Sega's answer to Nintendo's *Mario Kart* and features characters and locations from across the Sega universe. *Transformed* was the sequel to *Sonic Racing* but as sequels always need to try and improve upon the original its unique selling point was transforming your kart into a boat and an aeroplane!

Once again, defining the track data was the place to start and the concept of the track being made up of a series of quads remained. However, the tracks in a kart racing game tend to be a little bit wackier than your average racer and this was no different – loop-de-loops, racing upside down, and right-angle corners were all commonplace. The tracks were also very much three dimensional. All the games discussed in this chapter were also three dimensional, but the track data could be treated as though they were only in two dimensions. In fact, the algorithm used for generating baseline racing lines worked with 2D maths. Generating a racing line on a loop-de-loop would not work and thus required the algorithm to be modified somewhat.

For *Sonic All Stars Racing Transformed*, a tool was developed to help author tracks. This tool allowed the designers to lay down track data using splines, not segments as was done in the previous titles. From these splines you could then generate track data in the format the AI required, which was a much simpler process than anything done before. Taking the time to develop such a tool was repaid many times over as it sped up the iteration process of track design, provided an additional bonus of immediately validating the data, whilst also allowing designers to modify the track without any programmer input. With the simple click of a button new AI could be generated.

Navigating the track was achieved in much the same way as the previous titles discussed, where this game differed was when it came to cornering. *Sonic All Stars Racing Transformed* allowed for drifting! Drifting was a core mechanic of a kart's movement which meant that whilst a corner signified a need to slow down, it also meant a vehicle could drift. There was also the bonus that drifting could be achieved at full speed. This meant that in theory, the AI could get a kart around a track at full speed.

The next thing to consider were the two other modes of transport – boats and planes. Boats, it turns out, can be made to handle in a very similar fashion to cars. This was achievable due to a common interface between all three vehicle types. So steering, acceleration, and braking were all handled the exact same way, although with different parameters for each. Transforming into a plane offered something different. The AI could now go up and down as well as left and right on the track. To facilitate this, the track data was modified to contain some height information so planes could fly off the ideal line to both the left and right as well as up and down. Image 8.5 illustrates the change to three dimensions. It was essentially the same data as was used for a kart or boat which allowed us to keep the track data consistent.

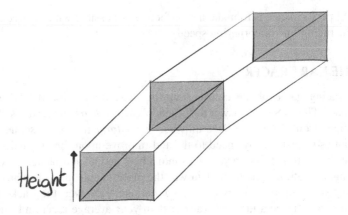

Height

IMAGE 8.5   3D track data to cater for flying.

Sonic All Stars Racing Transformed needed to take a different approach to avoidance that the other titles discussed in this chapter took. This game had power-ups, boost pads, and more, meaning that the racing line was not always the most optimal line to follow. Likewise, some of these things were dynamic so a way was needed to find the most optimal line at runtime. This was achieved using a simple A* search through the track data between our kart's position and the look ahead point. This was done by gathering all the racing line waypoints on the track, and if there was nothing of interest, the AI took the racing line as the line to follow. However, if there was something of interest, additional nodes were inserted into the graph to signify items such as power-ups and used this to modify the costs of the nodes so that this new dynamic section of the racing line encompassed the power-up the AI wanted to hit. Similarly, the AI could use the same approach for avoidance by adding in other racers based on their relative speed to ours. This approach is probably not as refined as splitting the track into sections as done on *F1 2009* or *Split/Second* but for a kart racer that allowed for vehicle contact, it worked brilliantly.

8.6   CONCLUSION

Every game is different, even if it is within the same genre. There are techniques that are transferable and plenty that are not, but that is half the fun of writing gameplay code, something that might work on one game might not work on another, but with some modifications, maybe you can adapt it to. Whatever the challenge, do not be afraid to experiment. There were plenty of gotchas in each of the games discussed in this chapter, but with some ingenuity and plenty of head scratching we solved them all.

REFERENCE

Manslow, J. (2004) *Fast and Efficient Approximation of Racing Lines. AI Game Programming Wisdom 2.* Edited by Steve Rabin. Charles River Media, pp. 485–488.

9 Believable Routes
A Pathfinding Acceptability Metric

Paul Roberts

9.1 INTRODUCTION

Much of pathfinding research focuses on the development of algorithms that attempt to calculate the optimal path – that is the mathematical shortest path. In video games, does it matter if a path is longer than the optimal path if it is a reasonable path for someone to take? To determine what paths are acceptable to a player, an approach was developed that uses player generated paths to create heatmaps with which a path generated by any search algorithm could be assessed. This chapter details the study conducted to generate these heatmaps and explains how an acceptability metric can be incorporated into path finding tests. The A* algorithm is used to demonstrate the usage of this metric.

9.2 BELIEVABILITY

The path an agent takes is a key component to ensuring characters are believable in games and is one of the primary behaviours with which the player can judge whether the actions of an agent are realistic or not. So, when a player is immersed in a game, any unexpected behaviour by a non-player character (NPC) noticed by the player could trigger suspicion, resulting in the immersion being destroyed and the believability being lost.

Player behaviour is closely intertwined with player experience. Player behaviour can be described as what a player does, whereas player experience is how the player feels. They are closely intertwined because what a player does will have an impact upon the experience of the player, which in turn impacts upon how they feel. Ultimately, if a pathfinding algorithm can exhibit the behaviour a player 'feels' is appropriate, this will in turn affect the immersion of the player. An agent's movement is more related to player behaviour, and it is the replication of this behaviour that will ultimately affect how the player feels. That is to say, if the AI character behaves in a manner expected by the player, then the player experience will be more immersive, and the illusion of intelligence held.

The study conducted for this chapter looks to build a metric with which AI character movement can be compared to human players' movement. The hypothesis being that if an NPC imitates human movement, the AI will then exhibit believable, human-like characteristics.

DOI: 10.1201/9781003324102-9

9.3   THE ACCEPTABILITY METRIC

The outcome of this chapter will be a new metric by which the acceptability of a path can be measured. This derived knowledge of player behaviour can then be used to help guide research in the development of pathfinding algorithms, which imitate human behaviour. Of the vast amount of data that could be recorded, such as positional data, reaction times, decision delay, and the like, the data of interest is the array of positions a human player takes when moving between two points in a real game environment. Timings are not taken into account, as it is a static overview of the entire path that is of interest to determine what a player thinks is an acceptable path. These tests are then combined to produce a heatmap, from which standard pathfinding approaches can be compared to rate their acceptability from a player's perspective. This takes the form of a percentage value, with 100% representing the calculated path completely within the acceptable route created by players.

9.4   METHODOLOGY

The player metrics extracted from these tests describe the player's behaviour whilst working their way through game maps. These metrics define the path that the player feels is most appropriate for an NPC to follow should they begin their journey from the start position and wish to move directly to the end location. Each participant in this study generated path data for each problem set. Once combined, all the participant's path data produced a heatmap which provides a detailed spatial location overview of the combined journeys.

9.4.1   MAP SELECTION

It would be great if we could develop a metric that works on every possible environment and every possible path within it. Unfortunately, this is not possible given the huge number of maps and the time it would take for participants to navigate each one. So, nine maps were selected from the benchmark tests created by Blizzard Games and which are compiled on the MovingAILab website for the Grid-Based Path-Planning competition (Sturtevant, 2012). All environments compiled in this database are from commercially available games from the real-time strategy (RTS) and role-playing game (RPG) genres, which usually use grid-based environments to describe the landscape. These benchmarks provide a wide variety of real game world environments, and those selected for this experiment were selected using an interquartile range boundary on the number of accessible cells, from maps sized at 512×512. Maps with the nearest accessible state count to the calculated value were used. This approach ensured a representative sample from the maps available. Of the four games provided, *Warcraft III*, *StarCraft I*, and *Baldur's Gate II* were used. The *Dragons Age* maps were not used as there are no consistent environments at the required 512×512 size and scaling was not desirable as it would change the environment from those available and make replication difficult. *StarCraft I* had an array of maps of varying sizes, but only those of size 512×512 were included in the calculation of the interquartile range. Table 9.1 details the number of accessible states for each environment at the extremes and the range that this results in.

TABLE 9.1
Calculating the Range to Determine Interquartile Ranges

Game	Environment with the Highest Number Accessible States	Environment with the Lowest Number Accessible States	Range
Warcraft III	131,403	36,462	94,941
Baldur's Gate II	231,469	17,587	213,882
StarCraft I	225,934	92,804	133,130

All test environments were rendered as black and white images, white representing accessible/walkable cells and black representing obstacles. This reduces any confusion that could arise for participants from the different coloured cells depicted in some of the original environments, and ensures all maps are consistent across all tests and games. The selection of environments offers a spread of complexity for a pathfinding algorithm or human participant to navigate. Table 9.2 details the environments chosen along with their accessible state count and the target interquartile range.

TABLE 9.2
Selected Maps That Are Nearest to the Interquartile Range

Game	Quartile Point (%)	# of Nodes at This Point	Chosen Map	# of Accessible Nodes on Map
Warcraft III	25	60,197.25	plaguelands	55,185
Warcraft III	50	83,932.5	isleofdread	83,111
Warcraft III	75	107,667.75	heart2heart	105,833
Baldur's Gate II	25	71,057.5	AR0309SR	70,757
Baldur's Gate II	50	124,528	AR0043SR	124,494
Baldur's Gate II	75	177,998.5	AR0042SR	146,967
StarCraft I	25	126,086.5	CrescentMoon	122,296
StarCraft I	50	159,369	WinterConquest	157,285
StarCraft I	75	192,651.5	OrbitalGully	197,371

9.4.2 PROBLEM SELECTION

Each environment selected was used for two different path searches. One starting from the left of the map and ending on the right side of the map. The second being a path starting from the bottom of the environment and ending at the top. The start and end points of these searches resulted in paths being produced that navigated all the way across the map and ensured a good coverage of each environment. The start and end positions were selected using the following criteria:

Search 1:

- **Left position:** The furthest left accessible cell on the map, which is centred in the largest vertical area of accessible cells.

- **Right position:** The furthest right accessible cell on the map, which is centred in the largest vertical area of accessible cells.

Search 2:

- **Bottom position:** The lowest accessible cell on the map, which is centred in the largest horizontal area of accessible cells.
- **Top position:** The highest accessible cell on the map, which is centred in the largest horizontal area of accessible cells.

The data describing the cells passed through in a search were saved out as an array of integers, with a value of 0 representing cells not encountered and a value of 1 representing a cell the participant had passed through. If a participant passed through the same cell multiple times, the integer at this position was still represented by 1.

9.5 PROCEDURE

Participants used a touch screen device and a stylus to draw a path from the start position to the end position. They could see the entire environment and had the ability to zoom in and out of the environment. They were under no time pressure constraints.

9.5.1 PROCESSING THE COLLECTED DATA

As each path generated by a participant was only a single pixel in width; overlaying multiple participant paths that run side by side and from a human perspective are the same route which would not be influencing each other. Image 9.1 depicts an environment constructed using the data from the MovingAILab website (Sturtevant, 2012) and shows this issue, where multiple paths (in different shades of grey) are essentially following the same route, but when these paths are overlaid, they appear to be different routes and create no interesting data.

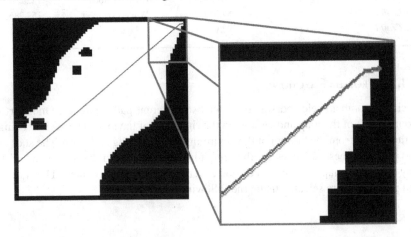

IMAGE 9.1   Overlaid participant paths.

Therefore, path widths were widened by ten pixels to create an acceptable *route* from the paths created by each participant, producing a single combined route. There is an argument for this kind of path widening to be done using a Gaussian distribution or some other approach, but this was unnecessary given when the results are combined into a single heatmap a drop-off is seen where *routes* do not overlap.

Each path is represented as an array the size of the environment (512 × 512). At each cell, a zero represents a space the player did not interact with, and a one on cells the player's path moves through. These arrays were then combined to create an overall array of values. This can be viewed as a heatmap, which is simply a visual interpretation of the values in the combined array, where the colours are calculated based upon how high the value is at a given cell. The more people moved on a particular cell, the darker grey it will be. Image 9.2 depicts an example heatmap, with a zoomed in portion to show the values at that location. As can be seen, the darkest portions represent an underlying value of 35, meaning that all 35 participant *routes* passed over those cells.

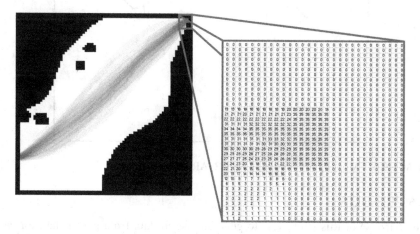

IMAGE 9.2   Heatmap example.

9.5.2   Calculating the Acceptable Route Metric Benchmark

To test the results of this study and to calculate a benchmark with which other path-finding algorithms could be compared, the paths generated by the A* algorithm in the test environments, from the same start and end positions, were generated. The Euclidean distance was used to calculate the heuristic and octile movement was allowed.

The A* path for each environment was saved out as an image. This was then overlaid onto the acceptable route heatmap, and for each cell that the path goes through:

- Add up the values in each of these cells.
- Divide the total by the number of cells that overlapped.
- Divide this by the highest scoring cell in the heatmap.

This results in a value between 0 and 100, which will be called a *confidence* value, which demonstrates the acceptance of the player of the path generated. Image 9.3 shows an example path, which is generated for the *Baldur's Gate* map bg512_AR0309SR, for a Search 1 (Left to Right) problem.

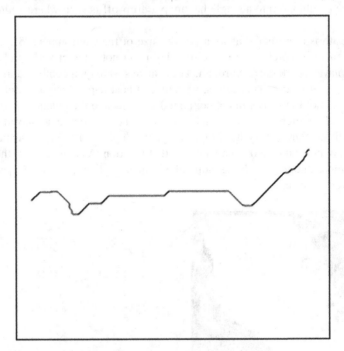

IMAGE 9.3   A* path in environment: bg512_AR0309SR.

9.6   RESULTS

The purpose of this study was to generate useful data from player data for each of the search problems detailed. The creation of heatmaps to depict this data is a great way to visualise this data. An example is shown in Images 9.4 and 9.5 of the search problem bg512_AR0309SR(25Percent_70757States)_1. The darker the colour the higher the value at a particular cell. This example shows that there are multiple *routes* through the maze-like environment, and all of them are acceptable from a player perspective; however, the *confidence* rating of a particular route will differ. To give this some real-world context, imagine going to a festival and camping. Throughout the weekend, the festival goers will repeatedly navigate their way through the thousands of tents to get to the various entrances and exits. As they do this the grass gets trampled. The more that people follow the same routes, the more the grass is trampled and the clearer the path. At the end of the festival, when everyone has packed up and gone home, an aerial view would show the routes that were used the most being more pronounced, which is the same as the darker greys depicting routes in the image. This is not to say that the *routes* less travelled are incorrect, but they are certainly *routes* that fewer people have used and those travelled more frequently can easily be identified as appropriate paths to follow.

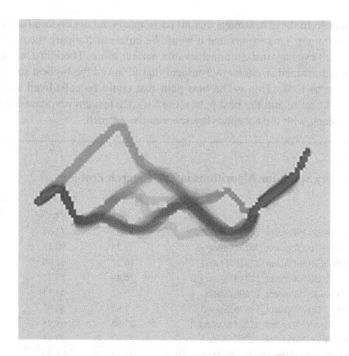

IMAGE 9.4   Heatmap for problem: bg512_AR0309SR(25Percent_70757States)_1.

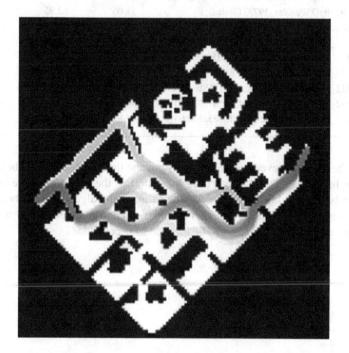

IMAGE 9.5   Heatmap overlaid on constructed map for problem: bg512_AR0309SR(25Per cent_70757States)_1.

It is clear from these heatmaps that all participants did not choose the exact same *route* to the target. This means that it would be unfair to compare the results the A* algorithm achieves against an unachievable perfect route. Therefore, an acceptable route was determined in each environment that followed the highest scoring routes the participants took. This is the best path that could be calculated via the heatmaps. The A* score and the best path score for each test environment are shown in Table 9.3, along with the acceptability score of the A* path.

TABLE 9.3

Acceptability Score for Algorithms in Each Search Problem

Map	A* Score (%)	Best Path Score (%)	Acceptability of A* (%)
bg512_AR0309SR(25Percent_70757States)_1	47.27	73.68	64.15
bg512_AR0309SR(25Percent_70757States)_2	58.25	90.12	64.63
bg512_AR0043SR(50Percent_124494States)_1	10.77	62.60	17.20
bg512_AR0043SR(50Percent_124494States)_2	36.49	57.72	63.21
bg512_AR0042SR(75Percent_146967States)_1	9.42	45.11	20.88
bg512_AR0042SR(75Percent_146967States)_2	7.95	66.66	11.92
sc1_CrescentMoon(25Percent_122296States)_1	27.98	69.95	40.00
sc1_CrescentMoon(25Percent_122296States)_2	27.97	73.94	37.82
sc1_WinterConquest(50Percent_157285States)_1	36.34	85.90	42.30
sc1_WinterConquest(50Percent_157285States)_2	54.92	81.01	67.79
sc1_OrbitalGully(75Percent_197371States)_1	51.06	62.95	81.11
sc1_OrbitalGully(75Percent_197371States)_2	68.30	89.21	76.56
wc3maps512_plaguelands(25percent_55185States)_1	64.81	91.91	70.51
wc3maps512_plaguelands(25percent_55185States)_2	37.50	79.34	47.26
wc3maps512_isleofdread(50Percent_83111States)_1	17.95	86.88	20.66
wc3maps512_isleofdread(50Percent_83111States)_2	47.76	79.36	60.18
wc3maps512_heart2heart(75Percent_105833States)_1	54.70	83.44	65.55
wc3maps512_heart2heart(75Percent_105833States)_2	69.61	87.36	79.68

Both the score achieved by the A* algorithm and the best path via the heatmap are shown in Image 9.6. The A* algorithm falls short of the best path score calculated using the heatmaps, but given the A* algorithm is the algorithm of choice in the games industry, it is this algorithm that should be used to generate the bar with which other algorithms need to surpass to be deemed as acceptable.

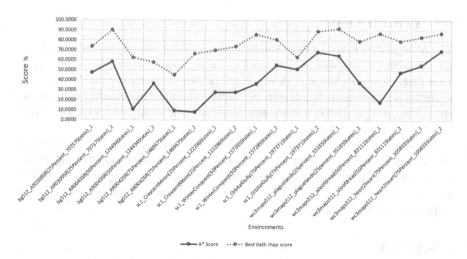

IMAGE 9.6 Scores achieved by the A* algorithm and the best path (generated by participant data).

Taking an average from the scores achieved by the A* algorithm and dividing it by the average scored by the best path score, and then multiplying it by 100 results in an acceptability score of 53.32% for the A* algorithm. This has been drawn on Image 9.7 as a dotted line along with the acceptability scores for A* in each environment (the last column in Table 9.3). In individual environments, the A* algorithm performs extremely well, but in others, it performs not so well. Each of these environments offered different challenges, and the acceptability score calculated for the A* algorithm using this metric is an average over all environments.

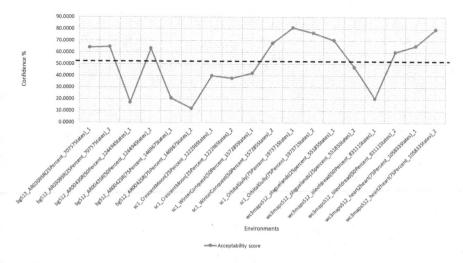

IMAGE 9.7 Acceptability score for the A* algorithm in each Search Problem.

9.7   CONCLUSION

The A* algorithm is used a lot in video games. This chapter and the metric discussed are not meant in any way as a criticism of the approach, but to add to the body of knowledge. The conclusion of developing this metric and testing the A* algorithm against it is that when testing future approaches, we should be including believability (from a player's perspective) as a metric along with the usual metrics such as length, time, expansions, and the like.

The score of 53.32% that was reached through the average scores of the results of the A* algorithm should be viewed as an initial starting point. As other algorithms use this metric, the bar should be raised to ensure that the cutting edge of pathfinding research for video games always has the player's believability as one of the most important metrics for comparison.

REFERENCE

Sturtevant, N.R. (2012) Benchmarks for grid-based pathfinding. *Transactions on Computational Intelligence and AI in Games,* 4(2), pp. 144–148.

10 AI Under Lockdown
Various Approaches to NPC Tethering

Laurent Couvidou

10.1 INTRODUCTION

This chapter goes over various ways of restricting AI navigation to certain areas of a game world, a notion often referred to as *tethering* non-player characters (NPCs). Why would you want to place NPCs under lockdown instead of letting them move freely anywhere? Unless your game is about simulating pandemics there is no sanitary reason to do so.

A common motivation in combat design is that you may need to prevent players from gathering too much *aggro* as they navigate around the world. Having too many enemies chasing or fighting a player can feel overwhelming for them, so it is common practice to try and limit the number of aggressive NPCs to keep the gameplay balanced. This is where tethering helps: if NPCs are prevented from going everywhere, they eventually give up the fight and either return home, or de-spawn, whenever their target gets out of reach.

Level design can be a motivation as well. In some cases, NPCs with certain abilities are not adapted to specific areas. For example, in a highly systemic game, you might not want your NPCs equipped with firearms to step into a highly flammable refinery – as firing their guns might blow up the building.

Finally, tethering may also be motivated by performance concerns. Aggressive NPCs often weigh higher on hardware resources than idle ones. In games where AI perceptions are simulated, environmental queries are used to detect targets and find positions to attack. These often use physics requests such as line-of-sight checks, whose cost can quickly add up. Usually, pathfinding is also put under more stress as the designated targets move and NPCs need to adapt their own positioning. Add hit detection, visual effects, sound effects, and the like into the mix, and aggressive behaviours start to take their toll and show up in profiler traces. So, beyond design questions, using tethering can also be beneficial to the game framerate as it allows us to limit the number of NPCs fighting simultaneously.

The goals you are pursuing with tethering will probably be a mix of those described above. How to implement tethering will highly depend on the details of your requirements. There is no silver bullet. This chapter will go through different approaches and explain what they are good for and the issues they bring. Once you have read the full cookbook, you should know about the trade-offs and be able to come up with your own recipes.

DOI: 10.1201/9781003324102-10

In this chapter, it is assumed that NPCs use a navigation mesh and find paths using the A* algorithm. Your game may use a different type of navigation, but the chances are that you can still use the information provided by adapting it to your needs.

10.2   DATA STRUCTURE

For most of the approaches that follow, it is assumed that you have *tethering areas* available in the game world. These are spatially delimited zones that NPCs are supposed to stick to. They will usually be implemented using bounding boxes/spheres, binary space partition (BSP) brushes, or any other volume primitive that your engine has to offer. This means more work for the level designers, but at some point, someone must make the call as to where to constrain the NPCs, and this should probably be the job of the folks that lay out the levels. It is important to have a team discussion on whether these tethering areas should be their own separate entity, or if they should be shared with another type of volume to lighten the burden. For instance, one could imagine having areas used not only for tethering, but also to provide spatial semantics (indoors spaces vs. outdoors spaces) or associated with sound propagation settings (muffled room vs. resonating hallway). The preferred approach will depend on the level design requirements and the workflow that the team follows, so your mileage may vary.

It is also assumed that NPCs are somehow assigned to one or several tethering areas. A way to do this is to work with tags. To do this, first, tag all the volumes that are logically part of the same tethering area with an identifier. Then assign a set of tags to NPCs at runtime to tell them where they are allowed to be. Image 10.1 depicts how this would work with multiple NPCs across multiple tethering areas.

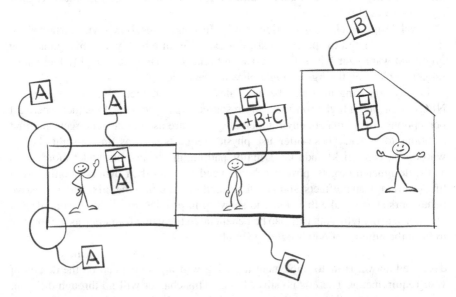

IMAGE 10.1   Areas tagged A, B, and C. Area A is the combination of three volumes. On the left: NPC tethered to area A. On the right: NPC tethered to area B. In the middle: NPC tethered to the three combined areas.

If you associate a bit to each tethering area in your level, you can use a bit set to represent a combination of areas and record the assignments for each NPC.

Furthermore, you can do the same for all spatial structures that are used for AI spatial reasoning. Navigation frameworks often offer a way to define *materials* or *user data* on the atomic element of their spatial structures, for example, a navigation mesh face, a navigation volume voxel, an influence map cell, and the like. This is where you can store your tethering area information as bit sets. Such user data is usually 4 bytes so you can either store the bit set directly or, if your needs go beyond tethering, point to a more elaborate data structure that contains it.

Checking whether a location is allowed then boils down to a simple bit mask between the NPC's bit set assignment, and the bit set at the location that you need to check. This helps in making the data cache friendly. The data is compact and 100% local if stored directly in the spatial structures. Alternatively, it can be stored in a continuous buffer that fits into a cache line. This approach also prevents you from having to run geometric checks all the time.

10.3   DEALING WITH ENVIRONMENTAL QUERIES

One important aspect of decision-making in game AI is picking the right location for an NPC to move to. This topic is tightly related to our topic of how to *restrict* their movement as we want to forbid locations that are outside that NPC's tethering areas. Sometimes, NPCs follow scripted directions such as patrol routes. So, it is possible to check for errors offline. For instance, a level editor can warn level designers when an NPC is assigned to a patrol point that is outside their tethering area. But as soon as NPCs move systemically, it is necessary to poll the environment at runtime to find the best location for their behaviour.

A common type of environmental query consists of collecting a set of points in the NPC surroundings and scoring them relative to the goals they are trying to achieve. For example: in a military shooter game, engaging soldiers need to find a location that provides them with a line of fire towards their target, within the attack range of their weapon, and preferably behind cover. The scoring will weigh these factors to try and find the best possible position to attack from.

There are other ways to query the environment: navigation mesh line checks, influence map propagation, radial combat placement, and the like, but all these environmental queries have the goal of finding the *best* location that is then used as a goal for a pathfinding request. Some tethering approaches are based on pathfinding (Sections 10.4.1–10.4.3 below) which will make this request fail if the goal is outside the NPC's tethering area. With no further logic, that NPC will stay stuck, repeatedly trying to reach that same location until the situation changes, as shown in Image 10.2. This is a highly undesirable outcome. A motionless NPC feels *buggy* and will break the suspension of disbelief, especially when the gameplay is based around action.

IMAGE 10.2 The NPC on the left tries to get near the player on the right (wearing the P hat). Pathfinding fails as they are constrained to stay inside their tethering area.

A naïve solution to the problem is to run pathfinding on all potential locations before making the decision. This can work up to a point but is not something that will scale well in terms of performance. Pathfinding is still one of the most expensive AI tasks in that regard and should be used as sparingly as possible. It is unrealistic to consider using pathfinding for every polled point in an environmental query. Fortunately, there are possible optimisations for this problem that better integrate tethering with environmental queries, which will be addressed later. Just keep in mind that this is an open problem.

10.4 TETHERING APPROACHES

The first approach is the most restrictive one, with NPCs unable to leave their spawn area at all. Subsequent approaches allow for more slack on where an NPC can go, in and around their tethered areas.

10.4.1 STATIC NAVIGATION ISLANDS

The most basic and most restrictive approach to tethering is to have statically isolated navigation mesh *islands*. Provided there is no teleporting, and there is no link between *islands* whatsoever, pathfinding will never jump from one to another. This effectively constrains NPCs to their spawn area as depicted in Image 10.3.

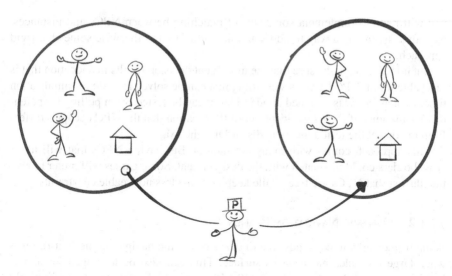

IMAGE 10.3 NPCs are constrained to their tethering area, while the player can freely navigate between them.

Any reasonably featured level editor offers volumes to define where the navigation mesh gets generated from physics. So, instead of encompassing the entire world with a single volume, you can generate navigation mesh *islands* by using several non-overlapping volumes. It is also common to be able to flag the physics surfaces that should or should not be used to generate the navigation mesh. This is something else that you can leverage to create navigation *islands* if the volumes approach is not available or convenient.

If you do not have any of these things readily available, you will have to create your own tethering volumes and make sure that the navigation mesh is only generated inside them.

On a positive note, this approach is probably the most cost-effective way of doing tethering. It comes with absolutely zero runtime cost; possibly even improving the overall AI runtime cost as small *islands* will effectively limit the expansion of pathfinding.

Some games make this one of the subtleties players must learn to play with. For example: games in the *Dark Souls* series seem to have such *islands* and although NPCs may temporarily exit them with melee attacks that use root motion, they will always return home as soon as their path following triggers. So, this is something that players can exploit to play around the notorious difficulty of these games.

You do not necessarily need to stick to the same distribution of *islands* for all NPCs. For instance, if design requires one specific faction that is allowed to move around the world freely, it is generally possible to support a separate navigation mesh *layer* or *instance* to handle that case. To reuse the example of the introduction, you could make sure that NPCs with firearms are forbidden access inside the refinery, while other NPCs would still be allowed in. This adds complexity as these different instances will have to be generated with distinct settings and you will need to implement some sort of matching between NPCs and instances. Nonetheless, this is a way to add some flexibility to an otherwise somewhat rigid approach.

But how do you make sure that the movement decision results in a location that is reachable for an NPC? This is something that can be solved at build or initialisation time. If each *island* is assigned an identifier, it can be tested when polling for potential destinations. If the *island* identifier of the location that the NPC occupies differs from the one at the tested location, discard it right away.

This approach comes with many advantages. But having NPCs that will never cross borders could mismatch with the design intent. Some games will prefer to give the illusion that NPCs are free, while keeping some less noticeable constraints.

10.4.2 DYNAMIC NAVIGATION ISLANDS

Some frameworks make it possible to *carve* or *cut* the navigation mesh at runtime when large obstacles move on its surface. This can also be leveraged for tethering. For instance, depicted in Image 10.4 is a mediaeval castle that can effectively become an *island* by cutting off the navigation mesh underneath when the player and their allies have entered, and the gates are closed.

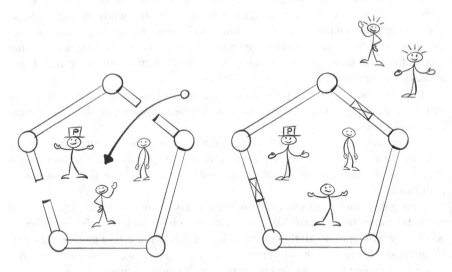

IMAGE 10.4 A player and allied NPCs enter a castle. The castle gates close behind them to prevent enemies from joining them.

Once the threat is gone, the gates reopen, and the mesh is welded, allowing NPCs to freely enter and exit. Carving the navigation mesh is not free though. Unlike the previous approach, it comes with a runtime cost. But it allows you to restrict NPC freedom temporarily instead of permanently. In other words, you can close the gates only at times when tethering is needed. Used wisely, this can also be a great tool for designers.

An additional consideration with this approach is to make sure that environmental queries result only in locations that are reachable for a given NPC. It is no longer possible to assign static identifiers to navigation *islands* as they can change at any time. Some frameworks already support hierarchical pathfinding which might provide a way to perform cheap connectivity tests between *clusters* or *tiles* at a coarser level of granularity. If the performance of this is reasonably good, and if it adapts to dynamic carving, you might want to consider using it to enforce the reachability of the locations tested by environmental queries.

If there is no hierarchical pathfinding available, or if it does not work with carving, an ad-hoc option is to implement a connectivity cache. This can be implemented with the following algorithm:

1. When a pathfinding request fails, flood fill the navigation mesh around its goal location and add the result to a temporary set of unreachable faces.
2. For the next environmental queries, exclude the locations that match with faces in the set, so they are never picked.
3. Clear this set whenever the navigation mesh is modified.

This solution has the advantage that it recomputes connectivity only where and when it is necessary.

This approach can also help in solving another problem. Sometimes pathfinding requests fail because some sort of limit was reached – a maximum duration or iteration count for example. In these cases, there might be actual connectivity to the destination, but the level is very intricate, and it would probably not make sense to send an NPC to follow a very long and twisted path. So, it is possible to consider these locations as *virtually* unreachable and thus make sure that future environmental queries discard them.

Dynamic navigation *islands* come with a few downsides and require more work to implement. Nonetheless, they have the big advantage that they make tethering more believable, or more diegetic. Players and NPCs may be able to traverse a gate until some limiting condition triggers, at which time the gate closes, blocking the path. This gives players a visible explanation as to why no one else goes through, while keeping some flexibility in the NPC distribution.

10.4.3 Pathfinding Filtering

Instead of relying on separated *islands*, it is possible to give NPCs some slack by moving the restrictions to another level. The example that follows takes place on a continuous navigation mesh and will directly affect the pathfinding instead.

Pathfinding frameworks typically offer the ability to implement a custom *cost modifier* of *filter* functions that will affect the A* cost of traversing faces. We can exploit this to implement tethering by testing whether these faces are part of the NPC's tethering area or not. If the source face is inside the tethering area and the destination face is not, it returns a score of zero and the connection is discarded. Note that directionality is important. If an NPC stands outside their tethering zone, you probably want them to be able to come back inside. This could happen in the event of an NPC being thrown there by an inconsiderate player.

This makes things 100% strict. In other words, it completely forbids paths that exit tethering boundaries. This effectively reintroduces dynamic navigation *islands* as seen with the previous approach. These are *virtual islands*, as they do not exist in the actual navigation mesh topology, but only because of the restrictions applied to pathfinding. It is possible to apply these restrictions to some types of NPCs but not others while keeping a single navigation mesh, keeping those guns outside of our refinery as shown in Image 10.5.

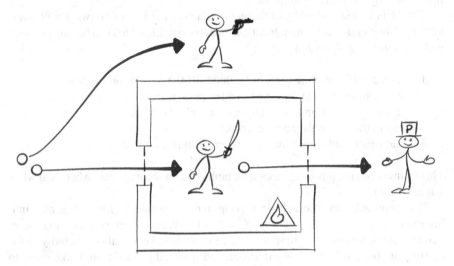

IMAGE 10.5   Two NPCs follow the player. The one equipped with a sword can path across the flammable refinery. The one with a gun must take a detour.

It is also possible to partially lift the restriction by only multiplying the cost by some factor. NPCs equipped with guns can be allowed to take the risk of entering the refinery only if it is the only way to engage a player that must be killed no matter what. Image 10.6 depicts this change.

IMAGE 10.6   Both NPCs follow the player inside the refinery, as it is the only way to engage them.

The downside here is that a cost modifier may become a performance bottleneck as it is a hot function in the A* algorithm. It gets called every time the algorithm steps from one face to another, which is a frequent operation. If the scoring or filtering is poorly optimised, this type of approach can quickly ruin pathfinding performance. This is where baking tethering information directly into the navigation mesh user data can really make a difference.

Then comes the usual problem with environmental queries of how to make sure they do not produce locations that will result in pathfinding failures. With this approach you rely neither on static *island* identifiers, nor on hierarchical information as it is now cost modifiers that drive the logic. So, you may choose to implement some sort of connectivity cache as described in the previous section. If you go with this route, note that it is important to also clear the cache when the filtering logic is changed, as it potentially implies a change in the distribution of *virtual islands*. If your data structures allow for it, you can also choose to bit mask the queried location versus the NPC tethering assignments, as is presented in Section 10.2.

This approach comes with a lot of constraints but can still be useful in cases where design requires a strict spatial limit. You do not want NPCs that accidentally end up in the refinery, so you must make sure that its *borders* are respected. Sometimes though, it is OK to not respect borders. When there is no level design constraint to keep NPCs in perfectly delimited areas, it becomes possible to use other approaches.

10.4.4 DESTINATION FILTERING

The approaches discussed in Sections 10.4.1–10.4.3 are all part of the same family as they always act at the pathfinding level, in one way or another. Destination filtering achieves similar results without the pathfinding constraints.

As was brought up several times, when it is time to pick a new destination for an NPC, environmental queries need to take tethering into account to produce valid destinations. It turns out that this is enough to implement a variant of tethering. If every destination produced by the movement decision-making is within an NPC's tethering area, they will necessarily always end up in a spot that is allowed for them. They *might* step outside on the way if their tethering area is concave and there is a gap to cross, or if blocking geometry forces them to a detour, but this is only temporary. An example of this is shown in Image 10.7.

IMAGE 10.7 NPC temporarily gets outside the U-shaped building they are tethered to.

In many cases (convex area, or no blocking geometry), this even gives the exact same result as the previous approach with a much lighter cost, as the pathfinding runs freely.

This approach is valid in many situations. The constraints are still relatively strong as it is unlikely that NPCs would move very far from home unless the level is absurdly complex. Even if the leash is a little looser, it is still there, so you are still in control of the number of NPCs in a roughly delimited area. If the tethering information is directly baked into the navigation mesh, as described in Section 10.2, there is a relatively low cost to pay when doing environmental queries. So, if strict spatial limits are not a requirement, it is an approach that makes a lot of sense. This approach was used successfully in *Deathloop*.

Note that you might want to implement a safeguard so that no environmental query that ignores the tethering area is ever added. A simple assert to check the goal of all pathfinding requests will handily catch outliers.

10.4.5 BEHAVIOUR FILTERING

Behaviour filtering is quite different from all the previous approaches as it is a very light constraint and is designed to be unnoticeable by players. It does not impose any limitation on pathfinding nor on environmental queries. Instead, it simply tracks whether the current NPC location is still within their tethering area or not. An NPC that ventured outside their home area will be flagged and known as such, but not acted upon immediately. This could happen with an NPC allowed to wander without any restrictions and is named appropriately as a *wanderer*. As discussed in the introduction, the most performance intensive NPCs are often the aggressive ones. To accommodate this, a threshold of NPCs that are allowed to run such a behaviour simultaneously is maintained. If at any given time, this threshold is passed, and if there is a *wanderer* among the group, it is sent *back home* to its tethering area. This should be done when they are out of sight of players, to make this almost unnoticeable. Image 10.8 shows an NPC out of the player's view, who then gets teleported home.

IMAGE 10.8 An NPC returns home as soon as line-of-sight breaks, as it is one too many to fight the player.

Checking line of sight to every NPC from the player point of view might not be efficient, but there is another option that works great in single player games. Instead of checking their visibility from the player's point of view, you can trigger the return home behaviour when *they* lose sight of the player. It is not 100% accurate but this type of sensory information should always be readily available. The goal location for the return home request can be a random point in the tethering area, or if this is not something easy to compute their spawn location or initial patrol point.

This approach works great when the number of active NPCs must stay controlled, but level design does not require them to strictly stick to their tethering areas. It is very light on system resources as it has no impact on environmental queries or on pathfinding. NPCs can move virtually anywhere unless there are too many of them *attached* to the player. So, this approach will not work in the refinery versus firearms type of situations. This is the approach used in games such as *Dishonored* and *Dishonored 2*.

10.4.6 Summary

As a quick summary of the pros and cons of the five approaches discussed in this chapter, take a look at Table 10.1. This is a very high-level overview but should help when deciding which approach is most suitable to your specific game scenario. The three columns convey a different aspect to consider when choosing an approach. These are:

- Impacts env. queries: Whether the approach requires special handling in environmental queries or not.
- Constraint strength: How strictly does the approach maintain tethering borders that NPCs will not cross (by themselves).
- Runtime perf. cost: A rough estimate of how heavy the approach is on system resources (CPU, mostly).

TABLE 10.1

Overview of the Described Approaches

Approach	Impacts Env. Queries	Constraint Strength	Runtime Perf. Cost
1. Static navigation islands	Yes	*****	None
2. Dynamic navigation islands	Yes	****	Medium
3. Pathfinding filtering	Yes	***	High
4. Destination filtering	Yes	**	Medium
5. Behaviour filtering	No	*	Low

10.5 CONCLUSION

In this chapter, five different ways of implementing NPC tethering in games were discussed. These approaches answer to design requirements, what cost they imply on system resources, and how they constrain AI movement.

Like many things in game development, coming up with a solution is often akin to cooking a meal. You need to try out different things to see what works for your taste. Feel free to mix and match the ingredients and maybe find some more, and, as you come up with your own recipes, you will find a flavour of NPC tethering that fits with your very own requirements. Happy cooking!

11 Low-Cost, Mutable Path-Planning Spaces

Steven Dalton

11.1 INTRODUCTION

During early development of a not yet announced sandbox game, set in the universe of and sharing many similarities with Team17's *The Escapists* and *The Survivalists*, a requirement was identified for every non-player character (NPC) to have their own unique interpretation of the game world, specifically areas to avoid or to consider differently when navigating. This was driven both by the NPC archetype's traversal preferences and by their knowledge of navigation cost modifying in-game events. NPCs should be free to navigate to and from any unblocked location in their 2D, grid-based world. Simple, nothing new, A* does the job and then some. Complications arise when NPCs are expected to avoid bespoke areas relative to temporal events that they have either encountered first-hand using their visual and audible sensory systems or have gained awareness of following the slow knowledge propagation between NPCs (barks & gossip). This knowledge could theoretically be different for every single NPC in the game, meaning that every NPC would have their own interpretation of the search-space over which they request and generate paths. This chapter details the solutions that were considered and those implemented to provide a robust, fast, and reliable path-planner for a specific game type, created for multiple limited platforms.

11.2 THE PROBLEM

Since the content of the game cannot be discussed we will consider these problems as if they were in the World of *The Escapists*, with a subset of NPC archetypes: Prisoners and Prison Guards. A level has a maximum number of NPCs set at 120, made up of roughly 100 Prisoners and 20 Guards. It should also be noted that each level in the game world clocks in at around 800×600 tiles on average, with an absolute limit of 800×800.

The in-game events that cause NPCs to consider areas differently are multiple but will be distilled into a single effect in the interest of simplicity and relatability: a hazard in the form of fire that will significantly increase the cost of traversing an area that it affects. A fire can start anywhere in the game's world, will burn for a short amount of time, and will burn out leaving the area it occupied as navigable as it was before the blaze began. NPCs can be aware of any number of these events, including zero, even if their world hosts many. Upon discovering an event it is added to an NPC's working memory in the form of a description of the area affected (commonly a primitive shape such as a circle or rectangle) and the associated traversal cost multiplier. Once added

DOI: 10.1201/9781003324102-11

to an NPC working memory it remains until the world event expires, at which time it will be 'forgotten', and removed from the NPC's working memory.

11.3   THE WORLD AND WORKSPACE

Before getting into the real content, a definition of the world snapshot that is used to demonstrate ideas and develop prototypes should be discussed. This case will be confined to a very small and simple sandbox area as outlined in Image 11.1, a relatively simple building containing multiple routes between two rooms through naive corridors and doorways.

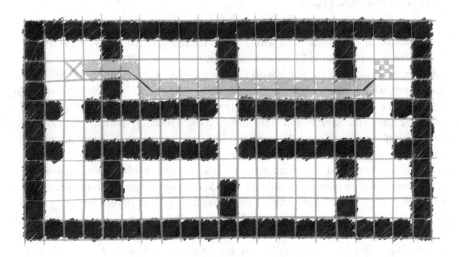

IMAGE 11.1   A sandbox area demonstrating the optimal path between two areas.

11.3.1   THE SEARCH-SPACE

Given the desire for this game to be playable on limited platforms (limited in both memory and CPU speed) it was decided early in the prototyping phase to give particular attention to data locality and cache coherence. A search-space representation was generated so that each grid cell, or node, contained not only the cost of traversing the node, but also a mutable search state used by the pathfinding algorithm and updated as nodes are considered, discarded, and consumed. Storing this data per node rather than in one or more additional data structures promotes cache coherence, meaning the data representing a node, and its close neighbours that are likely to be considered next sit happily within the lightning fast L1 cache.

11.3.2   WORLD STATE DATA

11.3.2.1   Traversal Cost

Each node needs, first and foremost, a default cost for traversing it. This cost is never used to make nodes un-traversable but is used by level designers to specify the cost of traversing a node as being anywhere from "cheap" to "expensive". Given a desire to keep the search-space small and quick to operate over, combined with the allowance for a wide range of values, an integer value between 1 and 63 is used to denote the traversal cost, with 16 being the default, meaning that the highest traversal cost for a tile is near-enough 4 times more expensive than the default (7 bits).

11.3.2.2 Blocked or Unblocked
A single flag was used to denote whether a node is traversable or not (1 bit).

11.3.3 SEARCH-STATE DATA

11.3.3.1 Open-Set
One of the two node-sets maintained during an A* path find is the *open-set*, a collection of all nodes that have had a neighbour explored and are next in line to be explored themselves. This collection is usually implemented in the form of a priority queue with the nodes estimated to be the cheapest (the distance from start and estimated distance to goal combined) being at the head of the queue. A flag on each node is assigned to identify whether the node is on the *open-set*. When a node is added to the *open-set* this flag is set to true (1 bit). This did not however eliminate the need for a separately maintained *open-set* data structure.

11.3.3.2 Closed-Set
The other of the two commonly maintained sets is the *closed-set*, used to store which nodes have already been expanded. This ensures nodes that are arrived at in multiple ways to be discarded as having already been explored, therefore, not added to the *open-set* again. Another bit per node was assigned to tag a node as being closed. This is set to true when a node is explored, far cheaper than maintaining and searching a list of all closed nodes (1 bit).

11.3.3.3 Costs
During a search, each considered node is updated with the cheapest cost of being reached from the start. This is calculated as the cost of reaching the previous node added to the traversal cost of the current node, multiplied by 1.414 if reached diagonally. This cost is updated per node and truncated into an integer. Given an 800×800 node search-space in which every node cost is at the maximum of 63, the highest theoretical cost is 20,185,200, given the layout in Image 11.2 expanded to 800×800 tiles. Accounting for this theoretical maximum cost, 25 bits are assigned to store this value, giving an absolute maximum value of 33,554,431, more than ample and even allowing for level dimension increases.

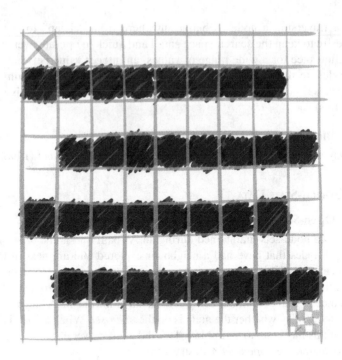

IMAGE 11.2   The longest possible route from start to goal tiles on a uniform grid.

Estimated Cost to Goal: To determine the total cost of a node when using the A*
algorithm, an estimated cost to reach the goal from the node being explored must be
calculated. The two approaches considered were Manhattan and Octile. The calculation of these heuristics is similar, but the results are significant. For a grid-based
environment, the formula for the Manhattan distance is $X + Y$, where X is the number
of cells between the start cell and the target cell on the horizontal axis, and Y is the
number of cells between the start cell and the target cell on the vertical axis. The
formula for the Octile distance is $Y + (X - Y)$. The X and Y values are calculated in
the same manner as was done for the Manhattan approach.

Taking a look at the environment depicted in Image 11.3, you can see there are six
cells in a column, giving Y a value of 6, and there are nine cells in a row, giving X a
value of 9. Using these values, the result for the Manhattan heuristic is $9 + 6 = 15$. The
result for the Octile heuristic is $6 + (9 - 6) = 9$.

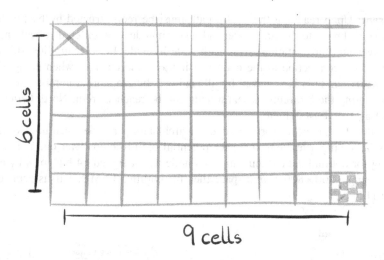

IMAGE 11.3   Distance of movement from the start cell to the target cell on the horizontal and vertical axis.

These results are compared in Image 11.4. The Manhattan heuristic had a value of 15, whereas counting the cells in the path in Image 11.4 (left) you can see that there are only 13 cells. This means that the Manhattan heuristic overestimates the distance. The Octile heuristic had a value of 9, and if you count the cells in the path in Image 11.4 (right) you can see that this is correct. There are nine cells in the path. Given that the Manhattan distance allows for sub-optimal paths to be returned, the Octile distance was chosen.

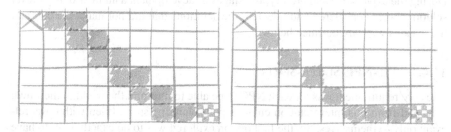

IMAGE 11.4   Left: Estimated paths from start to target nodes using the Manhattan distance. Right: Octile heuristic making evident the difference in path length and accuracy.

The maximum distance between the two furthest nodes in an 800×800 search-space is 800 nodes when using Octile distance, and 1,599 when using Manhattan. To allow for different heuristics to be swapped out or experimented with, the maximum of these two values was used. Again, allowing each tile to host the maximum traversal cost of 63, this gives a maximum theoretical traversal cost of 100,737 ($1,599 \times 63$) between the two furthest nodes. Another 17 bits are allocated to contain this value, allowing for a maximum estimate of 131,071, plenty of elbowroom again for level dimensions to be increased significantly.

Parent: Upon reaching the goal a path must be reconstructed by backtracking from the goal node to the start node, adding each node to an ordered collection, giving a reversed representation of the path node by node. In order to allow this each node stores a connection to the node that it was explored from when being added to the *open-set*. This is achieved by allocating 3 bits to store a number from 0 to 7 representing the 8 directions that a node can be reached from. North being 000, North-East 010, East 011, etc.

To allocate the above world state and search state per node, each node requires 55 bits. Allowing a few bits spare for potential optimisations later on, and adding padding for optimal data alignment, each node was assigned 64 bits, or 8 bytes, in total. A single 800×800 search-space then fits within 5.12 MB. This is depicted in Image 11.5.

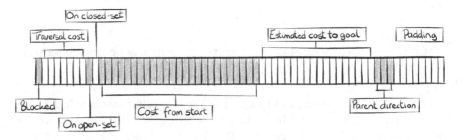

IMAGE 11.5   A breakdown of the 64 bits representing a single node.

11.4   CONSIDERATIONS

During the explorative and prototyping stages of development a number of high-level solutions were considered and rejected; the solutions that did not make the cut, and the reasons why, are outlined below:

11.4.1   PER-NPC SEARCH-SPACES

The core requirement was for each NPC to be able to interpret the world in their own way, and from this interpretation create a path-planning space filled with costs relevant only to themselves. So, the first option explored was to do exactly that, to have each NPC own and maintain their own path-planning search-space. Nothing was shared, events such as the discovery of a fire were consumed and the related modified traversal costs were permanently applied to their path-planning space, until the event expired at which time it was then removed.

It worked, but at a cost. 120 NPCs each owning an instance of the maximum size 800×800 tile search-space with each tile weighing in at 8 bytes

$$120 \times (800 \times 800) \times 8 = 614,400,000 \text{ bytes, or just over } 586 \text{ MB.}$$

Given the arbitrary, but quite generous budget of 250 MB for all runtime AI content, this was well out of scope.

11.4.2 Universal Search-Space with a Per-Tile Cost Query

Since it is likely that in most cases only a few, small areas would have their traversal costs altered, a solution was proposed in which the default search-space would be used by every NPC, and an additional step would be added when querying the cost of a node. For every explored node there would be a check to see if it is in any of the areas affected by the cost changing events in our NPC working memory. This was initially implemented by passing an array of primitive shapes, each with a traversal cost multiplier, into the path-planning system and having each explored node check if it was contained by, or intersected any, of these shapes upon being considered. Alongside the already expensive A* algorithm, this introduces an intersection test every time a node is explored, for every shape in the array. The performance took a hit and this solution seemed to be dead in the water until a pretty significant optimisation was employed.

With the 9 bits of padding per node currently serving no purpose, it was decided to use 7 of those bits to cache a modified traversal cost per node. Two solutions were written: Firstly, if the start and goal nodes were far apart, then every single one of the regions that applied a traversal cost multiplier was fed to the search-space and the assigned 7 bits were used to store any modified traversal costs after iterating this array of modifiers. If these 7 bits contained a non-zero value, then it must be a modified cost; otherwise, the original traversal cost is used. This could at times be wasteful as modified traversal costs were being painted into the search-space but were never used. The second option was employed if the start and goal nodes were not far apart. Each time a node was added to the *open-set* the traversal cost and any modifications would be cached in the spare 7 bits. This extra work was then guaranteed to be done only when necessary.

11.4.3 Known Issues

There are issues with the way data is stored and updated directly on each node. The main issue, a big hit on performance, was that after every path find a pass must be made over the entire search-space to reset all of the mutable data. While this could be done quickly, doing so for every node on an 800×800 level is expensive! The method used to mitigate this issue was to perform a bitwise operation that retained all but the 8 bits that contained the original traversal cost and the 'is blocked' flag. This was further improved by keeping track of the minimum and maximum bounds encompassing all nodes touched within a search, and then iterating over the area defined by these extremes, as shown in Code Listing 11.1.

Code Listing 11.1: A required post-path find pass over the search-space to reset any of the search-specific data that had been modified as part of the previous search. Optimised to only reset the rectangular region touched by the search.

```
// World state represented by rightmost 8 bits (0 - 7)
static const ulong k_worldStateMask = 0xFF; // 255
```

```
// Reset everything but the World state bits
for (int x = min.x; x <= max.x; ++x)
{
    for (int y = min.y; y <= max.y; ++y)
    {
        int nodeIndex = (y * width) + x;
        nodes[nodeIndex] &= k_worldStateMask;
    }
}
```

A second issue, known when the proposition for in-place search-state data within nodes was put forward, was that only one search at a time could be performed on the search-space. Since a search updated data within each node, it was required that this data remain until the search was complete, and another search could only be performed once the current search, and the reset pass over the search-space, were performed. Parallelised path finds were out of the question without taking the hit of duplicating the search-space.

11.5   THE SOLUTION

11.5.1   Cloning the Universal Search-Space and Applying Diffs

A happy medium between a single, global search-space, and an instance of the search-space per NPC was eventually selected. The original 8 bytes per tile search-space was retained as the global representation but was never modified during a search. Instead, this original search-space was copied to another pre-allocated buffer, the working search-space. Following this copy, the NPC-specific traversal cost modifications (or the *diffs*) were applied to the working search-space and then the search was performed on this spatial representation, unique to the querying NPC.

Since the buffer will be utilised again for the next path find, it does not matter what state it is left in as the original search-space would once again be copied into the buffer for the next path find, overwriting all data used and modified for the previous one. The obvious downsides to this approach are that the memory requirement is now doubled, and a pre-path find step is required to copy the entire search-space every time a path find is requested. This is however compensated by the removal of the requirement for a post-path find step to reset any data modified during a search.

11.5.2   Hierarchical Path-Planner

One way to significantly reduce the space that a search will be performed on is to make said search hierarchical, performing multiple passes over search-spaces increasing in resolution (Rabin, 2000). Since each level is already composed of rooms and corridors it was relatively easy to further break these rooms into composite sections, as close to square as possible, and to connect these sections to any neighbouring sections, resulting in a second, lower resolution graph on which a path find could be executed. Following this, the path-planning system was adjusted to perform multiple passes, first over the graph containing these new sections to narrow down the individual tiles to be explored, and then over only the tiles within these sections that made up the higher-level path.

The major complication with this approach arose when introducing the traversal cost modifications that occupied just parts of sections or spanned multiple sections at joining points. This was addressed by modifying the traversal cost of a section by a percentage of the modifier, relative to the coverage of the overlapping traversal cost modifier's shape. For instance, a section with just a third of its tiles covered by an event that applied a 2× modification was modified proportionally, multiplied by an adjusted amount of 1.33×.

As already discussed, the prototype for the cloned search-space saw a single buffer at the same size as the original search-space (800×800 tiles), with the entire search-space copied before every single path find request. As you are probably already imagining, this copy was a significant bottleneck, second only to running the A* search itself. Fortunately, a solution was already planned for phase 2 to leverage the result of this new top-level hierarchical search.

The top-level of the hierarchical search allowed us to, in most cases, drastically reduce the search-space that needed to be operated upon during the second pass, reducing the amount of data that needed to be copied from the global search-space to the working search-space. This reduction in the number of tiles to be copied can be seen in Images 11.6 and 11.7.

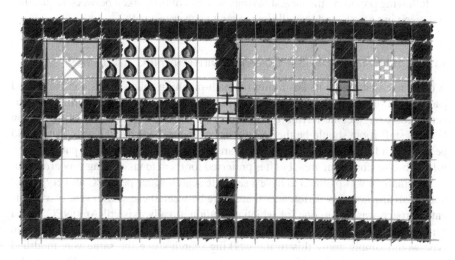

IMAGE 11.6 A completed hierarchical path find, the connected shaded sections show the high-level path from the start section to goal.

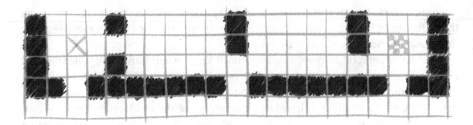

IMAGE 11.7 An outline showing the entire 19×5 node region to be copied to the path-finder's workspace buffer.

This optimisation brought with it another significant benefit; it allowed multiple path finds to be executed in parallel by pushing many of these smaller working search-spaces into the pre-allocated buffer until it was filled. All that was required was an accompanying struct that would outline the start and end index of each entry into the working search-space along with the region's dimension. In the end the size of the workspace buffer was doubled to 800×1,600 nodes, allowing even more of these smaller workspace regions to be copied before the buffer was exhausted.

11.6   OPTIMISATIONS

Over the course of a few months, many prototypes were proposed and trialled, with the following providing the largest savings in terms of time taken between requesting and receiving a path, and overall time taken to generate a path.

11.6.1   DIFFERENT TRAVERSAL COSTS FOR DIFFERENT NPC ARCHETYPES

A challenge that reared its head after the path-planning solution was confirmed and had been implemented, was the need to allow NPC archetypes to have different traversal costs for specific terrain types. For example, the traversal cost of the Prison Guard's staff room should be the default, or lower, for the Prison Guards, but should be very high for Prisoners. The Prisoner archetype can still generate a path through this high-cost (for them) area, but it is preferred for them to take a long way around it.

Originally it was planned to have a separate search-space per NPC archetype, but upon realising how few differences there were between these search-spaces a different approach was taken, one for which a solution already existed! Any NPC with a traversal cost for a terrain type that was different to the world's default for that terrain type would simply apply this to the working search-space the same way modified traversal costs are applied (from their working memory), as a *diff* in the form of a traversal modifier. To re-use the above example, the Prisoner archetype would have a persistent event in their working memory that applied a 4× cost increase to every region deemed a *restricted* or *staff only* area.

11.6.2 Insta-Paths

Another quick win came when generating short paths across a single section of a room. Before buffering a path find request a check for the start and goal tiles being in the same section was performed. If this were the case then this request would be handled immediately, skipping the hierarchical path find. Instead, this section's worth of tiles was copied into a very small, pre-allocated buffer, and the search was performed immediately. In most cases this worked fine, until NPCs were observed walking through fire to get across the area when it would have been more sensible for them to walk around the hazard by traversing a slightly longer route through another section. This issue was resolved by limiting the immediately processed requests to those not only constrained to a single section, but also to sections with no traversal cost modifiers to be applied within them. If either of the above two cases did not apply, then the path find was submitted and queued as normal.

11.6.3 Partial Path Generation

The last optimisation put in place was a real game-changer. Once a hierarchical path find stage was completed, it was possible to split a single path find request into many partial path requests. Initially a path would be generated from the start node to the exit point of the second section in the higher-level path and the hierarchical route cached. Then, upon an NPC reaching the entry point for the second section, the path from its exit point to the exit point of the third section would be generated. This was repeated for every section until the final section was reached, with at most a path through two sections generated and in memory at any given time. This resulted in a significantly larger number of path find requests being submitted and performed, but dramatically cut down the amount of time spent running the A* algorithm as paths were being generated over search-spaces no larger than 8×8 nodes and the time spent exploring nodes within the A* algorithm was dramatically reduced.

Not only did this reduce the time spent running the pathfinding algorithm, but also drastically reduced the number of nodes being copied to the working search-space. In all but the rarest of cases, in which every NPC requested a new path on the same frame, all path find requests were queued, their search-spaces buffered and modified, paths generated, and results returned within a single frame. It was such an improvement that the bottleneck became the execution of the hierarchical path find, an element that rarely showed up when profiling previous iterations of the solution.

11.7 CONCLUSION

The initial solution and subsequent evolutions discussed in this chapter, related to search-space data being stored in a manner heavily promoting cache coherence, prove that the approach taken caused no burdensome limitations. It did require a different approach to solve the pathfinding problems when they were coupled with a requirement for NPCs to have a unique and different representation of the search-space.

While initial implementations proved restrictive in that they would allow only one active path find at a time or required a costly post-path find pass to clean up modified data, these restrictions were quickly eliminated with a little experimentation and some non-invasive code changes.

While the solution discussed is one that all parties were happy with, there are still ideas floating around that could further improve it. An interesting example would be the concept of path caching; since the paths being generated are very small, most frequently just from the entrance of a room to its exit, the same path is being generated frequently when a large number of NPCs are heading in the same general direction. With some clever heuristics related to statistics such as an area's population density and the likelihood of mass transit in a specific direction, it *could* be advantageous to cache generated paths between these points, at least for a short amount of time, for other navigators to use provided the room being navigated contained no navigation cost modifying events. These cached paths could remain in memory for as long as there is a high chance of their re-use, or until something in the room changed such as a navigation cost modifying event, or an obstacle being removed or replaced.

REFERENCE

Rabin, S. (2000) A* speed optimizations, *Game Programming Gems*. Edited by Mark DeLoura. Charles River Media.

12 Auto-Generating Navigation Link Data

Dale Green

12.1 INTRODUCTION

Agents do not see the game world in the same way we do. Where we see the fruits of designers and artists, they see only data. Regardless of how advanced their behaviours or decision-making is, they can only ever be as good as the data they are working with. Navigation data gives our agents sight, allowing them to move through a world with purpose; so it is critical this data is correct.

Navigation meshes are used to approximate world geometry and give agents a surface upon which to move. Navigation links act to connect separate areas of a navmesh, letting an agent know that it is possible to move between them. While navigation meshes are generated automatically as standard, that is not the case for navigation links. This means that the data is generally hand-crafted, making it prone to error and becoming out-dated.

In this chapter we are going to look at the reasons why you might want to auto-generate nav-links, along with some limitations and considerations. An approach to generation will then be presented with a worked example. Implementation details are left sparse in favour of a more theoretical approach as a project's needs and technologies can be so varied, that supplying this detail would be counterproductive.

12.2 WHY AUTO-GENERATE?

Games development, especially toward the start of the process, is a very iterative process. Designers and artists are constantly fettling, resulting in levels shifting frequently. For the AI to keep up with these changes, navigation data needs to be equally as agile. Thankfully, this is not an issue for navigation meshes as they are generated automatically as standard, but that is unfortunately not the case for navigation links. As a result, this data usually needs updating by hand in response to world changes.

This process is not trivial, it adds manual overhead to such changes, and often results in the data becoming stale. It can be difficult to spot this, so the first sign is usually misbehaving AI. If auto-generated, however, nav-link data becomes as agile as nav-mesh data, hopefully greatly reducing the need for manual data corrections after geometry changes, bringing stability, and consistency to this vital data.

DOI: 10.1201/9781003324102-12

12.3   CONSIDERATIONS

It is difficult to generate data algorithmically and maintain the same level of contextual awareness that a developer brings. Algorithms define fixed limits and rule sets which can result in clinical, non-nuanced data. Unfortunately, nuance is often required, so it is unlikely that a single auto-generation process will entirely remove the need for manual navigation link data. It should however help establish a core data set that is robust to level changes, reducing manual data to special use-cases.

The various overheads of building such a system should also be considered. To auto-generate this data, there is the initial overhead of tool development, followed by continued maintenance, improvements, bug fixing, and increased build times. These factors need weighing up on a per-project basis to determine if auto-generation is the correct move.

If it is still the answer, it is wise to start conservatively. Navigation links affect both nav-data size and resulting agent behaviour since they are used when determining paths. Starting with a more rigid ruleset first, generating fewer, higher confidence links, is preferable to over generation, which could result in redundant or erroneous data. It is also wise to build an exclusion volume that will suppress generation within its bounds as early as possible. This is your 'Get out of jail free' card, and you will be very happy to have it should you need it.

12.4   GENERATING NAV-LINKS

The approach to generating navigation links presented in this chapter is an overview of one possible approach. Implementation specifics are omitted due to the fact that each project is highly unique, such as their needs. Instead, key ideas are presented alongside a running example.

The process has been split into the following distinct phases:

- **Gathering Data**: Boundary edges are gathered and validated.
- **Generating Simplified Edges**: Approximations of groups of suitable boundary edges are made to reduce the amount of data being processed.
- **Identifying Edge Pairs**: Pairs of simplified edges that are suitable candidates for links are identified.
- **Link Location Generation**: Potential link locations are identified for each edge pair.
- **Physics Checks**: Physics checks now made for each potential link. Any that fail are removed, meaning those that are left are valid locations for links.

The following example is provided such that the results of each step can be visualised. This is not real-world data but has been created to serve as an example. The example is shown in Image 12.1. It depicts a small environment containing two hexagonal platforms with three unconnected areas of nav-mesh. As each stage of the process is described, the results will be shown on this environment.

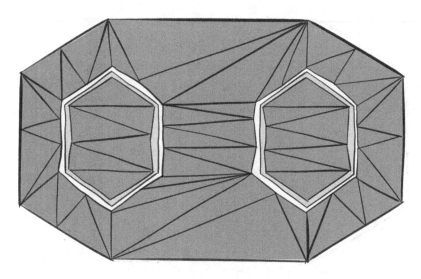

IMAGE 12.1   Example data that will be used throughout.

12.4.1   GATHERING DATA – FINDING BOUNDARY EDGES

The first step in this process is to gather all boundary edges that are to be considered for linking. A boundary edge is an edge on the exterior of a poly, not an internal edge that connects two polys. The details of how you query these edges will depend on the navigation library being used.

There are several options for scoping how this data is gathered. The first option is to gather all boundary edges from across the entire game world indiscriminately. This requires no level markup; it will however result in the largest data set, increasing workload and generation time. It is also unlikely that you want to generate nav-links everywhere you have a mesh, potentially resulting in redundant data.

The second option is a more targeted approach whereby volumes within which to gather boundary edges are placed into the world. This option avoids the potential issues of generating links where you do not want them, reducing the issue of redundant data. It does, however, introduce level markup which then needs to be maintained to ensure that it continues to encapsulate the correct area(s).

The third option is a highly targeted approach, in which you supply individual volumes to gather start and end edges separately. This option brings with it the most level markup, now having two volumes to maintain per area where you want to generate links. It does, however, remove the need to pair edges algorithmically since that has already been done by whomever placed the volumes in the game world.

Once gathered, it is worth doing a quick pass to ensure that no duplicate edges have been found. These can cause issues later in the process, so it is best they are identified and discarded now. Image 12.2 shows the example environment with all boundary edges highlighted.

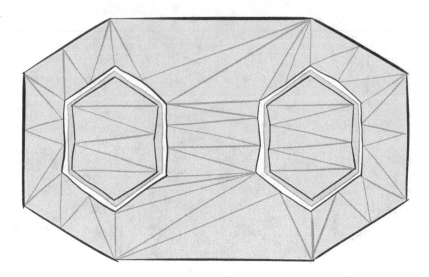

IMAGE 12.2   Boundary edges are highlighted as heavier lines.

12.4.2   GATHERING DATA – EDGE WINDING

When gathering edges, it is important to make sure that they are all wound the same way. This means that the vertices of each edge are laid out in a consistent manner, such that all edge normals are consistent in orientation. Edge normals provide important information about the direction of an edge so it is crucial that they are uniform. Image 12.3 shows two examples of poly edge normals. These were calculated using edge start – end crossed with world up vector. The platform on the left of the example has mixed edge winding, while those on the right are consistent. The edge normals on the left are not consistent, while those on the right are consistent. Inconsistent edge winding should only be a potential issue if you gather edges using different query methods, but it is something to be aware of and fix if present. An easy way to tell is to add some simple debug that will draw the edge normals.

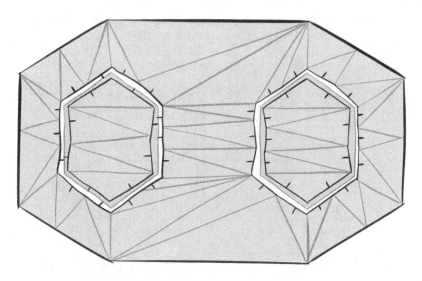

IMAGE 12.3   Mixed (left) and consistent (right) edge winding.

12.4.3   GENERATING SIMPLIFIED EDGES – IDENTIFYING EDGE LOOPS

Navigation meshes rarely mirror the geometry from which they are generated. Even a perfectly square platform will seldom produce a mesh consisting of four perfectly matching boundary edges per side. Instead, multiple boundary edges will make up what we might consider to be a 'single edge' when viewed in the context of geometry. This can be seen in the right platform of the example data shown in Image 12.3. Image 12.4 shows an enlarged look at the same data. The edges highlighted here are not a direct match. The single, straight edge of the geometry has resulted in three smaller boundary edges of nav-mesh. While the effect is exaggerated here, it is common. To reduce the amount of data to process, and to help generate more uniform links, a simplified edge that approximates the level geometry more closely can be generated.

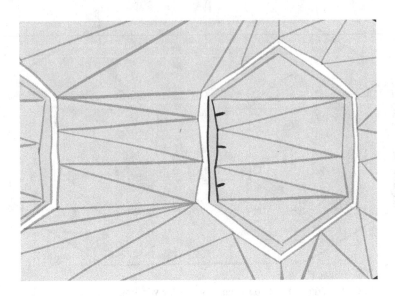

IMAGE 12.4 Example of how nav-edges do not always match geometry.

The first stage in doing this is to gather contiguous boundary edges. Two edges are considered contiguous if they share a common vertex. Boundary edges denote the exterior of polygons; so finding complete runs of contiguous edges in this way is identifying the inner and outer perimeters of navigation islands. These are referred to henceforth as edge loops. A navigation island refers to sections of mesh contained by a complete perimeter. To generate these edge loops, two boundary edges are compared, and if contiguous, they are grouped into an edge loop object. The next boundary edge is then checked, seeing if it fits with any existing loops, and if so, it is appended to the loop maintaining contiguity. If at any point an edge does not find a match, it starts its own group. This process may require multiple passes to ensure all boundary edges are correctly sorted. Image 12.5 shows the edge loops identified in the example data. Five distinct edge loops have been identified here, each shown by a different line style. It is clear to see that they outline the inner and outer perimeters of the navigation islands. As well as containing a set of contiguous boundary edges, each edge loop object also gets assigned a unique ID. This will be used later to differentiate between loops.

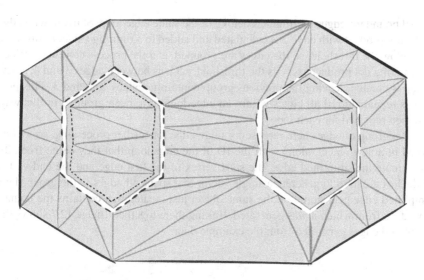

IMAGE 12.5 Identified edge loops in the example scenario.

12.4.4 GENERATING SIMPLIFIED EDGES – EDGE SIMPLIFICATION

With edge loops identified, the edges within can be further grouped by their relative directions to one another. These will then be used to generate a single, simplified edge. To determine these subgroups, each edge within an edge loop is checked against its neighbour. The dot product between them is calculated and stored in an accumulator. If this value remains below a determined threshold, the two edges are grouped, and the next edge is evaluated. If the threshold is exceeded at any point, the edge starts its own new group. Image 12.6 shows an example of this process.

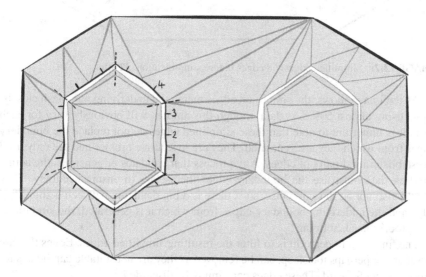

IMAGE 12.6 Identifying contiguous edges that are straight enough.

All boundary edges highlighted belong to the same edge loop. Starting with edge 1, the dot product with edge 2 is calculated and added to a running value. In this case it is below the threshold, so the edges are grouped, and the process continues. When the running dot product exceeds the threshold, such as between edges 3 and 4, a new group is created, leaving the previous group containing edges 1, 2, and 3. This process is repeated until all edges within an edge loop have been grouped in this way, and then repeated for each loop.

Each group of edges here represents a nav-edge for further processing, so will be stored in a new object, along with the ID of the edge loop that they came from. To then create the simplified edge, the start vertex of the first edge and the end vertex of the last are used to generate a single vector that spans all edges in the group. This simplified edge gets stored on the same object just created that contains the boundary edges from which it was generated, linking them together. Image 12.7 shows the simplified edges generated from the example data.

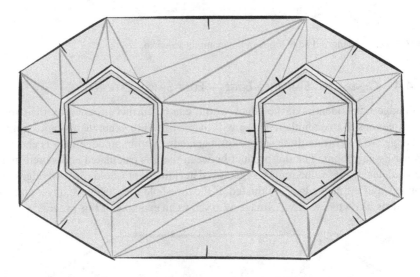

IMAGE 12.7 Simplified edges. 58 edges before simplification, 32 after.

As the image shows, the simplified edges match the underlying nav-mesh closely, while using almost 50% less data, though this amount will obviously vary for each case. It is important to note that these simplified edges do not replace the boundary edges from which they are generated. They are inaccurate proxies and are only used to establish initial pairs of edges. Any process that validates or generates the actual nav-link data must use the boundary edges themselves to ensure accuracy. They should also not be too imprecise, so if there is a big deviation between a simplified edge and the underlying boundary edges from which it is generated, the simplification process needs refining.

The final step to perform is to filter the resulting simplified edges. Edges that are too short, or perhaps too steep, can be removed as they are not suitable candidates for links moving forward. These edges can simply be discarded.

12.4.5   IDENTIFYING EDGE PAIRS

With simplified edge approximations generated, they can now be paired together as candidates for link generation. In this phase, checks are made that validate the relationship between two edges; level geometry is not considered at this stage. Two edges will be considered as a valid edge pair if:

- They belong to edge loops with different IDs. If they do not, they would come from the same nav-island and it is unlikely they would need to be linked.
- The distance between the edges is within valid limits.
- The two edges are parallel enough with one another.
- The direction of travel between the edges is correct.

Most of these checks are trivial to make, but the direction of travel can be complex. Consistent edge winding was identified earlier as important to establish, and that is because the edge normal can be used to determine the direction of travel relative to the poly. Image 12.8 shows edges with their normals shown, and dotted arrows have been added to denote the directions of travel through the edge pairs.

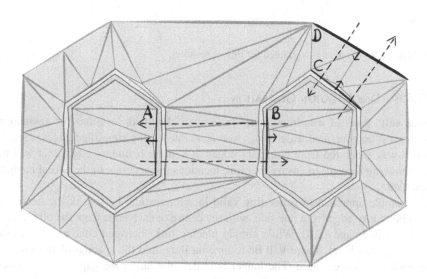

IMAGE 12.8   Examples of valid and invalid edge pairs based on the direction of travel.

If an agent passes through an edge in the opposite direction as the normal, they would be leaving a poly. If, however, they pass through an edge in the same direction as the edge normal, they would be entering a poly. This can be seen visually in Image 12.8 by following any dotted arrow and looking at the relationship between it and the normal of the edge it is passing through. For a link to be valid, an agent must leave a poly, and then re-enter a different one. The dot product can be used to determine this, with a dot>0 denoting 'same direction', and therefore entering a poly. Applying this to the data shown in Image 12.8, the links between edges A and B are valid. The links between C and D, however, are invalid.

Any two simplified edges that pass all these checks are suitable candidates for link generation. Image 12.9 shows the link candidates that have been generated in the example.

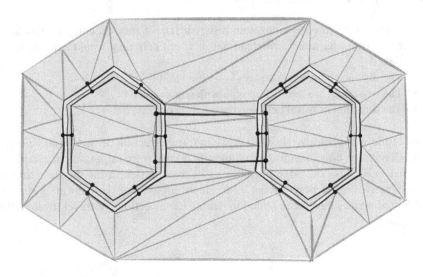

IMAGE 12.9   Edge pairs validated for link generation.

12.4.6   LINK LOCATION GENERATION

Once valid pairs of simplified edges have been identified, locations for navigation links must be generated. Edge pairs were generated using simplified edges, each of which was generated from boundary edges. It is these boundary edges that will be used moving forward to ensure that link locations are accurate to the actual navigation data.

A simple approach to generating valid locations would be to link the centre of each boundary edge from one side, with the centre of each edge from the other. This is shown in Image 12.10. While simply placing links between edge centres might work, it is not ideal. There will be redundant data, and the spacing of the links is dependent on edge length. The longer the edge, the larger the gaps between links which could result in agents taking circuitous paths to use them.

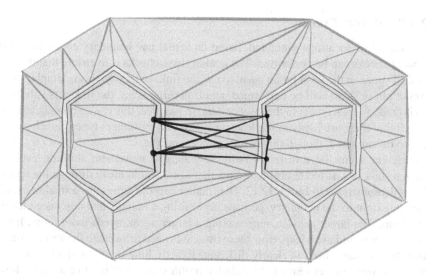

IMAGE 12.10 Example of simple linking of each boundary edge.

A better approach is to calculate the total length of the boundary edges on each side and determine how many links could be placed while maintaining a minimum spacing. This is done for both sides, and the minimum value was taken to ensure an even number of locations on each edge. An example of this improvement can be seen in Image 12.11. Assume that the edges of A have a total length of 80 units and the edges of B have a total length of 100 units. With a minimum distance of 20 units between links, the edges at A could fit 5 links, while the edges at B could fit 6. The minimum of 5 would be used, and each set of edges gets that number of links spread evenly across them. This has the benefit of having less data than the previous example, the links are more uniform, and it does not matter that the number of boundary edges is different at either side. The edges can be spread uniformly amongst them with some simple maths.

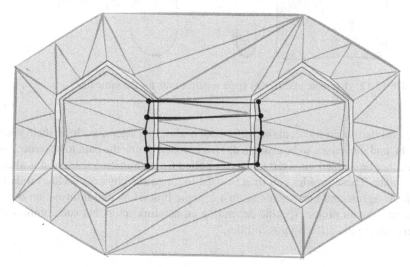

IMAGE 12.11 Better method for evenly spreading links.

12.4.7 PHYSICS CHECKS

With valid link locations generated, based on actual nav boundary edges, the final round of checks can be performed. The goal of these checks is to ensure that there is physical space in the level for an agent to use the link. In theory, this is simple; some form of physics cast will be performed, and if nothing is hit, the link gets validated and is ready for placement in the level or data. In practice, this can be complicated by the fact that there are likely multiple agent types, and movement types, which would need to be validated, though this is very project specific.

Different agents have different radii, heights, and movement abilities, each of which results in a different profile of how that agent would move through the space. This is demonstrated in Image 12.12. The smaller capsule represents a smaller agent. They stay tight to the geometry, perhaps performing a mantle, and don't need much headroom. The larger capsule, representing a larger agent, needs more room, however, as they would use a leap. How these two cases need to validate the space around them, for the same link, is clearly different. Exactly how this is best handled will depend on your project setup, but validation profiles can be of use to determine how different agents use links.

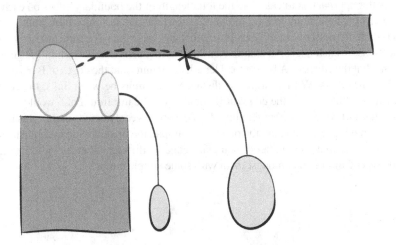

IMAGE 12.12 Example of different agent requirements for the same link.

A validation profile contains information about an agent, such as their width, height, and movement to be evaluated. This needs to define the path to be traced, and can either be defined via fixed targets, or pulled from animation data, so it is always up to date. These profiles can then be used to guide the physics checks, validating multiple agents and movements against a single link. How that information is then applied is again project specific depending on nav-link setup, but such profiles can help evaluate the different possibilities.

However multiple agent types and movements are handled, the physics casts will be performed, and any that fail will be removed as bad links. To demonstrate this, Image 12.13 shows a small physics object added to the example environment that would invalidate several links.

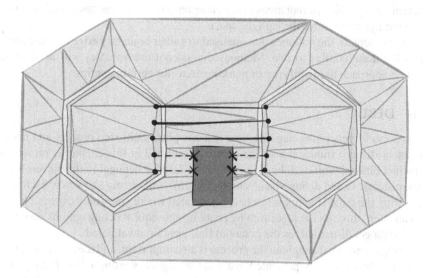

IMAGE 12.13   Image showing failed physics checks.

The dotted lines in Image 12.13 show links that would have failed the physics casts and so have been discounted. All remaining links are valid and ready to be added to the nav-data. For completion, the final nav-link data generated for the example environment is shown in Image 12.14.

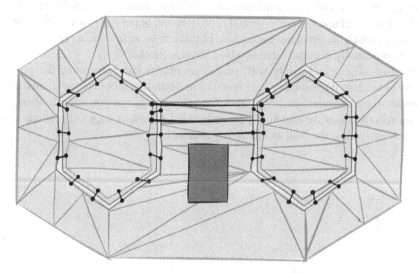

IMAGE 12.14   Final nav-link data generated in the example scenario.

12.5 CONFIG FILES

There are various places in the generation process where thresholds are defined. These values are best defined through config files so that auto-generation remains flexible, and some level of curation is maintained. For example: you could provide different configs for different areas of the game based on their geometry and how you want your agents to move through the space.

If implemented, the volumes that are used to gather boundary edge data are good places for these configs to live. Methods that do not use volumes will need some alternate approach to identifying or marking areas for certain configs.

12.6 DEBUG

The process of generating nav-link data is a complex, multi-step process and needs competent debug visualisations. The approach outlined in this chapter is presented in distinct phases, with each being a good candidate for debugging the current state of the process. Gated debug visualisations like this will clearly show how each step is affecting the data. If a link is not being generated where you would expect it to be, you can 'step' through the algorithm by enabling subsequent debug options until you see the data get discarded, or the potential link location invalidated.

Adding telemetry throughout the process is also important, and the phases through which the algorithm was presented again act as a good starting point. Having this information available is important as generating navigation data can already be an intensive process and any benefits of generation need to be fairly weighed against compromises such as increases in build times.

12.7 CONCLUSION

Auto-generating nav-link data can bring many benefits, including consistency of data, less manual work, and resilience of nav-data to iterative design. The approach outlined in this chapter is one potential approach, and hopefully gives inspiration for how to approach the problem. Each phase of this can be adapted to a project's needs, such as potentially needing more involved physics checks.

Starting off conservatively with generation efforts can help refine the process before generating redundant or incorrect data and building an exclusion volume early is highly recommended, as it will be a valuable tool should you need it. Plenty of debug visualisations are also highly recommended at various stages of generation, so that you can follow the data and track any anomalies.

13 Fluid Movement

Johan Holthausen

13.1 INTRODUCTION

Game worlds have become vast and complex over the years. Filled to the brim with objects and non-player characters (NPCs) to help bring the world to life. To improve the player's immersion, NPCs need to be able to navigate the world without walking into each other and/or other objects.

This chapter will look at how a game world can be translated into clear data for NPCs (interchangeable with 'agent' from now on) and shows some examples of how these can be navigated in a natural looking fashion.

13.2 NAVIGABLE SPACE

Navigable space is the translation of a game world into a set of convex shapes scaled by the agent's size to indicate a guaranteed area of movement without the need to check for static collisions. Its common implementations are nav-meshes, graphs, and grids. Each of these approaches is visualised in Image 13.1.

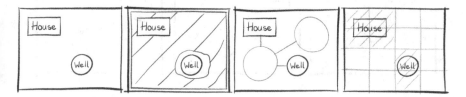

IMAGE 13.1 Navigable space represented (from left to right) as visual, nav-mesh, graph, and grid.

13.2.1 CREATION

Creating navigable space is done by taking the game world's (static) data and creating regions that can fit an agent, using attributes such as radius, height, step height, and the like. To provide a uniform representation, the size of the space is downsized by the radius of the agent, translating the agent into a single point location. This removes the need for calculating distances from obstacles when planning a path.

This process creates navigable regions with relation to their neighbouring regions. Each region is convex to ensure that they are collision free as the agent needs to be able to move from one location to another without hindrance.

DOI: 10.1201/9781003324102-13

13.3 PATH PLANNING

With navigable space, the set of generated regions can be represented in the form of a directed graph. Each vertex represents a region, and each edge represents a corridor between them. Edges contain data such as direction, size, costs, and other heuristics. Through the use of this graph, we can quickly find a desired path from our agent's location to its desired target. There are many approaches for finding the correct path to fit a given criteria, but common practice will often use a form of Dijkstra or A* to find the shortest path in the fastest amount of time.

A common problem path planning suffers from is scalability. As the navigable search space increases in size so does the number of potential solutions. Techniques such as sub-graphs, node-sets, or constraining distances can be used to help scaling. There is no need to search everywhere if the AI is not allowed to move to certain areas. This creates a set of path data containing the vertices to walk to and the edges providing information to reach them.

13.3.1 STRING PULLING

When the path planner has found the ideal path, it has only found which regions to traverse to and from. To make the agent take the truest shortest path and provide a more natural move, a post process of string pulling is applied to the path, as illustrated in Image 13.2.

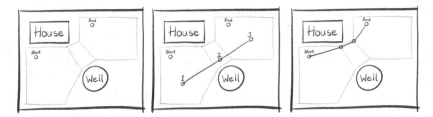

IMAGE 13.2   String pulling to find the shortest path between navigable regions.

String pulling starts by storing the start location of the agent as the first anchor point. It then tries to find the furthest corridor it can cast a line to that intersects all corridors in between. At worst, this will be the next corridor in the path. The location of the intersection is then stored as a new anchor point. This process is repeated using the last anchor point until the end location is reached.

Although this approach is most commonly used on paths generated by nav-meshes, it can still be applied to other data structures based on dynamic criteria. For example: a graph representation using a door for a corridor or a special grid tile that changes to indicate a ledge.

13.4 PATH FOLLOWING

We now have a path for our agent to follow in the form of a set of world locations, with the assurance of freedom of movement. The agent will traverse its path by providing a velocity update with each tick to follow the current path segment, made up of the next two locations of the path. Upon reaching the end point of the current segment, the next point in the path is used to create the next segment to follow.

13.4.1 PROXY AGENT

In some instances, it can be desired to have a sublayer between the agent and the path following. In these cases, a proxy agent can be introduced. This proxy behaves as a virtual, invisible agent, having its own movement constraints and other criteria. The proxy will follow the path and the agent will follow a target within the proxy. The agent will be tethered to this proxy and is given the insurance that the proxy will react to in-world events. A common reason for using a proxy is to allow multiple agents to walk as a group, as illustrated in Image 13.3. The proxy takes care of any avoidance and turns, and the agents will align themselves to this.

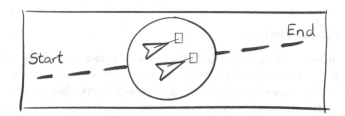

IMAGE 13.3   Two agents (triangles) following positions (squares) within a proxy (circle).

13.5 COLLISION

Until now we have described how a single AI agent can move through the world and avoid static geometry. However, a world will rarely be empty and will often contain all kinds of dynamic obstacles for our AI to avoid, such as the player, other agents, and dynamic terrain (rockslides, falling trees, and the like). These obstacles can be separated into two distinct categories: Pre-planned and Variable.

13.5.1 PRE-PLANNED OBSTACLES

Pre-planned obstacles are objects in the world that have a fixed location, impacting the navigation and the agent. Once the correct gameplay state is active these obstacles will come into effect, or even disappear. For example: a rock that can be removed by the player, allowing the connection of two regions or a cinematic creating a fire wall, blocking two regions.

When we know when and where there is an interaction with a 'dynamic' obstacle we can incorporate them with the creation of navigable space, creating a modular graph structure that allows the swapping of connections between nodes. Take a look at Image 13.4 for a depiction of this process. After a swapping of connection occurs, the active (proxy) agents will be notified and trigger a path replanning, making them reactionary from a more basic ground level.

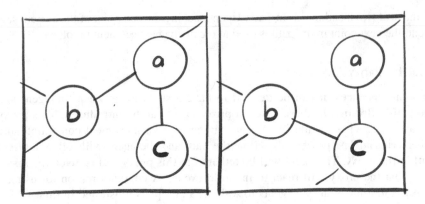

IMAGE 13.4   A modular graph block where a section of the graph can be swapped to ignore or create new connections.

13.5.2   VARIABLE OBSTACLES

Variable collisions are those that are influenced by more dynamic gameplay events. Most commonly being the avoidance of other agents. These collisions can be reacted to when they are about to happen or could potentially be predicted depending on the type. Even though the agent is following a path, it is technically only moving towards the end of its current path segment. This allows for deviation from said path if it is within the moveable space. After the deviation, the agent will resume heading toward its target location.

13.5.3   HEAD-ON COLLISIONS

One of the more primitive solutions to handling collisions is to delegate this to the physics system. As two agents intersect with each other the colliders will prevent clipping and push them away from one another. As most agents have a spherical collider, this creates the effect of them sliding against each other while passing, until they no longer collide.

13.5.3.1   Virtual Collisions

Commonly used with the implementation of proxy agent is the concept of virtual collision with other (proxy) agents. As two proxies come within range of each other, the proxies will repel one another and move past each other as with the physics collision. As the agent follows the proxy, it will not be impacted by this collision and will not be displaced. Instead, the agent simply aligns to its target position within the proxy. Having the head-on collisions hidden by the proxy allows the agent to maintain its location and reduce the chance of odd artefacts like foot sliding.

13.6   PREDICTING FUTURE COLLISIONS

Other than head-on collisions, it is also possible to anticipate any potential collision in the future and modify an agent's path accordingly.

13.6.1 STEERING

As the agent is moving along a path it continuously checks its current forward direction for any dynamic obstacles, ignoring any static ones as these have already been incorporated in the path generation. When an obstacle is detected, the agent will slowly steer away from the collision based on current velocity and distance to the collision.

In Code Listing 13.1, an example is shown where the agent will combine steering away from another agent while maintaining its course to its target. When interpolating with the current velocity, this creates a fluid momentum around the obstacle while maintaining a sense of direction towards the target path point. This algorithm is used for demonstration purposes as steering can incorporate many other factors, including other agent's heading and size.

Code Listing 13.1: Example of steering an agent away from an upcoming collision.

```
FVector CalculateAvoidanceVector(Agent agentA, Agent agentB)
{
    // Calculate strength based on distance to the other agent.
    // The closer, the stronger the impact.
    const float strength = 1.0f - (Distance(agentA.GetLocation() - agentB.GetLocation()) /
SteeringStartDistance);

    // Project a line from agent A to agent B and create a perpendicular
    // left/right vector depending on which side the target path point lies.
    const Line myLine (agentA.GetLocation(), agentB.GetLocation());
    const bool isLeft = IsPointLeftOfLine(myLine, agentA.GetCurrentPathLocation());

    const FVector directionToAgent = Normalise(agentB.GetLocation() - agentA.GetLocation());
    const FVector avoidanceVector = isLeft? LeftVectorFromForward(directionToAgent) :
RightVectorFromForward(directionToAgent);

    // Multiply the avoidance vector with the desired strength and add
    // this to the current path heading.
    return Normalise((avoidanceVector * strength) + agentA.GetPathHeading());
}
```

13.6.2 PATHFINDING WITH COLLISION ANTICIPATION

The navigation system will always be aware of the agents active in a world and what paths they are following. This could be utilised when planning a path, allowing the calculation in which sector a potential collision may occur. When following a path, the system can predict an agent's direction and location at any given time, allowing us to identify when multiple paths cross. If such an event were to occur, the current planning agent can treat the other agent as a temporary static obstacle for the purpose of path planning. By projecting an area around the obstructing agent, the path planner can string pull around this and generate a fluid path, free of obstacles, even if the object is in motion.

As illustrated in Image 13.5, an agent can predict a collision and adjusts its path at the path generation stage. This concept works under the assumption that each active agent will continue to follow their path. If an agent were to deviate from this motion it can result in agents trying to avoid nothing. This can be mitigated by applying the anticipation on a local level and only adjusting the path when nearing the agent or region.

IMAGE 13.5   Predictive collisions allow us to replan a path around the obstacle ahead of time.

13.7   CONCLUSION

Throughout the years we have seen games create worlds filled to the brim with NPCs that bring it to life. This chapter has explored how these NPCs can use various methods to navigate these worlds without stumbling into objects. A few examples of avoidance in a simulated world have been shown, which in the end will never be able to truly avoid one of the most unpredictable elements of the game: the player.

14 Combining Behaviour and Animation Systems in *Luna Abyss*

John Reynolds

14.1 INTRODUCTION

Creating behaviour systems that respond to a range of stimuli, all from different sources, is a complex challenge. Working with the animation system to set the appropriate trigger conditions, wait for blends, and query the current state, all while new stimulus events are arriving, adds to the challenge. It is important that the behaviour system maintains control of the character and that decisions or stimuli aren't lost because of the animation tree's current state, while respecting that the animations are the window to the behaviour system and the player can read a character's state through the way it moves. Decisions must also be made across all the team disciplines to ensure that the character reacts in a timely, convincing, and predictable way, both with the behaviour decisions and with the animation.

This chapter covers the decisions made while implementing the behaviour and character animation for one of the enemy characters, *Rawhed*, in the upcoming first-person game, *Luna Abyss*.

14.2 THE SOLE AUTHORITY

Decisions on behaviour can come from many sources. A behaviour tree can take a character through a flow of idle animations, patrolling, investigating shadows or noises, suspicion, enemy detection, attacking, reloading, moving to cover, and more. In addition to this, there can be higher-level team goals, such as advancing, retreating, flanking, or searching.

With an enemy within weapon range and a clear line-of-sight (LOS), the behaviour tree could make the decision that now is a good time to fire; however, there are other systems that could influence the decision to fire. The animation system could still be playing a key animation, such as a vault, which cannot be interrupted or blended out of; or the character could still be transitioning out of a run and back into its idle animation. So, the animation system may not be in a state where the character is ready to raise its gun. The behaviour tree will need to query the animation system to check if it is in a state where it is able to fire and have a fall-back plan if it is not. If the animation system confirms that it can transition into a fire animation, then that is great, and the character can fire. But if the animation system is not ready then we will

DOI: 10.1201/9781003324102-14

need to abandon the decision and re-evaluate again once the animation is complete. Modern engines make it very easy to add custom code and events to the animation system. This can be very useful as it allows for customisation of the animation system, but care must be taken to ensure that the animation system does not overrule the decision made by the behaviour tree.

When developing the *Rawhed* character, an animation of the character giving a battle cry was added, which was a great way of adding some depth to the character and some variety to its behaviour. However, this was added directly into the animation system based on a random number. After firing a volley of shots, the character would either move a few steps, to avoid being a static target, or randomly roar at the player. On the surface, this worked well, but there were situations where playing a roar, rather than moving, was inappropriate, such as when it was taking damage. So, the animation system code was changed to add some extra logic. After a few more situations where a roar was inappropriately played and additional exceptions were added to the animation system to address them, the animation system had gained its own set of behaviour logic.

Having to maintain this behaviour in two places is something that should be avoided at all costs. Keeping all the decision-making logic within the behaviour systems improves the maintainability of the game characters and avoids the inevitable confusion that results from having behaviour logic buried deep within other systems.

14.3   TRANSITIONS AND TIMERS

When designing an AI system, we can easily find ourselves focusing on the behaviour flow in isolation. This is particularly easy if we are using placeholder assets, with the actual models and animations coming later in the project. However, the behaviour tree should be created in a way that it responds well to tasks that take time. The decision to fire a weapon can mean that the character must first raise their gun, perhaps aim too, and maybe wait for a telegraphed event such as a 'charge-up' particle system. The behaviour tree must split the attack behaviour into raise weapon, fire shot, wait, fire second shot, and the like.

14.4   SUB-STATES

To achieve the task of firing a shot at the enemy, we need to differentiate between the high-level task and the steps required. Image 14.1 shows a visualisation of this process. Once the behaviour tree has decided upon an action, we can use sub-tasks, or states, to provide behaviours for all the time-based behaviours. This allows the character to remain in a firing behaviour while still proceeding through the sequence of steps that leads to the projectile being fired. The higher-level behaviour, such as the decision to fire, remains the active state. And while in this state, the character will step through all the animations and behaviours required to achieve this high-level behaviour. If an animation has not completed yet, the tasks will continue to wait, but the high-level state will remain the current state.

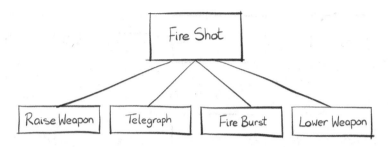

IMAGE 14.1 The sub-states of firing a weapon.

The behaviour system should remain in the current state until the task is complete, or a clear exit criterion has been met. This avoids animation issues when the AI system is moving quickly between choices. For example: when a decision is made to fire a weapon, the animation system begins raising the gun, but the enemy moves behind a pillar and so the behaviour system decides to move instead, and the character blends into a run. When the player reappears from behind the pillar, and a moment later, the decision is made to fire their weapon again. This results in undesirable behaviour where the arms appear to twitch as the character blends in and out of a run animation and the character moves a tiny distance.

By remaining in its state, the enemy will continue to fire. Having the enemy fire a volley of shots into a wall, just moments after the player has run behind it is an exciting way of affirming the player reached cover in time.

In *Luna Abyss*, when the *Rawhed* character had a valid target which they could see, the character entered a combat ready state, where the gun is raised, and the animation system is ready for the behaviour tree to send instructions to fire. These could be single events for single shots or burst start and burst stop events which used a looping fire animation. The combat ready state would only respond to a subset of animation events, such as flinching when taking damage, but the character would always remain ready to respond to instructions to fire its weapon.

14.5   WEAPON SEQUENCER

In *Luna Abyss*, there is a system called a *Weapon Sequencer*, which is used to control attack bursts. When an enemy fires, it is the weapon sequencer that decides on how many shots will be fired in the volley, the duration between shots, or whether a bullet pattern will be used. This is a great tool for the combat designer to use and each character's attacks can be choreographed and balanced. But this also means that there is another system that must be queried before deciding to begin an attack, and a system that must be considered when other stimuli come in. Image 14.2 shows how this worked in *Luna Abyss*.

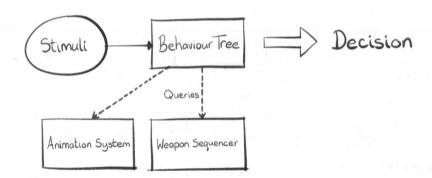

IMAGE 14.2   Behaviour Tree querying the animation system and weapon sequencer.

The weapon sequencer can be queried by the behaviour tree to determine how long is remaining before the next attack, or how long before the current attack burst completes. This allows the behaviour tree to evaluate whether there is time to do another behaviour before it is time to fire again.

For most of the enemy characters, the weapon sequencer was allowed to play out its attacks without interruption. If the character was shot by the player, it would trigger a flinch animation on the nearest bone and adjust the character material to make it flash white for a frame or two. For the *Rawhed* character, the weapon sequencer was used to fire short bursts at the player, during which *Rawhed* would remain focused on firing until the burst was complete. The firing behaviour is triggered by the behaviour tree itself, but the behaviour tree could also issue move commands independently of the firing behaviour. This allows *Rawhed* to move for a few seconds and stand still for a few seconds, regardless of whether the character is firing. Similarly, *Rawhed* can move to cover if they become injured without interrupting the weapon sequencer until they enter cover.

This slight disconnection between moving and firing led to a more dynamic character. We appreciated that there would have been value in allowing the player to understand that while *Rawhed* was moving they were safe, as the character would not fire. However, it was decided that this was an acceptable trade-off as the *Rawhed* was the lowest ranking enemy – a grunt or cannon fodder – and existed to provide a background threat while higher-powered enemies did their attacks. Having *Rawhed* move around the scene with their gun always raised and ready to fire, achieved what was required of that character.

It is important for the animation team to appreciate that the animation duration will affect the character's response time. An elaborate raise gun animation, where the character checks that the gun is cocked before carefully raising it and taking careful aim, will make a character's response sluggish. In *Far Cry 2*, characters would exit a vehicle using a convincing animation and would blend into their idle animation before entering combat. This made the enemy feel unresponsive and disconnected when they chased you down in their vehicle because it took a long time transitioning from driving and into combat.

Raising a weapon can be a good way of communicating to the player that the character is about to fire, but the animation team will need to work with the combat designer to ensure that the pacing of animations is suitable for the game and the responsiveness required. Animation playback speed can be adjusted at runtime, but usually by less than 20% to avoid the animations looking unconvincing.

14.6 CONCLUSION

As AI programmers, we should create systems where the AI system retains full control over the character's behaviour. The AI system can query other systems and send events, but we should avoid situations where behavioural decisions are being made outside the AI code. We should strive for clear boundaries and interfaces between these systems.

The behaviour systems should be developed with consideration for timings. Animations, particle systems, and combat systems can all require the AI system to wait for events. During these pauses, the character's behaviour must remain focused on the current high-level task. Only well-defined events should break a character out of its state. The *Rawhed* character in *Luna Abyss* went through a few changes during the lifetime of the project, but allowing the AI systems to maintain control made the character maintainable and allowed the tech, design, and animation teams, to focus their strengths on making the best character for the game.

15 How to Make Your AI Fireproof
25 Years of AI Firefighting

Andrea Schiel

15.1 INTRODUCTION

It is possible to build an AI system such that it is less prone to bugs, runs efficiently, and is easy to author for. In the intricate world of AI game design, the choice of architecture is a critical decision that can have a profound impact on the outcome of a project. The selection of an ill-suited architecture can trigger a cascade of issues that reverberate throughout the entire system, manifesting as bugs, inefficiencies, and a cumbersome development process. For example, if a rule-based system is used for a task that involves complex, non-linear relationships, it may struggle to produce accurate results and may require a lot of manual intervention to address edge cases. On the other hand, if a neural network is used for a task that involves explicit rules and logical reasoning, it may produce suboptimal results and be difficult to interpret and explain. Choosing the right architecture can also impact the performance of the system. Some architectures are more efficient than others and can process data faster or require fewer computational resources. This can be important in applications where speed or efficiency is a critical factor. Just as in biology, where a mismatch between an organism and its environment can lead to adverse consequences, the wrong choice of AI architecture can disrupt the delicate balance of a game's AI system. The consequences of such disruptions can be far-reaching, leading to delays, additional work, and increased costs. Therefore, it is crucial to choose an architecture that is aligned with the needs of the game to ensure a smooth and efficient AI development process.

Why do so many games end up with AI systems that do not quite fit the bill? Games built with suboptimal AI approaches are not uncommon, despite the potential negative impact of such decisions. The wrong AI system can be chosen in various ways, one of which is the lack of a deliberate choice in AI architecture, and instead, opting for pre-existing AI systems. How many times have you begun a project with the AI system that came with the engine, such as the behaviour tree in Unreal Engine (Epic Games, 2002)? Such a decision could be driven by the sunken cost fallacy (Kahneman, 2012), which suggests that the previous investment in a game or the availability of a pre-existing AI system should be the primary factor in the decision-making process. This approach is based on the false assumption that reusing or repurposing these AI systems would be faster, cheaper, or safer.

DOI: 10.1201/9781003324102-15

Unfortunately, the decision to build the AI based on sunk costs rather than game requirements can result in significant limitations in functionality and potential drawbacks in performance.

We also tend to feel more comfortable with systems that we know how to use, rather than taking the time to explore new options. Psychologists refer to this tendency as the availability heuristic (Lilienfeld & Lynn, 2014), where we assume something is true or right simply because it is familiar or comfortable to us. When a programmer or a designer chooses a scripted AI system simply because they are familiar with it, they may be making the mistake of assuming it is the best option without fully exploring other potential solutions that may be better suited for the game's AI requirements. This sort of suboptimal decision-making can have negative consequences for the development of the game.

Developing a new AI system can be a costly and time-consuming process, and it is very natural to stick with what you know and what has worked in the past. Due to the cost, the decision to abandon a proven system for a new one requires a deliberate and thoughtful evaluation of the potential benefits and drawbacks of each option. One possible approach is to assess whether the existing system can meet the specific requirements of the game's AI design. If it falls short or cannot be adapted to meet the game's needs, it may be necessary to explore new options. Additionally, it is important to consider whether new AI technologies or methods, such as deep learning or reinforcement learning, could offer significant advantages over the existing system. These techniques may be able to provide more advanced and adaptable AI behaviours that can elevate the game's overall experience. Ultimately, the decision to adopt a new system should be based on a careful and objective analysis of the available options, rather than relying solely on familiarity or past success.

Objectively comparing AI approaches using quantitative properties helps avoid natural biases in the decision process by providing a systematic and data-driven approach to evaluate different AI systems. By focusing on specific quantitative properties such as scalability, efficiency, and adaptability, the evaluation process becomes less subjective and less prone to preconceived notions. Adopting a systematic approach to characterise the properties of the design requirements of the project at hand, and then evaluating a variety of AI approaches and their properties against the properties of the design, will allow programmers to make more informed decisions and avoid the pitfalls of relying on subjective biases or incomplete information.

This chapter will explore a process for quantifying AI architectures based on their underlying properties rather than their static metrics of implementation. Common AI approaches will be examined and described in terms of these properties. In addition, the process of extracting the properties of a game's design will be covered using examples from shipped titles. However, even with a thorough understanding of this process, there may still be resistance to overhauling or replacing a current system. Therefore, this chapter will start with how to measure the cost of having the wrong architecture to help convince decision-makers of the importance of objective evaluation.

15.2 CASE STUDIES

15.2.1 CASE STUDY 1: MEDAL OF HONOR HEROES I AND II

In 2006, EA released a game called *Medal of Honor Heroes I* based on the well-known and successful *Medal of Honor* franchise. Set in WWII, it was a first-person shooter (FPS) game designed for Sony's PSP handheld gaming platform, which was known for being memory, CPU, and GPU constrained compared to platforms like the Xbox. Unlike the original *Medal of Honor* game, which had a highly scripted campaign with little AI, *Heroes I* required its AI to move around the level and make use of cover in a sandbox skirmish mode. The only available AI system was a scripted system, designed for campaigns, which did little more than spawn an AI agent that could shoot at the player until it was killed. To measure the impact of the pre-existing scripted AI system, the time to write a script and to hand-place agents for a typical *Heroes I* level was measured. During run time, the average lifetime or time to AI death (TTD) was measured, as was the system's performance (CPU). The resulting tests showed that the authoring of scripts for sandbox levels would take too long, and result in a poor, repetitive AI experience since the script would set up the same scenario every time. This is an extreme case where the pre-existing AI system did not meet the needs of the AI design requirements and was too cumbersome to continue to use.

15.2.2 CASE STUDY 2: AGE OF EMPIRES IV

Published by Microsoft in 2021 for the PC, *Age of Empires IV* was built on top of the *Relic* Essence Engine. This same engine had been used with great success for previous real-time strategy (RTS) games. However, in this case it was recognised that the scope of *Age of Empires* was much larger than previous titles, so a lot of changes were made. One requirement was a method for the AI players to find enemy walls. An initial prototype system was put in place. The cost of reworking this prototype would require significant time from both the gameplay and AI development teams and as such the work was pushed out. This is a slightly different case of sunken cost that happens despite the best of intentions. In this case, a prototype of a system was left rather than reworked. The thinking was the same though – that it was "cheaper" to keep it and fix the bugs as they came in, rather than to rework it. To finally make a case for fixing this, bugs related to this (fixed or unfixed) were grouped. As new bugs came in that were caused by this, they were added to the group. A technical design for a proper system was made and estimated by both development teams. Once the number of bugs and the cost of fixing them started to outpace the cost of the rework, then production was able to justify the expense of fixing the system. It is not easy to project the cost of future bugs or to quantify the quality improvements. Nor was showing the poor runtime performance of the existing system despite having projected performance improvements for the proposed replacement. It was not enough to point out that there were things that could not be done with the prototype system. Unless those capabilities were a high priority, production had to have something more that they could measure that would help justify the cost. Prototypes that ship are an example of how the sunken cost fallacy can lead to a reluctance to change, even when it is necessary, and can result in wasted resources and time.

15.3 AVOIDING THE TRAP

To make unbiased decisions, it is crucial to take a quantitative approach to compare different options – especially when it comes to choosing an AI system. While it may not always be possible to compare runtime performance, any quantitative metrics should be used whenever feasible. For instance, in *Age IV*, it was possible to look at the runtime performance against a hypothetical approach, but the scale of the decision was smaller than an entire decision architecture.

To begin the comparison, the primary functional requirements should be met by each approach. This is a crucial step as each system has its own inherent properties. Planning systems solve planning problems, but they are not particularly reactive. Therefore, each system's ability to meet functional requirements, as well as the properties of the design and any quantitative metrics, must be compared. This process can be used during pre-production, production, or even as a post-mortem analysis. In the games as a service model, it can be used to identify technical debt that should be weighed against any new feature development. This process assumes that there is no existing system, and the current system becomes just another option to consider.

15.3.1 STEP 1 – GATHER THE COMPLETE DESIGN REQUIREMENTS

The first step is to go back to the design – to the requirements. It is possible that the design may be incompletely described. For example: in iterative titles, design is sometimes assumed to be the same as the last one with some minor tweaks. It is on the engineer to ensure they have a complete set of requirements. In games already live or in production, there may be parts of the design that were never met by the current approach and there may have been cut features – pieces of the design that were sacrificed to a lack of development time. Once the full set of requirements has been established, the next step is to characterise the properties of the design. By carefully comparing the properties of the design with the properties of a variety of approaches, developers can assess whether the current AI system is meeting those requirements or if there is a better approach that could be used.

The first place to start would be the original design spec. However, given that not every designer will know what questions the AI developer needs answered, it is best practice to follow up with design. Here are some key questions to ask that can help elicit a more complete design:

1. How long does the AI agent expect to live?
2. How many AI will be active at any one time?
3. What sort of decisions is the AI making?
4. Does the AI need to plan or strategise?
5. Who will be authoring the AI?

In the first question, you will want to know the complexity of the AI's response to a situation. In a sports title, the AI plays the entire game, so this question is less relevant. In a combat game, an AI that has an expected lifetime of 30 seconds does not need the complexity of a behaviour tree. The second and third questions help nail down the scale of the AI. This will inform how expensive the decision-making and perception systems can be. A game that runs armies of 400+ units needs an AI that runs efficiently and at scale. The fourth question is going to sort which approaches make sense. AIs that require planning will need some sort of planner approach. The fifth question also restrict the choice of system. If the system requires an expert to author, such as with an expert system (usually some sort of production rule system but these can be scripted as well) or with a machine learning model that needs training, and there is no expert, then these systems are not going to be good approaches.

To ensure that any missing or cut features are captured in a game already in development, production and the schedule can be consulted. In this case, the developer should be looking to answer the following:

1. What parts of the design had to be cut due to time constraints?
2. Which parts of the AI take the longest to tune or to author?
3. Which parts of the AI's current behaviour are functioning poorly?

Games that are even later in development, including live games, will have a history of runtime performance profiling data and an extensive bug database. Identifying areas that are slow at runtime, or that are very spiky, are good areas to consider that the design and the approach are not a good fit. The same could be said for subsystems that seem to always have bugs. In this case we are identifying features of the design that are not being met well.

15.3.2   Step 2 – Characterise the Design

The purpose of gathering requirements is to determine the scope and type of work. In this case, the scope and types of decision-making needed by the AI system. It is not enough to have a wish list from Design, but the design spec needs to be analysed or characterised.

The first quantitative property would be to find the most frequent tasks that the designers engage in. Production can help here by listing Design tasks by frequency. A key principle is to make the tasks most frequently done easy and everything else as easy as possible. So, the top tasks should be examined for how long and how easy they are for a designer to execute. It is not always easy to see how this relates to an architectural choice. In BioWare's *Dragon Age II*, it was thought that it would make it easier to expose the logic for targeting to the designer by representing it in the behaviour tree implementation. A few things happened: behaviour trees and decision trees are not meant to loop or iterate within their execution. You can apply whole trees to each member of a list, but you do break the intended flow of execution if you loop within a tree structure. This resulted in spikes in performance. For designers who wanted to tweak different numbers for different characters and to open the behaviour tree editor it turned out to be a cumbersome process. The task they did the most was not to change the logic flow but to mostly tune the numbers. The fix was to extract the targeting logic into another tool better suited to number tweaks. Behaviour trees and decision trees are approaches best used when the logic being used is complex. A simple table of numbers with a hard-coded logic is often more performant if you are just varying on stats. This is an example of how the choice of architecture was inappropriate for a sub-piece of the AI and how it impacted the development efficiency as well as runtime performance.

Another property is the expected lifetime of the AI. In the case of *Heroes II*, the original AI would last about 3–15 seconds, but the design was looking for an AI that could last for >30 seconds. Another design property was the expected set of behaviours and the requirement that the AI can chase the player was not being met by the current system. The AI could neither roam the level, nor pick a cover spot. The fix in this case was to replace the scripted AI with a limited priority queue that acted like a fuzzy finite state machine (fFSM) (Malik et al., 1994). While not as robust as a behaviour tree, fFSMs have both emergent properties and were reactive enough to extend the AI's lifetime to upwards of 2 minutes.

The scope of the AI should also be defined by this point. In *Age IV*, the engine, which had been designed for squads of 5–10 soldiers, had to be refactored to support armies of 200 units and for up to 8 players. Decisions that are made with a high frequency per unit would have to be cheap. Whereas with a game with only 1–10 AI enemies running could support the average runtime of a behaviour tree. As mentioned earlier, if the AI units do not need to live for more than 30 seconds, a behaviour tree is probably over engineered, and a simpler approach might be faster to develop with and execute, regardless of how many AI units need to be supported.

The design should also indicate which decisions require planning, which may require coordination, and which may require some emergence. For example, AI with a tech research tree in which there are constrained ways to research a technology could indicate the need for some planning. If there are a lot of ways to get to the same technology, though, a more opportunistic, greedy approach might make more sense.

Finally, the game design may indicate the idea of modes of gameplay or states that the game can be in. This refers to a state property. A first-person shooter can have two core modes: in combat or out of combat. It may also have other modes: in vehicular gameplay, on foot gameplay, and the like. This is indicative of obvious states that the AI could be in. Other games, such as a RTS, may not have aseasily identifiable states. This does not make them emergent, just that it could be hard to determine what state the game is in. In these cases, AI approaches involving state, such as Finite State Machines (FSM), may be expensive to do as determining the state could be non-performant and difficult.

These states will be examined more thoroughly in the next section. The process of characterising the properties of the design is to establish the requirements for the AI system in a systematic way. Once you have the properties of the design understood, the next step is to characterise the current AI system. If there is not a current system, then the next step is to pick some subset of AI systems to examine their native characteristics. In an ideal world, it should be obvious how to match AI approaches to the current design through their shared properties.

15.3.3 Step 3 – Define the Properties of the AI System

To compare how well the current AI system meets the needs of the design, it should be understood both functionally and at a system level. Most AI programmers will have mapped out the static layout of a system's major classes. There may be a data flow or an activity diagram of its update. These are excellent starting points for a functional understanding. At a system level, each AI system will have inherent properties. These properties describe how the system interacts with the game. The following is a list of the properties you might consider with respect to measuring both an existing approach and hypothetical approaches. That is, these properties exist outside of a specific implementation.

15.3.3.1   State Property

A FSM is stateful. It carves up the game into states and needs to determine a state to be in. A decision tree does not have state. It may be deciding what state the game is in, but it is interacting with the game's current properties to do so. It does this every frame so the tree itself does not hold state. The property of state is useful in two regards. First, it brings with it the need to be able to subdivide the problem into states. Secondly, the update of such systems tends to update the current state which can be a performance advantage or a disadvantage when the state changes with a high frequency. For a stateful approach to be usable, the game itself must lend itself to easily identifiable states.

15.3.3.2   Reactivity Property

Another property to consider is how reactive it is. One advantage to not holding state is that the system can react to what is happening right now. This makes such systems, such as decision trees, better at handling games where the state changes frequently. They are highly reactive. This is because they re-evaluate every update. FSMs are moderately reactive by comparison. Even if the FSM updates every frame, they do so only within their current state context. At the other extreme are planners. A full-order planner like Goal-Oriented Action Planner (GOAP) has a low reactivity. Planners work best when they have time to lay out a plan that is then followed. Working out the plan is usually relatively expensive and best when not executed every update. If plans are frequently interrupted, it can become very expensive as the planner will need to replan a lot.

15.3.3.3   Emergence Property

Another good property to look at is the system's emergence. Emergence in this case is referring to the possibility of unexpected behaviours. Most scripted AIs will have low emergence. This is highly variable depending on the scripting system and where the scripting is being used. *Age of Empires II* used a scripted AI that scripts the overall approach but is reactive at lower levels. A script with a lot of random events can still be quite emergent. The whole point, usually, of using a scripted approach is to take advantage of its fixed nature. In *Medal of Honor*, the scripts were to control the AI in a predictable fashion in line with the narrative elements of the story. For example: after a voice over, spawn three soldiers here and move them there. The reactive part, the system that makes them shoot was extremely limited. Overall, this system had low emergence. You could rely on the same three soldiers doing the exact same thing every time. A behaviour tree, on the other hand, can be quite emergent, especially if authored well. Utility systems are an approach that compares different outcomes based on a scoring system which can be highly emergent as well. If the design requires predictable, repeatable AI actions, then choosing a highly emergent system will mean a lot of edge case bugs.

15.3.3.4 Planning Property

Planners are a group of AI approaches that produce plans as their output. Other approaches produce behaviours (behaviour trees) or decisions (FSM, decision trees) or predictions (Bayesian networks, Deep neural networks). Planners can handle situations where the solution requires reasoning, searching, or decision-making under uncertainty. Most games will have some sort of implementation of A* as their navigation planning solution. If, instead of planning, the AI used a direct walk towards the goal, as was done in the game *Dead Reckoning*, it is possible for the AI agent to get stuck in a local optima dead end. Most other architectures do not consider the long-term consequences of the actions taken and may not result in the best overall solution. These approaches are more suitable for problems where the objective is to find a quick, satisfactory solution, rather than an optimal or near-optimal solution. In game AI architecture, using a non-planner approach for a planning problem could result in the AI making suboptimal decisions, which could hurt the game's overall experience. The planning property is really a subjective classification of the AI's overall problem. Does the game design or situation have a lot of "dead ends"? Does it require searching for a best or near-best solution? Can it take more than one update to "decide" what to do?

15.3.3.5 Expertise Property

This is the property design to capture how much expertise is needed by the author of the AI and is arguably the most overlooked property of them all. For example, production rule systems require someone to create rules. If the rules are authored by someone who is not a problem domain expert, will that be ok? A medical diagnosis system is not one that could be authored by a programmer as domain (medicine) expertise is needed. The same applies to rules-based systems for a first-person shooter or for a machine learning model mimicking a race car driver. Other expert guided approaches include expert systems, scripted systems applied to solve specific domain problems, fuzzy logic systems, decision trees, utility functions, neural and Bayesian networks using guided input, and genetic algorithms or reinforcement learning models using guided fitness functions. This means that if your research tree for a strategy game requires expert level decision-making, using a designer who is not an expert player to author one of these approaches will generate subpar AI experiences. If no expert is available, it would be better to consider a more generalised approach.

15.3.3.6 Machine Learning Properties

The properties for machine learning vary by the specific approach. One useful property is its data required for training. Reinforcement learning policies tend to require a large sample set, as do a lot of large-scale models. Some deep neural networks require smaller but clean data sets. Consider if the training could be done with synthetic data or how the model or policy is trained.

The reward or label property needs to be considered. Reinforcement learning (RL or DRL) requires a clear reward and operates best when the reward can be delivered frequently and relatively near, temporally, to the desired behaviour. Deep neural networks (DNNs) require labelled data to be trained. If the design makes understanding what an optimal move is at any given time difficult or ambiguous, it can be very expensive and very time consuming to train a model or policy.

15.3.3.7   Authored/Data Properties

It is possible that the current system is the most appropriate but that it has been misused. It may also be useful to look at the data or the current authoring of the system. For example, if a behaviour tree is being used, does it have any unusually long branches or is it very wide? Both are indicative of using the behaviour tree as a script. If the only nodes being used are selector nodes, the author may have a bias towards decision trees. When behaviour trees become riddled with interrupts, it may be being used as a finite state machine. The use of interrupts may also indicate that the system is not reactive enough for the design. If you suspect that the authoring is creating distinct properties, it would be good to list those as well though separate from the core properties.

15.3.3.8   Other Properties

Other properties for consideration, depending on your needs, include update cost, memory requirements, world scalability, cooperation modelling, and the level of expertise needed by the author. There is no official guide to how to rate the various known approaches and certainly there will be nothing on any custom AI approach. If there are several systems, the same process of outlining each of their properties should be done. The key here is to be honest about the advantages and disadvantages of the current approach.

There are other architectural properties discussed in literature that may not be as useful for this process. These include the concepts of cyclomatic complexity, cohesion, coupling, and so on. These sorts of properties are more useful for analysing if there is a problem with the specific implementation of any given architecture. The properties that are useful for architectural comparison, with regards to game design, tend to be ones that are fundamental to the particular system regardless of implementation. However, no property is entirely independent of either implementation or usage. Emergence may or may not be useful for example, since any system, if authored incorrectly, can become rigid and deterministic.

15.3.4   STEP 4 – DESIGN MEETS IMPLEMENTATION

The final stage is to compare the properties of the design with the properties of the current AI system and a couple of alternate systems. Even if everyone is determined that they know which system they want to implement, it is important to go through the comparison as a sanity check. As an example, the following case studies are presented. These are cases where the design called for the AI to have certain properties, but the wrong approach was used, or the right approach was used but in a poor manner.

15.3.4.1 Case Study 3: ReCore

Released in 2016, developed by Armature Studio, *ReCore* is a single player action-adventure game involving a young woman and her robot dog. Together they fight a series of diverse robotic opponents. *ReCore* used a hFSM for its AI enemies. Its properties might be those shown in Table 15.1.

TABLE 15.1

ReCore Used an hFSM for Its AI Enemies

Property	ReCore's hFSM
State	Yes
Reactive	High
Emergent	Low
Planner	No
Opportunistic/greedy	No
Handle complex world	No
Scales with number of agents	Linearly
Easy to create variants	Yes

ReCore's hFSM editor required the designer to be fairly technical, though the editor and debugger were excellent. As an example of authored data being an issue, some of the authored state trees, that is, its data, were built more like a behaviour tree. This is an example of when the data of a system has different properties than the system itself. In this case these trees were less predictable and tended to react to the current situation rather than have a defined behaviour in a set state. In other words, the properties of the data were those shown in Table 15.2.

TABLE 15.2

Properties of ReCore's hFSM

Property	ReCore's hFSM – Specific FSMs (Data)
State	Somewhat
Reactive	High
Emergent	Moderate
Planner	No
Opportunistic/greedy	Yes
Handle complex world	No
Scales with number of agents	Linearly
Easy to create variants	No

This resulted in a variety of edge cases with suboptimal experiences for the player. The fix here would have either been to reauthor the data to be more like a classical hFSM or to rework the tool to enforce more of a hFSM standard (preventing the issue in the first place). The design did not require the depth of behaviour that a behaviour tree offers.

15.3.4.2   Case Study 4: *Medal of Honor Heroes II* – Revisited

As an example of when a design change requires a new AI approach – in *Medal of Honor Heroes II*, the design specified an on-rails shooter mode. This mode required that the AI not move around and that it only do a limited set of actions. The AI needed to have low emergence, be highly predictable, not opportunistic, not intentional, and have high reactivity. The current AI system, from the first *Heroes* game, was a fFSM, and did not share these properties. The fFSM was emergent and varied. It was highly reactive. When the properties of the fFSM were compared with the design properties as can be seen in Table 15.3, it became apparent that the old script system was a better approach. Since *Heroes II* shipped with the skirmish mode as well, two AI approaches were used: the script-based system for the on-rail shooter and the fFSM was kept for skirmish.

TABLE 15.3

Comparing Two AI Systems between Games

Property	*MoH Heroes I* fFSM	*MoH Heroes II* Script
State	Somewhat	Yes
Reactive	High	High
Emergent	High	None
Planner	No	No
Opportunistic/greedy	Yes	No
Handle complex world	No	No
Scales with number of agents	Linearly	Linearly
Easy to create variants	No	No

15.3.4.3   Case Study 5: Optimisations Gone Bad

This is one of the most frequent causes for an AI "fire". In these cases, the system or approach was not necessarily the wrong one. It was just too expensive. As such, the system was altered through an optimisation. Optimisations can change the inherent properties of a system depending on what they do.

Many AI systems have an inherent update requirement. Highly reactive AI systems, like FSMs or decision trees, need to update every tick. In these sorts of systems, when the AI update is skipped, the AI will become less responsive and buggy.

Another form of optimisation bug is when a planning or search-based system, which is designed to run over many frames asynchronously, gets halted. For example, if the A* planning takes too many frames to deliver a path, often it is aborted as a time out. Graph searches such as A* do not work when capped. The current "partial" path is not necessarily guaranteed to be optimal. Intuitively, one would think that the current path might be the closest path that could currently be generated, but it is not. It could very well be a degenerate path going in the opposite direction. Another variant is when the game implements A* in a blocking fashion and just cuts it short after a certain number of opened nodes. This results in truly bizarre partial paths that are rarely useful (Martelli, 1977).

Finally, another common issue occurs when behaviour trees, which can be inherently expensive to evaluate, are evaluated every update. Behaviour trees are meant to select a behaviour and run that behaviour – re-evaluating rarely. Often this results in "unresponsive" AI agents and to fix this, the tree becomes littered with interrupts to force the tree to re-evaluate. In these cases, often the design implied a higher level of reactivity, which would have indicated a different approach, and the designer is fighting the behaviour tree and trying to work with it as a decision tree or FSM. When optimisation occurs, the trees are often made shallower as more and more logic is pulled out of the behaviours. This results in two quality issues. The behaviour tree loses its ability to backtrack, a core characteristic of behaviour trees that makes them more intelligent and robust, and the tree becomes very cumbersome to maintain. Reactivity should be handled at the behaviour level, not by interrupting the tree.

15.3.5 STEP 5 – FINDING THE RIGHT APPROACH

There is one last hurdle to overcome which is to create a table of candidate alternate systems. Though if the AI programmer has limited familiarity with other approaches, it can make it harder to compare. To that end, Tables 15.4–15.6 detail some of the properties from implementations in shipped titles. If there is a system that seems more appropriate, then at least this may provide some motivation to do more research. However, it is advisable to create your own table with the properties that make the most sense. Even if the current approach does seem to fit the design, there may be one that is less dependent on having an expert or one that is lighter weight at runtime.

TABLE 15.4

AI Approaches with State, Reactive and Emergence Properties from Shipped Titles

System	State	Reactive	Emergence
Simple decision tree	No	High	No
Limited action utility function	No	High	Moderate
Spatial placement utility function	No	Low	High
Fuzzy finite state machine	Yes	High	Moderate
Simple DNN	No	High	High
Production rules system	No	High	High
Goal-oriented action planner	Yes	Low	High
Behaviour tree	Yes	Moderate	Low
Simple finite state machine	Yes	High	No
Partial order planner	Yes	Moderate	High
Hierarchical task network	Yes	Moderate	Moderate
Scripted set of orders	Yes	Low	No
Reinforcement pathing policy	No	High	High

TABLE 15.5
AI Approaches with Author, Planning, and Complexity Properties from Shipped Titles

System	Type of Author	Planning	World Complexity
Simple decision tree	Anyone	No	Moderate
Limited action utility function	Anyone	No	Moderate
Spatial placement utility function	Technical	No	High
Fuzzy finite state machine	Anyone	No	Moderate
Simple DNN	Expert/technical	Predictive	High
Production rules system	Expert	Limited	Moderate
Goal-oriented action planner	Technical	Yes	Moderate
Behaviour tree	Technical	No	High
Simple finite state machine	Anyone	No	Low
Partial order planner	Technical	Yes	Moderate
Hierarchical task network	Expert/technical	Yes	High
Scripted set of orders	Expert	No	Low
Reinforcement pathing policy	Expert/technical	No	High

TABLE 15.6
AI Approaches with Coordination, Number of Agents, and Ease of Debugging Properties Seen in Shipped Titles

System	Supports Multiagent Coordination[a]	Supports Large Number of Agents	Easy to Debug
Simple decision tree	No	Yes	Easy
Limited action utility function	No	Moderate	Poor
Spatial placement utility function	Yes	Moderate	Poor
Fuzzy finite state machine	Yes	Moderate	Easy
Simple DNN	Yes	Moderate	Poor
Production rules system	Yes	No	Average
Goal-oriented action planner	No	No	Average
Behaviour tree	No	No	Average
Simple finite state machine	Yes	Moderate	Easy
Partial order planner	Yes	No	Moderate
Hierarchical task network	Yes	Moderate	Moderate
Scripted set of orders	Yes	Moderate	Moderate
Reinforcement pathing policy	Yes	Yes	Poor

[a] Supports multiagent coordination means the system does not require any additional work and can control multiple agents at the same time working on a task together.

This is by no means an exhaustive examination of all the possible approaches; it is just a subset from actual experience. The values for the various properties are reflective of the specific implementation for each. Decision trees, for example, can be used for planning. The decision tree referenced above is a simpler use case more commonly found in games. The next step here is to select a few candidates that might match the properties of the design. Laid side by side with the properties of the current approach, it should become clear if there are other approaches to consider.

In the end the reason for deciding on any approach for any given problem is:

1. Does this system solve the core problem?
2. What other problems does it solve well (without modification)?
3. Are there other (sub) problems that it does not solve?

Compare the current approach against any other candidates and so long as the result fits the rationale above, you should be well informed on doing a cost benefit analysis on any possible refactor.

15.4   CONCLUSION

The point of the process as outlined is to remove bias from any decision-making about which approach to use for an AI problem. It costs time and money to prototype a new system. Refactoring an existing system also takes time. By having a better handle on how a system solves the set of problems, edge cases and extra coding should be avoided. When authors do not have to fight a system to get their desired behaviours, bugs and development time are reduced. Run-tim performance usually follows when a system is used properly. Instead of falling into the trap of using what is there, but instead methodically choosing the right tool for the right job, many future headaches can be avoided. There is always more than one way to look at a problem. At the very least it is hoped that a more thoughtful consideration will be given towards why a given system is being used.

REFERENCES

Epic Games. (2022) *Behaviour Tree Quick Starter Guide*. Available at: https://docs.unrealengine.com/5.0/en-US/behavior-tree-in-unreal-engine---quick-start-guide.

Kahneman, D. (2012) *Thinking, Fast and Slow*. Penguin.

Lilienfeld, S.O., and Lynn, S.J. (2014) *Errors/Biases in Clinical Decision Making. Wiley Online Library*. Available at: https://onlinelibrary.wiley.com/doi/10.1002/9781118625392.wbecp567.

Malik, D.S., Mordeson, J.N., and Sen, M.K. (1994) On subsystems of a fuzzy finite state machine. *Fuzzy Sets and Systems*, 68(1), pp. 83–92. https://doi.org/10.1016/0165-0114(94)90274-7.

Martelli, A. (1977) On the complexity of admissable search algorithms. *Artificial Intelligence*, 8(1), pp. 1–13. https://doi.org/10.1016/0004-3702(77)90002-9.

16 Pedal Control for Cars
How to Maintain Speed, Change Speed, and Stop at a Point

Dr Nic Melder

16.1 INTRODUCTION

Controlling a car, maintaining speed, and slowing down and stopping are something that most experienced drivers do naturally without thought. But how can we get an AI to do this? This chapter will discuss some approaches, along with the challenges that go into making a car drive at a desired speed, accelerate (and decelerate) at a desired rate, and stop at a desired point. The techniques described have been implemented in multiple racing games throughout my career, including Codemasters' *Dirt*, *Grid* and *F1* series, as well as the Ubisoft's *Watch Dogs* series. These games represent a full range of different driving models, from arcade games (*Dirt Showdown*), through sim-cade (*Grid* and *Dirt* series) to simulation (*F1* and *Dirt Rally* series) and only minor modifications were needed to apply these techniques to all these different vehicle simulations.

16.2 TYPES OF VEHICLE SIMULATION

So how do we control our vehicle? Well, this depends upon two main things: the physics model of the vehicle and the type of vehicle AI we are creating. Typically, there are two different ways that you can simulate the movement of a vehicle:

The first is to use the physics system and for the AI to apply controller inputs directly. This means that the physics system is responsible for moving the car. This approach sees the AI using the same vehicle that the player does, with the same set of inputs.

The second approach is to use simple Newtonian mechanics to move the vehicles around. This simplified model can work for objects that move in three dimensions, but could also be applied to trains or even cars if they are just going to move along fixed splines.

So how do you control the speed of a vehicle? No matter what type of vehicle physics model used, you will need to apply the equations of motion in the initial calculations. These are:

DOI: 10.1201/9781003324102-16

$$v = u + at$$

$$s = ut + \tfrac{1}{2}at^2$$

$$s = \tfrac{1}{2}(u + v)t$$

$$v^2 = u^2 + 2as$$

$$s = vt - \tfrac{1}{2}at^2$$

where s is the distance, a is the acceleration, t is the time, u is the initial velocity, and v is the velocity at time t.

16.2.1 SIMPLE NEWTONIAN MODELS

For a simple vehicle that can be directly affected by any arbitrary force, you can simply apply forces directly to the body to affect its velocity and acceleration. All you need to know is its mass and then you can easily calculate the force required to generate an acceleration. Using the equations of motion, you can then calculate the acceleration required, and thus the force, to change from one speed to the next. Maintaining speed is truly trivial as you just do nothing!

But there are no vehicles that actually behave in this manner, are there? Imagine a spaceship travelling through space. There are no external forces being applied to the spaceship so the only forces that act upon it are the ones that are from the spaceship itself – the thrust. If you can apply a force from any direction to the spaceship, then you can easily control it. If you want to accelerate in a direction, you simply apply a force in that direction. This may require rotating the ship so that the engine is pointing in the correct direction, but this is trivial to calculate.

Even for earth bound vehicles, this may still be a valid method of control. Small flying creatures can be simulated very well by applying forces directly to their bodies. A flock of birds can be achieved using flocking algorithms that do just this.

16.2.2 TRAINS, PLANES, AND AUTOMOBILES (AND BOATS TOO)

Unlike our spaceship (or birds), ground-based vehicles are limited in the direction of their movement. You cannot just apply a force in an arbitrary direction and expect the vehicle to move in that direction. External forces are applied to these vehicles such as wind resistance, tyre forces, and gravity. However, you can still use the simple Newtonian methods detailed above to calculate what forces are needed to accelerate and decelerate the vehicle. There are just additional constraints to consider. For example: if you slow an aeroplane down too much, it will fall from the sky!

Provided your vehicles are simple and can be modelled as a simple mass that you can apply a force to, then you can easily control the speed and acceleration of the vehicle. Furthermore, you do not need to apply the force directly! If you are simulating a train that is constrained to movement along its track, or a vehicle that can only move along a fixed spline, you can skip the force entirely and just start with a desired acceleration. Using the equations of motion, it is easy to calculate the velocity every frame based upon a desired acceleration.

For example: $V_{new} = V_{old} + Acc * FrameTime$, where *FrameTime* is the duration of a single frame.

Compared with acceleration, maintaining the current speed is truly trivial; you just need to balance the forces on the vehicle. Or, if you are skipping forces and applying accelerations directly, you don't do anything. Or in other words, you just apply an acceleration of 0.

16.2.3 How to Stop at a Point/Slow Down in a Desired Distance

A car might need to stop at traffic lights or slow down to go around a corner. In both of these cases, the car needs to be at a given speed at a desired position. If you know the distance to the target speed, you can calculate the deceleration needed to reach that speed at that point. However, that is not a realistic way of driving. What you really want to do is for the car to drive normally, and then to slow down when it gets near to the point. But should it slow down when it reaches a desired distance to the point, or should it decelerate at a desired rate? Using the equations of motion again, you can do either! In practice though, you will want to decelerate at a desired rate, otherwise the car will be slamming on its brakes hard for some speed changes, and then just lifting off lightly for some others. You might also find yourself in a situation where the car reaches the marked brake point, but it cannot decelerate enough to achieve the desired speed!

So, typically you want to always slow down with a desired deceleration. This could either be a nice gentle deceleration because you are simulating traffic (for example: 3 m/s^2) or in a racing game it might be the best deceleration that the car could achieve (for example: 50 m/s^2 for an *F1* car). Using the equations of motion, you can determine when you need to start decelerating by rearranging the fourth formula: $v^2 = u^2 + 2as$ to get s (the distance). The rearranged formula is $s = (v^2 - u^2)/2a$. You just need to make sure that the deceleration is achievable for the vehicle.

Similarly, if you want to accelerate to a desired speed by a desired point, maybe to make a jump, or slot between cars merging onto a highway, then the maths is identical. Just remember that a deceleration is just a negative acceleration!

16.2.4 But Is This All Useful?

Described thus far has been how you can affect the motion of a simple body by applying forces or accelerations. There is not really anything particularly interesting, or complex about this so why even bother writing about it? Well, this simple system was used throughout the *Watch Dogs* series for simulating far away vehicles on roads as well as the trains and trams driving through the cities.

Vehicles were moved along the road splines directly and had very simple vehicle dynamic models applied to them. They were essentially just points on the spline that were either accelerating/decelerating, maintaining speed or stopped. Because they were fixed to the spline, they were essentially only ever moving in one dimension, and since they were far away, they did not need to exhibit complex dynamics like weight shift or tyre slip and the like. The spline direction and normals were used directly to set the orientation of the vehicles. This meant that using simple Newtonian motion was more than adequate to simulate them. Because they were so simple to simulate, they were easily parallelised (using SIMD instructions, or even passing to the GPU). In the *Watch Dogs* series of games, 10,000+ vehicles were able to be simulated for negligible cost.

16.3   COMPLEX SIMULATIONS AND REALISTIC DRIVING

The above method works great if your vehicles are simulated as simple systems but with complex simulations, to create vehicle AI that behaves in a realistic manner it is desirable to use the same inputs that the player uses. This is especially important in racing games where cheating can ruin the player's experience – everybody loves extreme rubber banding right? The AI cannot cheat if it is controlling the vehicle in the same manner that the player is! More importantly, with a complex vehicle simulation, the main benefit of using the same inputs and running the same underlying simulation is that the AI vehicle will behave in the same realistic manner, with the correct weight shifting, engine revs, tyre slides, and a multitude of other effects, as the player's vehicle does.

In the previous approach, you were applying forces to the vehicle to move it, with this approach you can only apply the throttle, the brake, the hand brake and turn the steering. So, how can you know when to apply the brake to slow down so the vehicle can stop nicely at the upcoming traffic lights? Or how do you control the throttle and/or brake to maintain a desired speed? Suddenly this has become a much harder problem than just applying the equations of motion!

16.3.1   MAKE IT A PHYSICS PROBLEM

The team who wrote the vehicle physics simulation should have a good idea of how the car interacts with the world and how the controls affect the vehicle. They also have much lower levels of information than the vehicle AI would ever have. With this in mind, it might be possible for them to control the car such that instead of the AI applying the brakes/throttle, it could request a desired acceleration/deceleration or speed and then the car internally sets the pedals to achieve this. Then, like the previous approach, you just need to decide what acceleration or speed you want to use and calculate when to apply it. Essentially this turns the low-level vehicle control from an AI problem to being a handling/physics problem. You might think that this is cheating, (well it kind of is) but there is already precedent for this with ABS braking, traction control, and stability control. AI programmers are not expected to write an ABS system to stop the wheels from locking up (ABS essentially works by detecting the wheel locking up and then reduces the brake amount to stop the lock) so you are not really cheating too much by getting the vehicle physics guys to do it for us. Of course, the physics programmers might be too busy (or too grouchy even), or it might be an external library where you do not have access to the code, so you, the AI programmer, will have to do it yourself by pressing the pedals.

16.3.2   VEHICLE DYNAMICS AND VEHICLE STATISTICS

If you want to be able to control a vehicle you need to understand how the vehicle reacts to the brake and throttle pedal. If you want to slow down to stop at a traffic light you now need to know when to press the brake, and by how much. If you are controlling a bus, you will not be applying the same amount of brake as if you were controlling a sports car. So, you will need some method to learn and catalogue this data. But what data do you need?

Using braking as a simple example. If the vehicle is travelling at 50 kph and you want to stop in 50 m, what do you need to know? What if you want to stop in 20 m? What if you want to decelerate at 3 m/s^2 to stop at a point 200 m away?

What you need to do is create a model of the vehicle's dynamics and how it responds to the pedals. You need to know what deceleration you get when you press the pedals, and you need to know what the deceleration would be if you pressed it 100%, 50%, or just 0%.

16.3.3   GENERATING VEHICLE STATISTICS

So, if your vehicle is driving at 20 m/s and you apply the brakes 100%, how long will it take to come to a stop? This sounds like a problem for the physics programmers again! They know the maths involved (they wrote the code after all) as well as the car handling setups, so surely, they can come up with some nice equation that links speed, brake pedal pressure, and stopping distance? Well, maybe they can do it, but the more complex the simulation the harder it is to estimate. In fact, in one game the physics team was asked to provide the AI team with an estimate of the braking, but it turned out that their estimate was wrong by over 400%. The actual stopping distance was approximately 6.5 m, but their estimate was closer to 35 m! So, it turns out that estimating based upon the handling setup and vehicle dynamics is really hard. But there is a much easier way that is guaranteed to give the correct results every time, within a small margin of error.

16.3.4   BRAKING DATA

Calculating the 'accurate' data is simply a matter of taking a vehicle and accelerating it to top speed, then applying the brakes, and logging the distance from initial brake to it fully stopping. You now know the braking distance from top speed to fully stopped! If you also log the distance and speed for every few metres after you start braking, you can then tell what the stopping distance is from any speed to fully stopped. But what is the distance it takes to slow down from one speed (v) to another, non-zero speed (u)?

If you know the distance to stop from speed v ($_{dist}v$), and the distance to stop from speed u ($_{dist}u$), then the distance to slow down from v to u is $_{dist}v - _{dist}u$. It really is that simple!

The full process to generate the braking statistics is as follows:

1. Place the vehicle at 0 speed on an infinite plane.
2. Lock steering angle to 0 (forward) and accelerate the vehicle until the speed no longer changes. This is the top speed.
3. Log this position (BrakeStart) and apply the brakes.
4. Every frame, log the distance travelled from BrakeStart along with the speed.
5. If the vehicle has stopped, then end, otherwise, go back to 4.
6. Once all data is generated, process it into speed–distance pairs.

It is important to note that the data you have generated is actually wrong. If you read the data right now, at top speed, you will have 0 distance, but at 0 speed you will have a large distance. Step 6 is needed to fix the data. You just need to take the stored data from the max stopping distance to get the actual braking distance. For performance reasons it is also recommended that the braking distance at whole speeds is saved and used which might require some trivial interpolation to calculate. With further testing you would probably find that you can reduce the amount of data you need and only store the speed–distance pairs at every 2 m/s (or 5 m/s) intervals. But memory is cheap, so this should be avoided. It is better to have all the data so you know that it is not a data/interpolation problem when things do not work. The (corrected) data generated should look like Image 16.1.

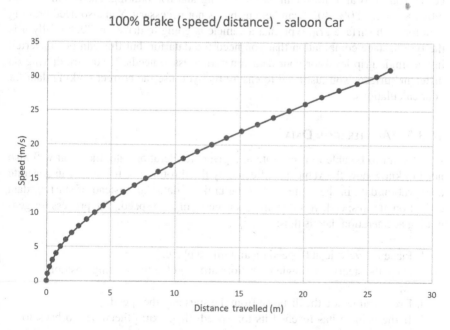

IMAGE 16.1 Graph showing the speed and distance travelled for a saloon car braking from top speed (31 m/s) with 100% brake applied.

When generating the data, it is important to wait until the vehicle has fully set-tled before starting the data generation. It is also desired that the time step is fixed. These two precautions should allow the data to be re-generated consistently each time assuming that the handling or physics has not changed. An added benefit of fix-ing the time step is that there is no longer the need to run in real time. Instead, you can run the test as fast as your computer can run. You are also not limited to running just a single vehicle at a time. If you disable all collisions on the vehicles, you should be able to generate all the vehicles at the same time. This might result in much worse frame rates than with a single vehicle. For example: with 90 different vehicles you would need 90 cars on screen at once to generate all the data. However, the fixed time rate should ensure the generated data is good, and the total time to generate all the data would be much lower than having to run the test 90 times separately.

There are a couple of problems to be aware of when doing this. The first is that it is imperative that the vehicles all run at full LODs otherwise the data generated will be useless. The second is that you need to ensure that the vehicle can complete its test without falling off the edge of the world! In some environments, generating an infinite plane may not be possible, so just make sure to generate a plane big enough that the vehicle can accelerate and stop in the available space.

To reduce the generation time, you could also place the vehicle at speed instead of stationary. If it is placed close to top speed, you reduce the time (and distance) required for the vehicle to hit top speed before it can start logging the braking data.

Now that you know how to generate the braking data, what data do you actually need? You need at a minimum 100% braking and 0% braking. Having more data (90%, 80%, …, 20%, 10%) can help us but is not necessary. You also need braking data for each surface grip type that a vehicle is going to drive on. Technically it is the tyre-surface combination that you need the data for, but this can be converted into a single grip level for your data generation/usage needs. If you are driving on different surfaces you just need to ensure that you use the correct braking data for your calculations.

16.3.5 Acceleration Data

If you want to be able to accelerate at a given acceleration rate, then you will also need to know how the vehicle is affected by the throttle. For this, you can generate acceleration data in the same way as the braking data, but instead of starting data collection at top speed, you start the distance from zero speed. The process for gen-erating acceleration data is thus:

1. Place the vehicle at 0 speed on an infinite plane.
2. Lock the steering to angle to 0° (forward) and log the starting position.
3. Apply the throttle.
4. Every frame, log the distance from the start and the speed.
5. If the vehicle has reached its top speed, then exit; otherwise, go back to step 4.
6. Once all data is generated, process it into speed–distance pairs.

Like the braking data, step 6 is needed to tidy up the data, so that you only save the data for the whole speeds. You also need to remove any extraneous distances when near to the top speed since the last few m/s of acceleration normally take the longest. In practice you will never really care about using the data at these high speeds, so it is ok to just stop the data sampling a few m/s below the actual top speed. Unlike the braking data though, you do not need to reverse the distances. However, the same caveats and suggestions for generating the braking data also apply to the acceleration data. The generated speed–distance data should have a similar shape to Image 16.2.

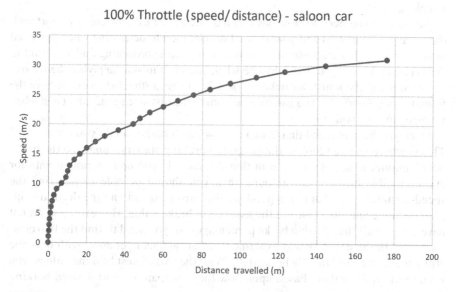

IMAGE 16.2   Graph showing the speed and distance travelled for a saloon car accelerating from stationary. The changes at 10 and 20 m/s are caused by the car changing gear.

For acceleration data, you need to generate the data with a good selection of throttle values. For example: at intervals of 10%, 20%, or 25%. The more data you have, the better a response you will be able to generate when you try to accelerate away at a desired acceleration rate.

16.3.6 VEHICLE PERFORMANCE DATA

By looking at how you generate the data, as well as the data itself, it should be obvious that you can grab some useful information out of the data. You can calculate 0–60 times, 0–100 times, top speeds, braking distances from fixed speeds, or the time it would take to brake a fixed distance or from a fixed speed. This information can be very helpful to the car handling designers as it can allow them to better balance their cars. It is trivial to add this extra data for their benefit, and as an added bonus, they will love you for it too.

16.3.7 SLOWING DOWN

So, how do these vehicle statistics aid in our driving? Since the data is a series of speed–distance pairs, when a vehicle is at a given speed, you can easily calculate the stopping distance using the data's associated amount of braking. Using this data, you can now easily determine the stopping distance for a vehicle's current speed, or any arbitrary speed, when using the brake value that the data was generated with. You can even slow down by a smaller amount. For example: when slowing down from 20 to 10 m/s, you need to find the stopping distance from 20 and 10 m/s and the difference is the distance to slow down from 20 to 10 m/s using that amount of brake. Simple really!

But what if you need to slow down at a desired rate? Like before, you start with the equations of motion and your desired deceleration to determine when you need to start braking. For example: if there is a stop point approaching and you want to decelerate at 5 m/s^2, you first calculate when you need to start applying the brakes. By rearranging the fourth formula: $v^2 = u^2 + 2as$ to get s (the distance), we have the formula: $s = (v^2 - u^2)/2a$. You can then determine the distance to the target and when you need to start braking.

Once you have reached that distance, how much brake should you use though? This is where you can look at the generated braking statistics and find the brake pedal amount necessary to stop in that distance. If you had generated data for every possible brake pedal amount, then you should be able to just find the speed–distance pair that corresponds to the current speed and the desired stopping distance and then just use the associated brake value. However, you do not have data for all the possible brake percentages, so you need to find the two closest values in the data. As was explained earlier, you can get away with only the 100% brake data and the 0% brake data. With the two closest braking values, you need to interpolate them based upon how they compare to your desired braking distance!

DesiredStoppingDistance = CurrentSpeed^2/2a
InterpolationFactor = (DesiredStoppingDistance − MaxBrakeDist)/
    (MaxBrakeDist − MinBrakeDist)

The calculated interpolation factor can then be used to scale the brake value to apply between the two data sets. The interpolation factor could be converted directly into a brake input (after clamping between 0 and 1) which would provide a linear interpolation between our two data sets, but in practice using an exponential interpolation seems to work best, such as: Brake Value = Interpolation Factor^{pow}, where pow is a constant. Using this exponential method of interpolation, a typical graph showing the brake usage and speed looks like Image 16.3.

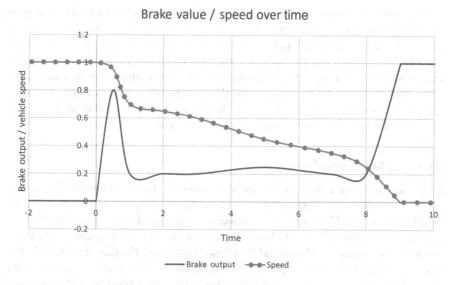

IMAGE 16.3 Graph showing how the brake is adjusted based upon how the vehicle speed changes. This is only using 100% and 0% data. Using more data sets (10%, 20%, etc.) would result in more consistent brake usage and smoother deceleration.

If you want to use the minimum stopping distance you can ignore all the calculations related to desired deceleration and equation of motion. Instead, you just calculate what the stopping distance is at 100% brake for our current speed, and if that distance is less than our target distance, then we apply 100% brake. This will give you the maximum braking for your vehicle, thus the shortest stopping distance. One issue with this method is that you will miss the target speed every time since the brakes were applied AFTER it was too late.

A couple of improvements would be to include a one frame distance adjustment into the calculations, so that you know the distance the vehicle would travel in one frame. Also, if your vehicle simulates the time it takes to press the pedal, this should also be taken into account.

16.3.8 SPEEDING UP

If you want to accelerate at a desired rate you need to use the acceleration data to determine how much throttle to apply. In a similar approach to braking, you need to determine what throttle value will give you the desired acceleration at a given speed. You can calculate the distance that the vehicle will need to travel to reach the desired speed with the desired acceleration and can then check the data to find the matching pedal value. However, although using the speed and distance you have already generated is sufficient, it might be easier to just store the acceleration in the data as it gets generated. It then becomes a simple case of finding the appropriate data set that has the desired acceleration at the current speed.

One thing to be aware of though is that there are numerous extra forces at play when trying to accelerate from a standstill. Even though your calculations might suggest that you should only apply a small amount of throttle, it might not be enough to get the vehicle moving. It is better to give all vehicles a minimum starting throttle that is needed to get the vehicle moving initially. For example: up to 1 m/s. This initial throttle value will be different for all vehicles, where a bus will need a larger value than a sports car. This data can be determined offline by either analysing the generated data, or you can get a designer to choose and set this number.

16.3.9 MAINTAINING SPEED

So, you can now make your vehicle speed up and slow down in a controlled manner, but how can you maintain speed? This sounds like the perfect task for our old friend the PID controller. There have been numerous papers and articles written describing what a PID controller is and how to tune them, so instead of repeating that here, check out the references Melder and Tomlinson (2013) and PIDExplained (2023), but in short, using a PID controller works by looking at the current speed vs the desired speed. This difference is the error. The error is then multiplied by a *Proportional* constant (*Kp*). The error is then collected (integrated) over time and multiplied by an *Integral* constant (*Ki*). The rate of change of the error is also calculated and then multiplied by a *Derivative* constant (*Kd*). These values are all added together to create the final output. The different components (*Proportional*, *Integral*, and *Derivative*) affect the speed that the error changes, and each needs to be tuned specifically for the system it is trying to control.

Using a PID controller to control the speed of a vehicle works well, but it does need some modifications. The primary issue is that the effect of the throttle and the brake on the vehicle can be vastly different. When close to the target speed it may be applying less than 10% throttle or brake, but 10% throttle will have a much smaller acceleration than 10% brake would. Because of this it can be necessary to apply dead zones to stop braking too much. For example: if the speed is a small amount over your target speed, then instead of applying any brake you just do nothing and let the vehicle naturally lose speed to engine braking. Another way to solve this problem is to have two different sets of PID parameters depending upon whether you are above the desired speed or below it. Even with these additional caveats, using a PID controller works very well for speed control.

16.4 CONCLUSION

This chapter has shown how you can control vehicles through two different methods based upon the vehicle physics setups: using a simple Newtonian model you can just apply forces and acceleration directly to the body, and a physics-based model where you can only apply inputs via the same control interface that the player has, such as throttle, brake, and steering. Using these techniques, especially the generation of vehicle statistics data, has made it much easier to build robust vehicle AI systems that work with large quantities of different vehicles, and different types of vehicles. *Watch Dogs: Legion* had over 50 different cars, and the *Grid* and *Dirt* games had over 90 different cars. Once the systems were set up, adding new vehicles to the game caused no extra work for the designers or AI programmers, other than needing to generate new data. And especially at the end of the project, if vehicles needed to be changed, it was a quick job to regenerate the data instead of needing to re-tune by hand any parameters. Another huge benefit was that the statistics data was used to help keep the cars balanced amongst their groups. It was easy to see that their top speeds and/or acceleration matched, or that their brakes were equally good. One side effect of looking at the data was that we were able to find issues with how the cars were set up themselves! During the development of *Watchdogs: Legion*, it was found that for many of the cars, using 10% throttle or 70% throttle would result in the same acceleration and same top speed! Similarly, it was found that the best acceleration was achieved using 90% throttle rather than 100%! As you can see, using vehicle statistics is very useful, both in making the vehicles drive well and in finding bugs in the vehicles themselves.

REFERENCES

Melder, N., and Tomlinson, S. (2013) Racing vehicle control systems using PID controllers, *Game AI Pro*, edited by Steve Rabin. CRC Press, pp. 491–500.

PIDExplained. (2023) *PID Explained*. Available at: https://pidexplained.com/how-to-tune-a-pid-controller/.

17 Bots for Testing

Jonas Gillberg

17.1 INTRODUCTION

Bots for testing have been implemented for many different games, studios, and engines, over the years, including at EA in titles such as *Battlefield 2042*, *Plants vs. Zombies: Battle for Neighborville*, and *Dead Space*. The details of those implementations vary but the fact that you can get very far with a bot that can move, aim, and press some buttons does not. Often developers wonder how to get started and if it is worth the effort for them. Often it feels like they imagine some very complex bots that can solve everything, and they imagine all the work that would be required and worry that they cannot prioritise that kind of effort. While it is true that bot and test automation solutions can get very big and complex over time, they should not start that way. This chapter will try to help you find the most important initial use case for your needs, share a few key points to get your bot started, and then cover a few things you might want to consider moving forward.

17.2 USE CASES

17.2.1 LARGE-SCALE MULTIPLAYER STABILITY

Large-scale multiplayer stability testing that requires tens, hundreds, or even thousands of players can be considered the canonical use case for test bots. It is simply too costly and time consuming to test all content and game mode combinations throughout production without the use of bots. You might not have enough capacity on the development team to test a full game session. In this case, some form of bots or simulation becomes necessary to develop the game. From a stability at scale perspective, bots that perform pseudo-random actions can go a long way. However, adding even a little more direction and control to such bots opens a wide range of test options by allowing the bots to play the game in a more representative way.

17.2.1.1 The Server Perspective

If the primary purpose of a test is to stress test the servers, then it is beneficial to have some form of minimal client, headless or similar, so that it is fast and inexpensive to run a lot of them. It is also good in this case to have all bot-related data and processing done on the client side.

17.2.1.2 The Client Perspective

It is also very likely that you will want to test the client in a full multiplayer scenario. In this case, it might be beneficial to run as much of the bot as possible on the server.

DOI: 10.1201/9781003324102-17

17.2.2 LOCAL MULTIPLAYER TESTING

It is possible to create bot solutions that allow a single developer to do at-desk multi-player testing. This can, for example, be achieved by using the test bots as virtual players on the server or through some form of minimal client or clients that can connect to the locally hosted server. This form of setup empowers developers to do their own multiplayer validation before code or content even leaves their machine. You might be tempted to think of this primarily as a tool for engineers, but many forms of content, such as visual effects or audio, scale or behave differently in a multiplayer scenario.

17.2.3 CRITICAL PATH TESTING

At some point in the production cycle, especially for a single-player game, it might make sense to have bots run through the critical path of the game as it is being worked on to make sure that there are no blockers. You might also find it useful to capture other forms of data in a representative in-game context such as how cinematics and the transition to them look when they are triggered during gameplay. Or, if you are really ambitious and have a serious data and bot setup, you might be able to test if it is possible to complete all achievements or secrets.

17.2.4 CLIENT PERFORMANCE TESTING

Camera flythroughs or similar techniques are very common when it comes to client performance testing. They can easily be combined with automated playtests performed by bots to get even more accurate data. Since such automated playtests do not require excessive amounts of staff hours, you can even set up automation scenarios where a whole range of settings and configurations are automatically explored. Data collected during client performance tests is also commonly used to generate heatmaps to better visualise hotspots.

17.2.5 FUNCTIONAL TESTING

One thing that often comes up is whether or not the bots should be used for simple functional tests or if simple scripting should be used. It can potentially save a lot of time and maintenance to direct a bot rather than to manually calculate inputs if player movement and navigation is involved as part of the functional test. You might however end up in situations where internal bot logic fights the test setup, such as potentially invalidating a target the functional test wants the bot to attack. It generally comes down to a simple question: does the autonomous nature of the bot help or hinder the test?

17.2.6 OTHER SCENARIOS

Once you have a sufficiently capable bot setup, test automation, and data collection, a lot of different scenarios open up. Bots can, for example, be instructed to explore the entire world, climb, and navigate things in different ways in order to find crashes or blockers not found during normal gameplay, but that could potentially happen to a player regardless.

17.3   MINIMAL TEST BOT

Once you have figured out a use case that you think will provide value, it is time to take the next step – building a bot. It is important to start small with the sole focus on building something minimal that works which can then be iterated on, even if that means taking on some technical debt. If the bot can control a single client that can move, aim, and press buttons, that will go really far. Once this is in place, it should immediately begin to save time or otherwise generate value, which might help generate the necessary buy-in from other stakeholders. More importantly, it will let you quickly find where it breaks to better inform your decisions moving forward, so you do not waste time on things you will not need. This section will try to show in a practical way just how small an initial implementation can be.

17.3.1   MINIMAL SETUP DESCRIPTION

To reinforce just how minimal a bot setup can be, let us start with a small description of code that could be placed where input is generated. This would need to be expanded to be more robust but hopefully it illustrates the point nonetheless. Some possible expansions include being able to maintain its state so that it does not have to generate a new target every frame, to be able to express more states than combat and to be able to follow paths returned by a navigation mesh query.

Somewhere inside an input injection function:

- Get the player's position, direction, and view (aim), possibly as positions, rotations, or transforms.
- Get the closest valid enemy, this could possibly include line-of-sight checks to see if the enemy is behind the player, and more.
- If you do not have an enemy, do nothing; otherwise, continue with the input generation.
- Calculate the player's relative direction to the enemy's position and use this to set the Forward and Strafe input axes.
- Calculate the Yaw and Pitch based on the enemy position as well as the player view and use this to set Yaw and Pitch input axes. Input scaling matters a lot here.
- If you are close enough, press the attack button.
- Done.

17.3.2   INPUT DRIVEN BOTS

Bots that generate inputs in some form rather than interacting directly with game code or functions are preferable. The reason for this is that for the tests to have value you need to trust that what the bots do is representative of what players do and that the bugs and issues that they find are things that could also be experienced by players. It will be easier to trust that the bots do things in a representative way if the code follows the same paths. The bot will be built in three parts: Input Injection, Input Generation, and Basic Behaviour.

17.3.2.1 Input Injection

You will need to inject bot input after hardware inputs are processed and before input is processed by the game itself. Often there is a middle layer where hardware is mapped to some sort of abstract input such as Jump, Attack, and the like. The place in the code where it makes sense to inject your own input might be part of the update input or pre-process input for a player or player controller class. Whether or not it makes sense to generate this abstract input or to set the equivalent of key presses after first looking up which key press corresponds to a specific current action depends entirely on the game, engine, and context at hand. At this point you should focus on the task at hand which is to get to a bot that works as quickly as possible – worry about how to maintain this throughout production and as the game and key mappings change if and when it becomes an issue later. A good way to verify that the input works is to hard-code the forward or sideways axis to see that the character moves, and to similarly hard-code yaw and pitch to see that the character aims and turns as expected. Important to note here is that while they are called forward, sideways, yaw, and pitch in this text, depending on your engine, project input setup might be called something different like throttle, turn, lookup, etc. Finding the input mapping in the project settings or somewhere in code could give a lot of insight not only for appropriate axis names but also for what other actions are available and what they are named. It might be advantageous to set these up as runtime tweakable console variables if this is easy to do in your engine – and to set button press/release for some obvious action like shoot or jump. Once you have verified that input injection works, you can move on to making the bot generate the right inputs.

17.3.2.2 Input Generation

17.3.2.2.1 Movement

For standard analog stick movement, you can calculate the angle between the direction from the player to the target position and the player forward vector and convert that to the forward/sideways input. Assuming that these are given on the horizontal plane in 2D, and ignoring the up component of the positions in world space, for movement, the Forward component is set as follows: a target position straight ahead should generate a value of 1, a value of 0 for sideways, and a value of −1 for a target position behind. The Sideways component, which handles strafing, would be set to a value of 0. This is depicted in Image 17.1.

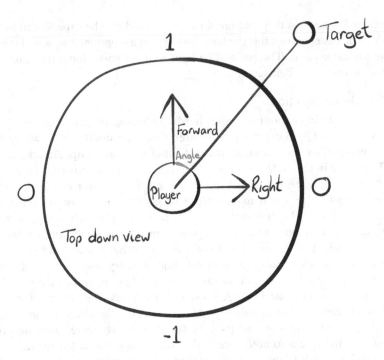

IMAGE 17.1 Top-down view of axis values for the forward component for a player with an angle between player forward and direction to the target.

For strafing only, the Sideways component is set as follows: 1°–180° to the left has a value of −1°, and 1°–180° to the right has a value of 1. The Forward component should be set to 0. This is depicted in Image 17.2.

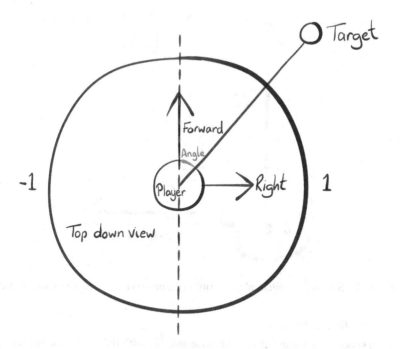

IMAGE 17.2 Top-down view of axis values for the sideways component for a player with an angle between player forward and direction to the target.

Another way to think about this is to use the angle between the player forward and the target and use that to rotate a 2D vector with the values (1,0) which represent forward and sideways respectively. To easily verify that this is correct, generate positions at known angles relative to the player and check that the calculation returns the expected results. Make sure to double check that the character strafes in the intended direction.

17.3.2.2.2 Aim

To turn the character, or 'yaw', you can use the same angle between the character forward and the target position in the horizontal plane as was done with movement. One important difference is that often yaw and pitch expect input on a much smaller scale than movement. So even if the target is completely behind the player a full −1 or 1 value for yaw might cause the player to turn much too fast, even if the character input accepts values in this range. This is especially true for small angles when the aim is almost correct. You will need to convert or scale the angle such that it does not overshoot the target in a single frame, while at the same time is fast enough, especially when the player needs to turn a lot (see Section 17.3.2.3.1).

To have the character look up or down, or 'pitch', you instead need to calculate in the vertical plane. So, instead of the angle around the Up axis relative to the Forward direction, you use the angle around the Sideways axis as shown in Image 17.3.

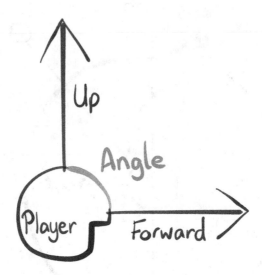

IMAGE 17.3 Side view of pitch calculated using the up axis relative to the forward direction.

17.3.2.2.3 Button Presses

To jump, shoot, pick things up or otherwise interact with the world, the bot will have to press buttons. Depending on the desired action the button may have to be held for different amounts of time which is something that needs to be managed with some form of timer. If the same action is repeated without pause, you might end up with a continuous press when what you want is button spam. Remember to add some time between actions so that the button can be released.

17.3.2.2.4 First-/Third-Person Perspective

For games with a first-person perspective aim and movement can often be quite straightforward, for games with a third-person perspective, however, how aim and movement relate to the avatar and view can vary. Often the movement is relative to the camera which tends to place the actual player avatar slightly to the side. To achieve good-quality aim and movement, this relationship should in the third-person case be figured out in detail; one good way to start is to discuss this with whoever implemented that player character controller. Do not get stuck on this step, if there are parallax issues with the aim or character to the side, make a note of it, possibly make a small, hard-coded offset that works in most cases, and move on. Sometimes it is even possible to switch to a first-person mode even if it is not the default one. The important thing is to stay focused to get to a bot that works in game as soon as possible.

17.3.2.3 Basic Behaviour

Pick a place in the game that is very easy to launch and iterate on, like an empty level with flat terrain. Then generate a list of targets, move, and aim positions, some high and some low, so that it is easy to tweak and verify aim and movement sensitivity. The move should be associated with a radius so that you know when you have arrived at the destination. At this point, the bot should work even if it must constantly adjust its aim. Constant aim correction can sometimes be visually jarring so it might be worth the effort to have a constant minimal threshold on the input it generates to prevent this. Later it might make sense to base aim tolerance on the angle between the current aim direction and the desired one or on the closest Euclidean distance between the current aim and the target aim position.

17.3.2.3.1 Calibration and Debugging

If you have a good way to debug, draw the target positions, visualise the inputs the bot is trying to press, and the like, now is a very good time to implement that. Try to find a sweet spot where aim and turn are fast without oscillation as it gets close to the target. Aim and yaw jumping back and forth can be very uncomfortable to look at and may result in occasions when the bot cannot hit a target because the aim is too sensitive. Often it is also desirable to aim faster when the target is far from the cross hairs and slow down as it gets close, potentially compensating for relative movement, and adjusting sensitivity based on zoom levels and the like. Once again, this is something that can be improved upon later. You should now have a bot that can move between hard-coded positions which might be enough to get through very simple content. However, to demonstrate this well, you need to add an attack or interaction support depending on the game.

17.3.2.3.2 Interactions

Interacting with something in a game is simply a matter of going to a position, aiming at a position, and pressing a button for some time. The bot should already have the tools to do this. Sometimes you can get away with the aim and move positions being one and the same, but most of the time, it is preferable to generate two different positions based on the interactable object. The aim position might be exactly where the object is but the position to move to can be offset. For example: the offset is set as the forward vector of the interactable, scaled such that the bot stands some distance away.

17.3.2.3.3 Combat

Attacking an enemy can be thought of as a somewhat difficult interaction where the interaction parameters are decided by the weapon at hand and with an interaction position that moves. Hardcoding the values for combat distance, time to hold the fire button, and the like is the way to go initially. Loop through all valid enemies and pick the closest one, if the enemy is too far to shoot at, use the enemy position as a move position, and move towards it. If you are close enough to shoot, use the enemy position as the aim position and aim at it and press the shoot button repeatedly. There are many ways to improve this. One example is a target standing behind something – in which case you need to check for line-of-sight before you can successfully shoot the target, but more importantly you need to be able to walk around the obstacle. If the enemy is a non-player character (NPC), that NPC most likely has a way to get to the player such as pathfinding using a nav-mesh. If it does, figure out how to query that underlying system so that you can generate the next waypoint for the player to follow. It is important to note that you might not need pathfinding at this point. With a bot that can move towards enemies or interactions, aim, and shoot, you can already create a lot of test cases or demos. You could launch multiple clients and potentially stress test a multiplayer scenario or walk the bot through a shooting gallery using a list of hard-coded waypoints showcasing some really fast head shot combat. Imperfect aim, navigation, better encapsulation, scripting support, and the like can all be added later. Starting simple makes it easier for others to understand why it works which makes it easier for others to trust the results.

17.4   GOING FORWARD

Once you have a minimal bot that works, it is time to make it as useful as can be. Let the context in which the bots will be used dictate the level of effort you put into the architecture and the complexity of the solution. If all you need is a bot that can get through levels and survive combat, maybe the tiny bot you have already created, coupled with a scripted way to tell the bot where to go, where to aim, and when to press a button, is sufficient. All it requires then is a way to hook into the input generation process at the right level of abstraction in a way that exercises player code in a manner similar to the way a human would play.

Once you reach this stage, there are a number of considerations on many levels to make:

- Who will create and maintain the tests?
- You might have some idea of what types of tests you think will be most beneficial already, but whether that is a single-player walkthrough or a full-scale multiplayer solution, it is important to know who the end user of the bots will be.
- Will the tests be scripted and maintained by technical testers well versed in automation, or is the hope that all developers will be able to contribute to both the tests and the test bot capabilities as well? Either way, one of the first things you look at after putting together the basic bot building blocks is how to provide that bot with directions.

17.4.1   EMPOWER PEOPLE

Consider building a system that empowers non-engineers to build tests and expand the bot's capabilities. Exposing just a few basic goals to the script system, like movement and world interactions, and making it possible to control combat, will potentially allow others to build custom scenarios at a high level which frees up engineering time for other things. It is often possible to fill in small capability gaps the bots may initially have with such scripting as well. One thing that is important if scripting is used to fill those gaps, is to provide sustainable replacements for any brittle or otherwise bad script patterns, or you might not be able to take advantage of the bots' autonomous nature.

17.4.2   On Using Game AI as Test Bots or Test Bots as Game AI

If you have bots for gameplay, you should absolutely see if they can also be used for testing or if there is some sort of tech sharing that can be accomplished. A word of caution though, the game always wins. What that means is that if some changes required to ship a game feature breaks parts of the test bot functionality it is very likely that it will be allowed to do so and that your test bot will be worse off for it. This in turn might be a slippery slope where the test functionality of the bots degrades over time, which means that they become less of a factor when making decisions for the game bots, which in turns means that they degrade even faster.

17.4.3   Data

One thing to highlight is that when developing bot capabilities and new tests, it is important to track their functionality such that you can base your decisions on data. Initially the bots might have enough eyes on them and be simple enough that broken aim or bad behaviours will be noticed. If things go well, they will be used in an unattended way to generate performance metrics, crash reports, gameplay blockers, and more. You will want to be able to look at data to quickly see that they are still behaving as expected. Tracking player positions, view direction, and ability use are a good first step as it allows you to see if abilities are unused. Create bot position heat maps to see if they are moving in the wrong places or do more detailed deep dives of a playthrough.

17.4.4   Use Shortcuts and Cheats If You Can

As for the way to think about features and issues themselves and how to implement solutions for the bot, it can be useful to think of it as if you were testing the game yourself. Think "What would be ok to do?". In this scenario it often makes sense to cheat if that makes things simpler. Good ways to cheat can be things such as invulnerable mode, infinite ammo, and teleports. The purpose is to build scenarios that test things in a way that generates bugs or other data in a way that is actionable and trustworthy.

17.5   CONCLUSION

This chapter has demonstrated the value of bots for testing, how easy it can be to get started, and some things to think about moving forward. It has covered some details on a possible implementation order, input injection, input generation, and basic bot behaviour. Furthermore, it has called out things that can wait until later as well as shortcuts like teleports that work even better for test bots than gameplay bots. It is important to stay on the critical path, especially initially. The most important takeaway is to just start, and to start small. That way the needs of the project and the best ways to leverage the team's skill set can help guide the work the rest of the way.

18 Infinite Axis Utility System and Hierarchical State Machines

David Wooldridge

18.1 INTRODUCTION

Developing realistic characters for role playing games (RPG) is a difficult task. Most non-player characters (NPC) are typically non-interactive and are just used as window dressing to fill up a world and make it feel more active than it is. For AI to take the next step in believable character creation, all NPCs should behave and act as realistically as possible. This means that they need to have their own personalities and day-to-day activities while being able to interact with each other and the player, responding to any actions another NPC or the player makes and adapt to any changes within the game world.

A complex set of behaviours is needed to achieve this, which poses a problem to not only the performance and flexibility of the behaviours, but also modelling and organising of these behaviours. This chapter will look at two methods of AI decision making architectures used in video games. The first will be Hierarchical Finite State Machines (hFSM), followed by a utility focused approach that is increasing in popularity called Infinite Axis Utility System (IAUS) (Graham, 2013). Next, this chapter will show how you can combine both methods to produce a system that can both organise behaviours from high-level states down to individual actions while maintaining high levels of reusability and speeding up development time.

18.2 HIERARCHICAL FINITE STATE MACHINES

hFSMs derive from Finite State Machines (FSM). These are used to model sequential logic where the problem is defined as abstract states, and the transitions between them. Such an approach is reactive in nature, as states change in response to changes in the problem space (Basicevic et al., 2010). The use of FSMs in video games is very common. *Call of Duty: World at War* on the PS2 used a FSM as its decision making architecture and had three basic states: *Idle*, *Alert*, and *InCombat*. Image 18.1 depicts the simplicity of this architecture.

DOI: 10.1201/9781003324102-18

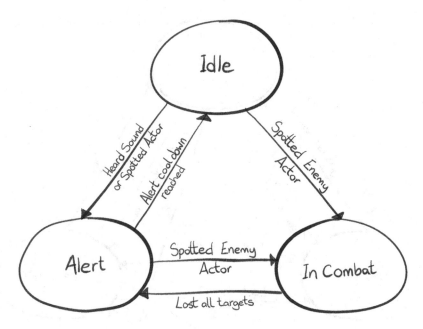

IMAGE 18.1   A simple agent finite state machine.

However, there are major issues with using FSMs, the most obvious of which is the complexity that occurs when additional states and state transitions are added to give an agent a wider choice of actions to perform. To demonstrate this, the two states *Alert* and *InCombat* seen in Image 18.1 will be split to create a more descriptive FSM and a more responsive, intelligent agent. The new states to be added are: *Investigate*, *TakeCover*, *FireWeapon*, and *Flee*. All actions a soldier would need to do. Taking a look at Image 18.2, which visualises the modified FSM, you can see how it quickly becomes more complex and unmanageable (Dawe et al., 2013).

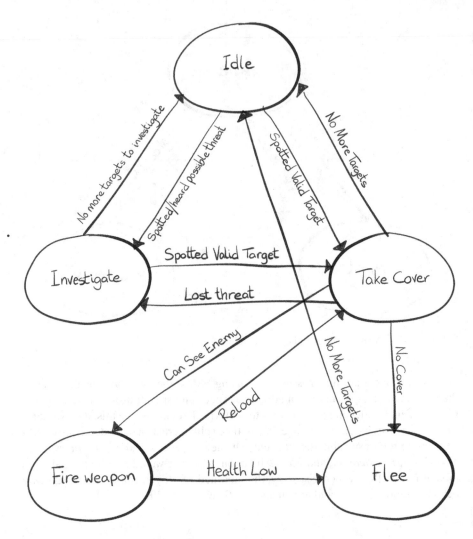

IMAGE 18.2 A more complex NPC behaviour.

hFSMs attempt to address this issue by grouping states together into a higher-level state that contain sub-child states. This results in fewer transitions and makes it easier for more than one developer to work on the architecture, where each developer would work on a higher-level group of states independent from each other. A well-known variation on the hFSM architecture was developed for *Halo 2* (Isla, 2005), which formed the basis of what is now called 'behaviour trees'. Behaviour trees were an attempt to reduce the complexity of a FSM, but there are some disadvantages to using hFSM such as behaviour trees requiring the designer to know about basic programming concepts such as sequence, selection, and iteration, which can lead to inefficient behaviours (memory, CPU time) and an increased workload for the programmer who is required to implement, fix, and manage these problems.

None of the approaches discussed thus far can cope with the complex behaviours needed for a more realistic open world game. IAUS leverages hFSMs to construct complex yet easy to manage behaviours and will be discussed next.

18.3   INFINITE AXIS UTILITY SYSTEM

Utility is the notion of worth over value and is commonly used within economics and game theory. IAUS takes this concept to trigger the best possible action as measured by the utility for any possible outcome. This is done by splitting behaviours into four simple concepts: *Reasoners, Actions, Considerations,* and *Axis.*

Reasoners are the primary tool in which decisions are made; it does this by grouping possible choices together, with each one becoming a consideration that could be made. Each consideration is an outcome with an action attached to it. Each consideration contains an axis, which is a scored piece of data that has often been passed through a response graph (which is where the name axis comes from). The choice of response graph is an important consideration to make when designing a IAUS behaviour, because it will determine the actual action choice (Lewis, 2017). The consideration will total up the scores from all the axes, and the reasoner will pick the consideration with the highest utility, which results in the highest scoring consideration's action being run.

18.4   CHARACTER UTILITY BEHAVIOUR GRAPHS

For the remainder of this chapter, the discussion will turn to Character Utility Behaviour Graphs (CUBG), which are a hybrid of hFSM and IAUS. There are many differences between CUBG and IAUS, which will be discussed shortly, but at a high-level CUBG treats reasoners as high-level states, contained within sub-states (considerations) which can either perform an action or link to another reasoner's higher-level state.

By chaining reasoners together, the agent's behaviour will move through high-level states (*AmIHungry* and *IsItWorkTime*) all the way down to low-level individual actions (*MoveToPosition* and *PlayAnimation*), organising complex behaviours into a heuristic plan on how to approach a given situation the NPC needs to simulate.

The differences between CUBG and the IAUS are explained below.

18.4.1   REASONERS (HIGH-LEVEL STATES)

As described above, reasoners in CUBG represent high-level groupings of lower-level states as a list of considerations. The reasoner will evaluate each consideration and choose one based on its utility score. This is usually the highest scoring consideration, but considerations may be chosen based on the requirements of the game. Variants could see the lowest scoring consideration chosen, or a consideration chosen based on its order within the reasoner. It all depends on the problem at hand. Reasoners that work in this way make CUBG much more expressive over hFSM and IAUS in which multiple behaviours can be designed.

18.4.2 CONSIDERATIONS (SUB-STATES)

Considerations generate a score that is associated with an action. It does this through the use of a data gatherer or multiple data gatherers. CUBG will have specialist considerations that allow its action to always be running regardless of its utility. This allows for multiple actions to be running in parallel and is used to perform common tasks, such as moving to a position and the like. CUBG system also uses considerations as a local data cache, which allows data gatherers to write data to considerations, giving the system the ability to reason about past decisions.

18.4.3 ACTIONS

Actions are the real-world result of a reasoner picking a consideration. This could be moving to cover, firing a weapon, fleeing, or something else. Specialist actions can be created by the CUBG system that allows actions to chain reasoners together. It is here where the hFSM structure is evident. See Image 18.5 for a depiction of a simple combat behaviour using this approach.

18.4.4 DATA GATHERERS (AXIS)

Data Gatherers are an evolution of the axis seen in IAUS. With CUBG, data gatherers are responsible for gathering the required information about the world the agent is in and writing it out to a blackboard/consideration as well as generating a utility score for that piece of knowledge. A piece of knowledge in this context could be – position of cover, health, who the agent is talking to, and the like.

The CUBG variation of a data gatherer will still use response graphs, as in their axis counterparts. An example graph can be seen in Image 18.3 depicting a simple fall-off graph to determine weapon choice based on the amount of damage it would produce at a given range.

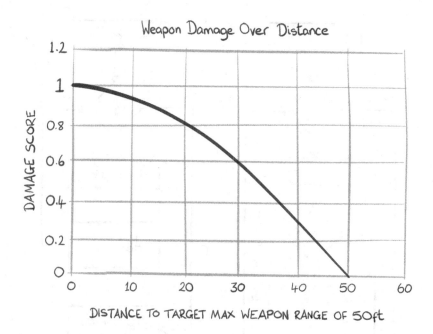

IMAGE 18.3   Weapon damage over range. The utility formula is $s = \sin(((a-b)/a) * (\pi/2))$, where s is the utility score, a is the max distance damage can be taken, and b is the distance to the target.

By compartmentalising knowledge gathering in this way it becomes modular. This means knowledge gathering is streamlined to the state(s) the current character is in or could transition to. By being modular in this way, knowledge gathering is highly reusable by allowing data gatherer nodes to be used multiple times for different considerations.

18.4.5   CUBG Example

The core loop for a CUBG system can be seen in Image 18.4. The way the core loop executes results in the hFSM self-updating without the need for a complex network of transitioning states. This can be seen in Image 18.5, which is an example of the FSM in Image 18.1 turned into a CUBG solution. There are four main reasoners:

1. *Root reasoner* (this is the entry point of the behaviour)
2. *NotInCombat reasoner*
3. *InCombat reasoner*
4. *Alerted reasoner.*

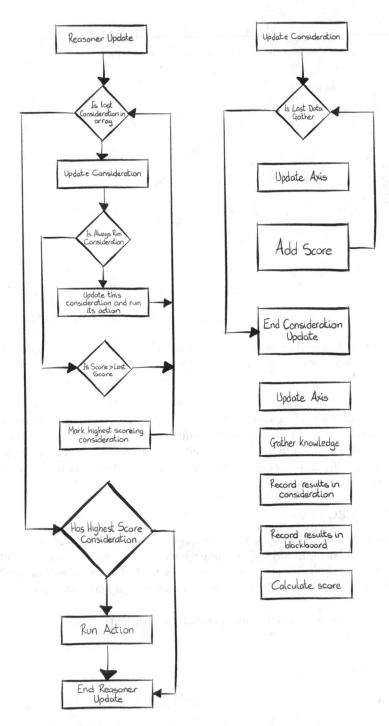

IMAGE 18.4   Character utility behaviour graph core loop.

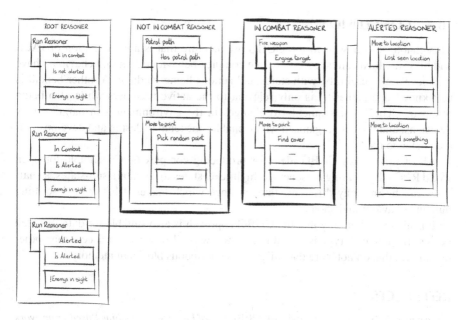

IMAGE 18.5 Example combat behaviour.

Image 18.5 shows the in-combat consideration within the root reasoner as activated and running the *InCombat* reasoner. It also shows that the *EngageTarget* consideration has been chosen and is running the *FireWeapon* action. This is the result of the *InCombat* sub-state (consideration) totalling up a higher utility score from *IsAlerted*, and *EnemiesInSight* data gatherers.

It should be noted that there are no transitions that move back to another reasoner, which would be needed in a FSM like that seen in Image 18.1. This is because the root reasoner, or any active reasoner, is always running.

Stepping through the logic of the CUBG architecture depicted in Image 18.4, if the *NotInCombat* consideration is scored higher than the *InCombat* consideration, a switch would be made to the *NotInCombat* reasoner. There is no transition precondition to make this switch, and it is automatically handled within the core loop (take another look at Image 18.4). For each switch that is made, the system needs to handle how actions and considerations are deactivated. There are multiple ways to do this, and the simplest approaches to do this would be to call an exit method or to fire an event.

What happens if all considerations have scored zero? To handle this scenario, a default reasoner should be designated as a backup, with the topmost consideration being selected. However, if the best result would be for the agent to do nothing, a specialist reasoner could be created that does just that.

18.5 CONCLUSION

This chapter has described the CUBG architecture that is a combination of IAUS and hFSM, which can be used to create complex behaviours. These behaviours have high levels of reusability, with states and actions being modular. Another benefit is that knowledge gathering is only relevant to the active reasoners while also being modular. CUBG reacts quickly to changes in the environment, can handle fuzzy decisions, and is easily organised which enables the team to design and develop complex behaviours.

All of this makes CUBG ideal for producing complex NPCs suitable for open world RPGs. By treating reasoners as high-level states that contain sub-states, a character can be in many different states at once which makes it better at describing human behaviour and choices.

It is also worth noting that the CUBG approach is also suitable for data-oriented design. If each node type is stored in arrays it will allow for faster access than other techniques that do not store data aligned as continuous blocks in memory.

REFERENCES

Basicevic, I., Velikic, I., and Popovic, M. (2010) *Use of Finite State Machine Based Framework in Implementation of Communication Protocols - A Case Study*, 2010 Sixth Advanced International Conference on Telecommunications, pp. 161–166. Doi: 10.1109/AICT.2010.12.

Dawe, M., Gargolinski, S., Dicken, L., Humphreys, T., and Mark, D. (2013) Behavior Selection Algorithms: An Overview, *Game AI Pro*, edited by Steve Rabin. CRC Press, pp. 47–60.

Graham, D. (2013) Breathing life into your background characters, Game AI Pro, edited by Steve Rabin. CRC Press, pp. 451–458.

Isla, D. (2005) *GDC 2005 Proceeding: Handling Complexity in the Halo 2 AI*, Retrieved January 14th, 2022 from: https://www.gamedeveloper.com/programming/gdc-2005-proceeding-handling-complexity-in-the-i-halo-2-i-ai.

Lewis, M. (2017) Choosing effective utility-based considerations, *Game AI Pro 3*, edited by Steve Rabin. CRC Press, pp. 167–178.

19 Tactical Positioning through Environmental Analysis

Michele Ermacora

19.1 INTRODUCTION

A central piece in making AI that is believable is finding a good position for an agent to move to, based on gameplay requirements. How to determine this location, though, is a complex task, because multiple factors need to be considered. For instance, if we want an agent to shoot while in cover, we want a position that is close, gives some protection, and has visibility to its target. Moreover, the performance cost of computing such a location, especially for huge amounts of agents in large environments, can quickly become a problem.

Different approaches have been used in the past such as those described in "Tactical Position Selection: An Architecture and Query Language" (Jack, 2013) and "Taming Spatial Queries – Tips for Natural Position Selection" (Johnson, 2021) from the *Game AI Pro* series of books, as well as Epic's *Environment Query System* (Epic Games, 2022) embedded in the Unreal Engine. With the aim to maximise its efficiency, this chapter presents a system that not only allows the sharing of results from expensive tests (such as line-of-sight checks) between multiple agents, but also to run the scoring of each one in parallel.

19.2 ENVIRONMENTAL POSITIONING SYSTEM

A visual depiction of the *Environmental Positioning System (EPS)* described in this chapter can be seen in Image 19.1. It is important to note that the system discretises the world by using points as locations, which it then feeds through to scoring functions.

DOI: 10.1201/9781003324102-19

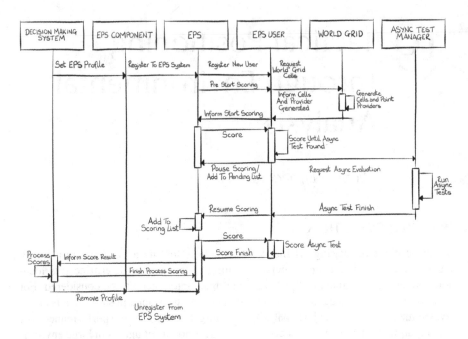

IMAGE 19.1   Overview of an *EPS* request.

The different elements composing the system are:

- The *EPS Component* which has the current *EPS Profile* that contains the *Queries* describing, among other things, how the points should be scored.
- The *EPS* itself which handles the requests from the agents and updates its users.
- The *EPS User* which represents an entity (usually AI controlled) currently using the system.
- The *World Grid* which generates points in the world that can be shared between multiple agents.
- The *Async Test Manager* which performs expensive tests in a centralised way.

The key elements of the system will be explored in detail in the following sections.

19.2.1   PROFILE

A *Profile* represents the set of data that expresses how we want to analyse the environment for a particular situation. It is set by the decision-making system we are using, which could be a finite state machine, a behaviour tree, a planner, or whatever approach you choose, and is continuously evaluated until a new one is set or the current one is unset. It is represented by a tree as illustrated in Image 19.2.

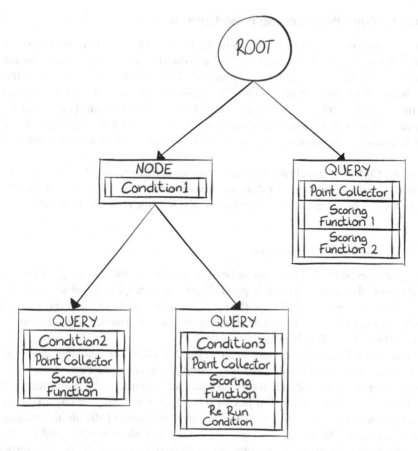

IMAGE 19.2   An example of *EPS Profile*.

The branches of the tree are formed by nodes that can store *Conditions*, which determines what branch is currently valid and therefore should be executed. The leaves of the tree are the *Queries*. These can also store *Conditions* to determine when they are valid. A *Query* contains the *Point Collector*, which has the information about how we want to generate or gather the points to score, as well as *Scoring Functions*, which decide how to score the points generated. For example: we can have a *Query* to generate a donut of a certain dimension around the player, populate it with points at specific intervals, and score them using line-of-sight tests and path distances. The *Query* can also contain *Re-Run Conditions* which, when met, will make it start another scoring process. For example: we can have a condition that can make the system re-evaluate the environment every *X* number of seconds.

Finally, the order of evaluation of the nodes is from left to right and stops at the first *Query* that passes all its conditions. This allows us to have a priority system in which nodes on the left of the tree have a higher priority than the ones on the right.

19.2.2 POINT PROVIDERS AND POINT COLLECTORS

Point Providers are classes that contain the list of points that have been generated following some criteria and that we can use during the scoring process. Its main purpose is to store different kinds of points while having the same interface to interact with during the scoring process. They also contain an ID so that we can refer to them. For example: we can have a *Point Provider* that contains points generated based on nav-mesh data and represented by a position and a nav-mesh polygon ID, while another could contain just handles to cover points which are managed by the cover system.

Point Collectors are classes owned by the current *Query*, which allow the system to gather and filter (by using volumes) points coming from the *Point Providers*, so that they can be scored. They contain a list of IDs of the *Point Providers* to use.

19.2.3 ASYNC TESTS MANAGER

In some cases, scoring functions can be too expensive to run in large quantities even if the code that executes them is parallelised. For example: line-of-sight can be a very expensive query and there will be a limit on how many of these checks can be performed each frame. The system that controls the performance costs of these tests is called the *Async Test Manager*.

The *Async Test Manager* spawns all *Async Test* classes that contain the logic of how to perform each of their tests. For example: you could have one *Async Test* in charge of performing physics traces and another responsible for performing pathfinding queries. Each *Async Test* has an ID and its own configuration. An example configuration could be an *Async Test* set to run a maximum of 100 physics traces per frame and up to 200 pathfinding queries. *Async Tests* also store the results of their tests by adding metadata to the points themselves so that the *EPS User* can retrieve the result.

The *EPS User* uses the system in the following way:

- When encountering a particular *Scoring Function* which is tagged to use the *Async Test Manager*, it sends the points currently evaluated to the appropriate *Async Test* (by using its ID) and receives back another ID. This will be used to identify the location of the metadata that the *Async Test* will use to store the result of the test.
- The *EPS User* stops the scoring process and waits until the *Async Test* notifies it that the points have all been evaluated.
- The *EPS User* wakes up again and, at the next scoring iteration, continues with the scoring of the points by reading the metadata associated with the ID received previously from the *Async Test*.

When an *Async Test* iterates through the points received, it will perform the test only if there is no metadata available for it or if the metadata currently stored does not pass a certain condition set in the *Scoring Function* that generated the request. For example: the *Scoring Function* could decide that if the metadata was generated or updated less than X seconds ago, the test can be skipped because the current cached data is considered still valid. This is a crucial aspect of the system because it is what allows us to skip tests. For example: if we have multiple agents trying to perform line-of-sight tests towards the player on the same physics channel and using the same points, in the same or closely related frames, we can perform those tests only once and then reuse the metadata.

To be able to share the results it is important that each type of *Async Test* defines what it means for the different *EPS User* requests to be considered equal. To give a real-world example, a line-of-sight test needs the start and end locations to be the same, as well as the type of physics channel used to perform the test for the results to be shared.

19.2.4 WORLD GRID

The *World Grid* represents a subdivision of the world using an infinite 3D grid and its main purpose is to easily share points between multiple agents. Each cell of the grid has a predefined size and contains the list of *Point Providers* that have been requested for it, so it can support different types of queries. For example: one query could work on cover points while another query works on nav-mesh points.

When a *Point Collector* wants to gather *World Grid* points, the area that it defines is converted into the list of grid cells with which it overlaps. If these cells are not present, the *World Grid* generates them together with the *Point Providers* required, which are populated with all the points that the cell can contain. While generating all the points is costlier than just generating the subset inside the area requested, it allows us to skip requests for points inside cells that have already been generated, which is likely to happen sooner or later. Each cell added will remain in memory until at least one agent needs it. An example of this process using two agents is depicted in Image 19.3. When Ai2 makes a request, the *World Grid* can skip the generation of all the cells inside the area with the dashed lines, since they were generated by Ai1.

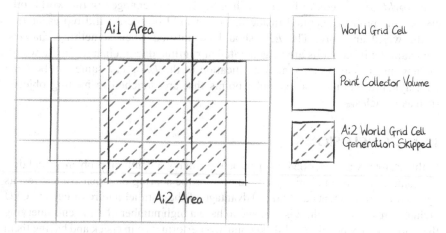

IMAGE 19.3 Ai2 makes a request to the *World Grid*. As Ai1 has already generated data that overlaps the area requested, and the overlapping area requests can be skipped.

It is important to select a good size for the cells. If they are too big, generating the points inside them becomes expensive, if they are too small it becomes too expensive to convert the area from the *Point Collector* to the cells and to iterate on them.

19.2.5 ENVIRONMENTAL POSITIONING USER

The *EPS User* contains the data representing the AI state inside the system. It also contains a set of private *Point Providers* that can be useful for storing points relevant only to that agent. For example: if by design there is only one agent that can perform melee attacks against the player, there is no need to share its points with the other agents.

19.2.6 PARALLELISM

The query selection, the gathering of the points, and its scoring can be run in parallel for multiple agents. However, making use of the scored lists by each *EPS Users* should be run from a single thread. This allows us to easily resolve any potential conflicts that may arise when multiple *Users* want to select the same *TPS Point*. This can happen if multiple users are close together and they each select the nearest point to them. Moreover, since they still have the list of points scored, if one user steals the point of another one, we can just pick the next best one, if any are available. We can also parallelise the different *Async Tests* because each of them works on a completely different set of data. The generation of points inside the *Point Providers* of the *World Grid* cells can be parallelised too. If we want to take things even further, the same can be done on a per *Point Provider* basis.

19.2.7 HANDLE WORLD CHANGES

The *World Grid* needs to be able to handle dynamic changes in the world; otherwise, the points generated inside its cells would not be a valid representation of the world anymore. The *EPS* should be notified when something changes. For example: if nav-cells are re-generated at runtime due to changes in the world, the nav-mesh system can send a notification to the *EPS*. The same can be done with dynamic points. For example: points that are attached to moving objects, such as vehicles.

19.3 CONCLUSION

In this chapter was described an approach to solving a common problem found during game development. This system allows for the sharing of expensive test results between multiple agents and takes advantage of the parallel nature of current CPU architectures. As a result, it is possible to have a high number of AI agents querying the world for new positions while keeping the performance in check and having them still behave in a responsive manner.

ACKNOWLEDGEMENTS

The author would like to thank Smilegate Barcelona for their assistance in writing this chapter. Thanks also to Sandra Alvarez, Jose Escribano, Mariano Trebino, Juan Albero, Hector Hesbri, and Ricard Pillosu.

REFERENCES

Epic Games. (2022) *Unreal Environment Query System*. Available online: https://docs.unrea-lengine.com/4.26/en-US/InteractiveExperiences/ArtificialIntelligence/EQS/.

Jack, M. (2013) Tactical Position Selection: An Architecture and Query Language, *Game AI Pro*, edited by Steve Rabin. CRC Press, pp. 241–252.

Johnson, E. (2021) Taming spatial queries - Tips for natural position selection, *Game AI Pro Online Edition*. Available online: https://www.gameaipro.com/GameAIProOnline Edition2021/GameAIProOnlineEdition2021_Chapter05_Taming_Spatial_Queries_ Tips_for_Natural_Position_Selection.pdf.

20 Level of Detail
Saving Crucial CPU Time

Bruno Rebaque

20.1 INTRODUCTION

This chapter will describe a system that enables a game to save some valuable CPU processing by efficiently handling the following questions in terms of AI:

- Who should be using the CPU at any given time?
- Why should the CPU usage change?
- When should the CPU usage change for each AI Agent in the game?

The system described in this chapter is a compilation of ideas tested and used in different very well-known games across the industry for both online and offline games. It is all based on the figure of a player and an overseer entity that will decide where resources should be used.

20.2 LEVEL OF DETAIL MANAGER

The same way a game can set the Level of Detail (LOD) on a texture or a mesh depending upon how far it is from the player's location (or camera frustum apex); it can also apply a LOD onto its AI Agent's functionality using the same criteria. This could be the distance to the closest player, or any other reference point that could fit the game's design. This chapter will stick to the distance to the closest player as the criteria because most games are developed around the figure of a player (even if it is just a camera) and it has been widely proven to be a good rule in different genres and games. A visual simplification of the concept can be found in Image 20.1.

DOI: 10.1201/9781003324102-20

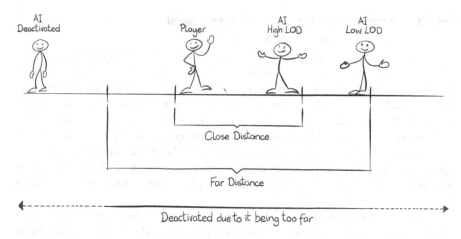

IMAGE 20.1 LOD calculation based on the distance to the closest player.

To handle LODs, the *LODManager* will run its logic in two conceptual steps:

1. Ask each AI Agent what LOD should it have.
2. Apply it.

The concept of *asking* and *applying* are achieved with the help of two interfaces: the LODRelevant and LODUser interfaces. Before these are explained, there is some core *LODManager* functionality that needs to be detailed for context.

20.2.1 REGISTERLODRELEVANT/UNREGISTERLODRELEVANT

The *LODManager* owns a container that holds all *LODRelevant* candidates. These could be actors, entities, prefabs, or anything else representing the AI Agent that will be iterated over when applying LODs. Registering or unregistering LOD relevant items to or from the container is the sole purpose of this function. The type of container used will be dependent upon the architecture, the needs of the game, and the programming language used, but for illustration purposes, it will be something like an array [] or a vector <>. There are two situations where this function will be used. The first is when creating or destroying a *LODRelevant* entity, and the second is when there is a need to pause or resume the *LODManager* from handling the LOD of a specific agent. For example: when sending agents to an object pool.

20.2.2 UPDATELODS (LOOPING/PERIODIC LOGIC)

The *LODManager* will, periodically, loop all the registered *LODRelevant* candidates and check if they need to change their current LOD level. It will be in this function where the *LODManager* will rely on the *LODRelevant* interface methods implemented in the agents. Initially, the system can loop all the registered *LODRelevant* candidates, but there are a couple of optimisations that will improve the processing speed.

20.2.2.1   Optimisation One: Not All Agents Need to Be Updated at the Same Rate

Agents that are very far away from the closest player will probably be ok staying in the wrong LOD for a few frames, while agents close to the closest player will need to change to the highest LOD as soon as possible to avoid unexpected behaviours that the player might perceive, such as the character not running their animations correctly. For example: an enemy that is far away from the player will have a low LOD on its animation resulting in a low animation update rate. When moving closer, this animation rate will need to increase allowing it to update animations more frequently. If the player moves from 1,000 to 970 metre distance, playing the wrong update ratio will be less noticeable than if the player moves from 90 to 60 metres from the same agent's perspective.

If this optimisation makes sense within the game's scope, the *LODRelevant* agents can be split into different containers depending on the distance to the closest player. Then they can update their LOD with more or less frequency depending on the container they are currently in. This means that, when checking on an agent's LOD, not all agents will iterate at the same time, but just the container(s) that needs to be updated based on the game's different distance-based update ratio.

20.2.2.2   Not All LODRelevant Agents Need to Be Updated on the Same Frame

Whether or not the *LODRelevant* entities are split into different containers, it is a good idea to limit how many are processed each frame. Especially if there is a high number of *LODRelevant* agents registered.

20.3   *LODRELEVANT* INTERFACE

This is the interface that will be added to each agent, be it an Actor in the Unreal engine, a prefab in the Unity engine or an Entity in any other engine that uses an Entity Component System (ECS). The concept of relevancy comes from the fact that the object itself, the AI Agent, will be what the *LODManager* will use as context when assessing an adequate LOD. This interface, at a minimum, will need the following functionality.

20.3.1   THE RegisterLODUser/UnRegisterLODUser Function

In the same way as the *LODManager* owns a container holding all *LODRelevant* entities, each *LODRelevant* entity has a container holding all *LODUsers* to which a *LODRelevant* entity will need to propagate its recently applied LOD. For example: in an ECS, the entity will be the *LODRelevant* and the components that qualify to have a LOD will be *LODUsers*.

20.3.2   THE CURRENT LOD LEVEL

A variable to store the current LOD level is needed for skipping unnecessary steps when checking whether the LOD can be applied in the *LODRelevant::CanApplyLOD()* function detailed below. This is where an enum will come in very handy.

Distance ranges can also be defined using an enum. It is also possible to combine the LOD enum and Distance as they represent the same concept. This being resource consumption based on distance to the closest player. For example: an enum representing *Distance_Close is* equal to an enum representing *LOD_High*. In the same way as an enum representing *Distance_Far* is equal to an enum representing *LOD_Low*.

20.3.3   THE CALCULATELOD FUNCTION

The *CalculateLOD()* function will return the LOD an agent should have based on the distance it is to the closest player. To the question *"how far is the closest player from this agent?"*, the answer should be something like: *Distance_Close, Distance_ Nearby* or *Distance_Far*. These can be predefined ranges with a minimum and a maximum distance. For example: close = 0 to 99, nearby = 100 to 300, and far >300. It is up to the specifications and needs of the game how many distance ranges are defined. Two is usually ok (close and far), but three is better for games that need more granularity – usually because the player can see agents from large distances away. Whatever number of ranges the system ends up with, one that represents a "null LOD" is also needed for an *Invalid_Distance*. That value will be the one assigned by default to the variable *LODRelevant::CurrentLOD*. It will help to avoid bugs with uninitialised values because if *CurrentLOD* is equal to *Invalid_Distance*, the AI Agent has not been processed yet by the *LODManager*.

It is within this function where a flag could also be read to lock the LOD on a *LODRelevant* entity. Sometimes it is needed that a certain agent keeps the highest LOD to always work at its full potential, no matter the distance to the closest player. For example: a boss, sniper enemies or a group/horde/ambush of enemies running towards the player from afar. A flag like *ForceLOD* can be set to true from some other system or data asset, forcing *LODRelevant::CalculateLOD* to always return whatever LOD the *LODRelevant* entity should have at all times; or at least while said flag is set to true.

20.3.4   THE CANAPPLYLOD FUNCTION

This function will retrieve a new LOD that should be applied to the *LODRelevant* entity, obtained from *LODRelevant::CalculateLOD* function, and it will return true only if its *LODRelevant::CurrentLOD* is different from the new LOD to be applied (to avoid re-applying a LOD) plus any other conditions the game might want to check. Remember, applying a LOD is not necessarily cheap to do, and it should be avoided when unnecessary. As was mentioned before, it is possible to lock a LOD on a *LODRelevant* entity by reading flags like *ForceLOD*. This function is a tempting alternative where flags can be read and simply return false, so the new LOD will not be applied. The counterpart of reading flags here instead of within *LODRelevant::CalculateLOD* is that, here, the LOD calculations have already run and, if the logic locks the LOD, said calculations could have been run for nothing.

20.3.5 THE APPLYLOD FUNCTION

The *ApplyLOD* function will apply the LOD returned by *LODRelevant::CalculateLOD* to the *LODRelevant* entity if *LODRelevant::CanApplyLOD* allows it. Applying in this case implies applying the LOD to not only the *LODRelevant* entity, but also to its registered *LODUsers*.

20.4 *LODUSER* INTERFACE

LODUser is the interface that will be added to each component within an agent. This will be the type of the references held by the *LODRelevant* container to which each *LODUser* registers itself through *LODRelevant::RegisterLODUser*. While *LODUsers* are servants that need to comply with whatever LOD the *LODRelevant* imposes upon them, they can have some independence. Their details are described in the following functions.

20.4.1 THE CANAPPLYLOD FUNCTION FOR A LODUSER

The functionality within *LODUser::CanApplyLOD* is much the same as that of *LODRelevant::CanApplyLOD*, but applied to the specifics of each *LODUser*. It is possible that there will be some exceptions required where a *LODUser* should not change the LOD depending on specific game-context rules, no matter what the *LODRelevant* owner LOD is. This is where the independence comes in. For example: there might be an enemy that is far away and to which a low LOD was applied, that, among other things, disables its sensorial perception (sight, hearing, touch, and the like). But a designer might want something like: *no matter how far away this enemy is, it should always react to players' gun noise*. In this case, when applying the low LOD to the owner *LODRelevant* entity, the perception component would skip it, meaning that the component is still up and running and able to react to the noise. The perception component will implement the *LODUser* interface and return false from *LODUser::CanApplyLOD* if the suggested LOD is lower than the one applied at *Distance_Close*.

20.4.2 THE APPLYLOD FUNCTION FOR A LODUSER

When a *LODRelevant* gets its *LODRelevant::ApplyLOD* called, it will iterate all the *LODUsers* in the container and call this function upon them to propagate the new LOD, assuming *LODUser::CanApplyLOD* returned true. It is here where things will be enabled, disabled, or tweaked for each specific component or subsystem.

20.5 THE LOD SYSTEM

The elements of the system have been described in detail in the previous sections, but to see it all brought together visually, look at Image 20.2.

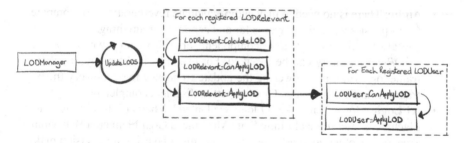

IMAGE 20.2 LOD update flow.

To detail the functionality depicted in Image 20.2 and to serve as a quick summary of the LOD components of this system:

- *LODManager* will have a function called *UpdateLODS* that executes periodically.
- *LODManager::UpdateLODS*, on each execution, will iterate over the collection where all *LODRelevant* entities are referenced within *LODManager*.
- *LODRelevant::CalculateLOD* will be called on each *LODRelevant* registered entity and calculate a LOD based on how far the *LODRelevant* entity is from the closest player.
- Then a call to *LODRelevant::CanApplyLOD* will happen to check whether we can apply the newly calculated LOD or not. If it returns true, *LODManager* will apply the new LOD to the *LODRelevant* by calling *LODRelevant::ApplyLOD*.
- When *LODRelevant::ApplyLOD* is called, the current processed *LODRelevant* entity will iterate over all its *LODUser* elements registered in its container, calling *LODUser::CanApplyLOD* and, if allowed, call *LODUser::ApplyLOD*, where the LOD will be applied to each owned component or system by the *LODRelevant* entity.

Building a LOD Manager in this fashion will help with CPU usage, but what should be enabled, disabled, or changed with the LODs? The answer is simply – it depends. It is all dependant on how efficient the engine you are working with is and how efficient the architecture of the game is, but there are some general areas that are good candidates for LOD optimisations:

- **Animation Updates**: How often the skeletal meshes are updated to match the animation pose expected, trigger events when specific keyframes are reached or computing physics for ragdolls.
- **Physics**: Many things can be set to sleeping states when not relevant to the gameplay and awoken when relevant. For example: there is no need to check collisions or check overlaps on trigger volumes within an agent when it is far from the action.
- **Visual Effects**: Update frequency, spawning, and VFX LOD itself.

- **Audio**: There is no need to play audio, calculate reverberations, or compute audio-physics when the player is far and cannot hear anything.
- **Updates**: Updating of any component or subsystem owned by the *LODRelevant* entity can be tweaked. For example: is there any on-every-frame logic running? Lowering the update frequency to once-every-thirty-frames is a good approach. Or even better, disable it completely.
- **AI Logic**: How often is the AI logic evaluated? Whether it is a Finite State Machine, a Hierarchical Finite State Machine, a Goal Planner, a Behaviour Tree, or any other approach that the game might be using for decision making, it can be tweaked or disabled at different distance ranges.
- **Perception Systems**: Sight, hearing, touching, damage, and the like can all be disabled when out of range. When an agent is far away and cannot possibly hear or see the player, there is no need to run logic to check if the player can be seen or heard behind objects.

There are some basic steps about how to track down if things are working in the best possible way, once the spawning system is up, which are worth explaining. The tips below assume that the LOD System implemented is based on distance to the closest player.

20.6 TESTING THE SYSTEM

To test the *LODManager*, all that is needed is a level with three things: a player, a very large floor that allows the player to be at a *Distance_Far* from an agent, and an agent at the end of the floor.

Start the game with the player as far as possible from the agent and start profiling. Move the player closer and closer to the agent and check how the *LODManager* starts enabling things the closer it gets. This should happen within the distance ranges mentioned previously.

Once the player is very close to the agent, start moving it further away again until it is at the furthest possible location. This will probably be the player's original starting location. Once done, the profiling results can be checked, and the following questions answered:

Was everything that could be off, actually off when the player was the furthest from the agent at the beginning?

When the player got back to the furthest position again, just before stopping the test, were the same things off in both cases? This will help to track what to turn off and to check if the flow is consistent.

When the player was close, was everything ok? Was everything that was expected to work, actually working? This could be animations, audio, VFX, behaviours, perception, and more.

If the game considers more than two possible distance ranges, answer these questions for all LODs.

20.7 FINAL CONSIDERATIONS

The *LODManager* can also tweak other aspects that are not relative to one actor or entity, but global, like how many AI Agents should be there in the game at any time. You could have a limit of 20 AI Agents and, when trying to add the 21st to the game, it could be stopped by the *LODManager* if all your 20 AI Agents are in *Distance_Close*. If only some of them are in *Distance_Close*, and enemy in *Distance_Far* could be reused, avoid spawning a new AI Agent.

The *LODManager* is not limited to AI Agents. There are other actors or entities in your game that can be optimised. If you have a special object that is used for spawning AI Agents for example, you could tweak which ones should be active. Or maybe you have gameplay objects for decorative reasons, like a windmill simulating its blades movement or physical objects that are to be moved when the player goes through them (like cardboard boxes, trash, and other debris) and that can be set to an asleep state until the player comes closer.

20.8 CONCLUSION

The intention of this chapter is to show one of those open secrets within the games industry for which little to no information is available: resource budget allocation for AI based on game conditions. Many games out there have this and yet, almost no articles or talks described how to do it exist.

This chapter presents a good base to optimise your game, which has been tested and delivered in commercially successful games. Since it is player-distance based, it also works in multiplayer games, whether they are online or not. Two players can be in different sections of the game world and only AI Agents relevant to them will be enabled. In conclusion, the techniques presented above will save a great deal in CPU budget, with a system easy to understand and expandable to other areas further than AI.

21 Agent Coordination
Designing a Generalised Coordination Layer

Dr Aitor Santamaría Ibirika

21.1 INTRODUCTION

AI characters in games have been constantly evolving and getting more complex since we started developing games. We have gone from characters taking simple decisions to agents that can express different emotions and take decisions based on a dynamically changing environment.

One of the main aspects that contributes to the feeling that AI agents are alive is that they are conscious of the existence of other agents and can take those agents into consideration when making decisions (Orkin, 2015). For example: imagine a situation where two enemies hear a sound. Without any coordination both enemies could play the same surprise reaction and then start independent investigations. This situation can be largely improved if both agents were able to take a coordinated approach. For example: they could play some dialogue and decide who goes to investigate, then the other waits in an alerted state for the investigator to return. When the investigator returns, they could play some dialogue before both standing down and going into an ambient state again.

This problem has been well explored for coordinated movement and there are several techniques that solve it for specific use cases (Pentheny, 2015) but generic, coordinated decisions that are not directly related to movement are a problem with a different set of issues. Most games usually face this problem from a pragmatic point of view, and they create their own systems that are closely related to their specific gameplay rules (Karlsson, 2021).

21.2 DESIGNING A GENERIC COORDINATION SYSTEM

21.2.1 GENERAL CONCEPTS AND INITIAL ASSUMPTIONS

Before discussing the details of the proposed coordination system, some common concepts must be established, and some assumptions made. The following concepts are expected to be present in many AI frameworks for games.

Agent: These are AI controlled game entities that can perceive the world, make informed decisions, and trigger different behaviours as reactions to these decisions.

DOI: 10.1201/9781003324102-21

World Representation: The local representation of the world in each agent's mind. It is everything that the agent knows about the world. This information can be incomplete or even incorrect.

Sensory System: This system reads in information from the world and stores it in the world representation of each agent. This is agent specific and based on what they alone can perceive through vision sensors, sound sensors, and the like.

Decision-Making Process: The decision-making process is assumed to have the following steps:

Sensory System > World Representation > Decision-Making Unit > Behaviour
First, the sensory system reads the world and creates data for the world representation of the agent. Second, the decision-making unit reads the world representation and selects an appropriate behaviour, and finally, the agent enacts the selected behaviour.

21.2.2 COORDINATION IN THE DECISION-MAKING PROCESS

One common practice for a coordination system is to directly assign orders to agents. In doing so, the coordination system is deciding to play a specific behaviour instead of letting the decision-making unit of the agent decide for itself. During development, it is easy to make this mistake because it simplifies the implementation of individual features, but it decentralises the decision-making process, and complicates the development process in the future.

To prevent this issue and to allow agents to decide everything in their own decision-making units, the coordination system should only be responsible for creating data for the world representation of the agents, so that they can decide for themselves whether to perform the coordinated behaviour in the same manner as they do for any other decision. This system is similar to a sensor system, and it gets its update at the same time in the process.

21.3 THE COORDINATION LAYER

The system presented in this article takes inspiration from the coordination system presented by Mika Vehkala in the GDC 2013 talk (De Pascale & Vehkala, 2013) and it is based on two main concepts: groups and roles.

Group: A group is a set of agents that are acting together in a coordinated way. Agents should be able to join and leave groups dynamically. Groups are defined by their *type* (investigation group, combat group, search group...), a set of *join conditions* that determine if an agent can join the group, a *decision-making unit* for the group (controls the state of the group), and a set of *roles* that groups assign to their members.

Role: Each member of the group has a role to play. Groups, depending on their type, will have a specific set of roles available. For example: a search group may have investigator roles that actively investigate, guard roles that move to points of interest to guard the area while the investigation is ongoing, and a list of bystander roles that will stay in place waiting for the group behaviour to complete.

Roles are defined by their *type* (investigator, guard, fighter, flanker, ...), a set of *assignment rules* that determine how agents are assigned to the role, and a set of *availability rules* that determine when a role is available to be assigned (some roles can be assigned at any time, even if they are already assigned, but other roles can only be assigned once).

Roles are assigned among the members of the group by evaluating the *assignment rules* against all agents in the group and selecting one of them. Finally, the group updates each agent's world representation to let them know which role they will play.

21.3.1 System Design

The coordination system detailed in the remainder of this chapter is divided into two parts: the first part describes constant data, and the second part describes the runtime data. This has been depicted in Image 21.1. Constant data contain the definition of each group and role type, whereas runtime data store the actual state of the system at any given time, such as active groups, group members, and slot assignments.

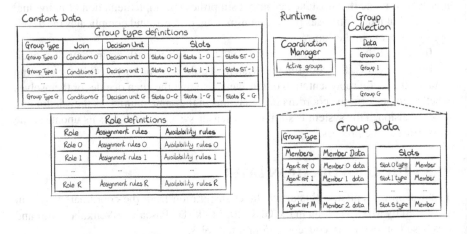

IMAGE 21.1 System diagram.

21.3.2 Constant Data

Some of the data stored in this section will depend upon the tools and engine used (the join conditions, the decision-making unit, the assignment rules, and the availability rules). Therefore, no detail about how this data is represented will be discussed. For this design, it is assumed there are pointers to a generic decision-making unit and to sets of custom functions for the join conditions, availability rules, and assignment rules.

21.3.2.1 Group Type Definitions

Group types are defined in a table with one entry per type. For example: combat group, investigation group, and the like. Ideally, the type is a data driven enumeration where designers can add new elements without code support. Each entry has a pointer to the join conditions, a pointer to the group's decision-making unit, and an array with a number of slots defining how many of each role this group will have when the group is created. This array contains one entry per role type in the role definition table and can be accessed directly by casting the role type to an index.

21.3.2.2   Role Definitions

Roles are defined in their own table. The first column is also a content driven enumeration to allow designers to add new roles in data. Each row represents a different type of role. For example: investigator, fighter, sniper, and the like. There is also a pointer to the assignment and availability rules.

21.3.3   GROUP MANAGEMENT

21.3.3.1   Group Collection

Active groups are stored in a sparse array of a predetermined size in order to keep the index of each group constant during its lifetime and to prevent any memory allocation. Each group contains information about their type, the members that are currently in the group, and the slots.

21.3.3.2   The Coordination Manager

This is the entry point of the system. It keeps an array with the indexes of all the groups that exist in the collection. This array is used to update the groups and is easily maintained because the manager is the only one that can create and destroy groups.

21.3.4   SYSTEM LIFECYCLE

21.3.4.1   Creating and Joining Groups

Decisions are always made in the decision-making unit of each agent, and the decision to join a group is no different. The process begins with an agent querying the existing groups and requesting to join one of them or to create a new one of a specific type. Then, the group system evaluates the join conditions of the group, and if the agent passes them, the agent will join the group. For example: combat groups would check that the agent wants to fight the same enemy as the group is already fighting. If the conditions are not met, the agent's decision-making unit will get notified back to act accordingly.

21.3.4.2   Group Update

First, the group evaluates its decision-making unit. This unit is responsible for updating the current state of the group, and it should set the slots and the conditions accordingly. This unit can be implemented with any system able to make decisions, such as behaviour trees or state machines.

Then, the system iterates through the slots and evaluates the availability rules of each role. If a slot is available, it will evaluate its assignment rules against all members of the group and will assign the selected member to this slot.

Finally, it will write in the world representation of this agent that from now on this is the role assigned to them.

21.3.4.3 Playing a Role

For agents, the role they have assigned to them is just another piece of data they have available when selecting which behaviour to enact. The group has also written what role everyone else in the group is playing. It is then up to each agent to decide how they want to play the roles assigned to them. For example: a swordsman assigned to a combatant role could try to get close to the enemy to attack, whereas an archer in the same role would try to find a good position out of harm's way from which to fire arrows.

Roles can easily be mapped to behaviour tree subtrees or specific Hierarchical Task Network planner (HTN planner) composite nodes. An efficient strategy for this is to create a default subtree/node for each role, and then create specific subtree/ nodes for each agent that needs a more special behaviour for those roles.

21.3.4.4 Leaving a Group

Agents can leave groups on their own if they find something more important to do. They must notify the coordination manager that they want to leave the group they are in.

21.3.4.5 Destroying a Group

A group is destroyed when its decision-making unit decides to terminate it, or when it does not have any more members in it. If there are members when it is destroyed, they are forced to leave after clearing the information from their world representation.

21.4 CONCLUSION

Building credible character AI is a complex process that requires complex systems. This is especially true when it comes to modelling coordinated behaviour between different characters. Having a solid coordination system is a must if you want to achieve a believable coordinated behaviour between agents.

The following bullet points summarise the key aspects of the system described in this chapter:

- The system is *gameplay agnostic*. There is no gameplay logic present in the system.
- The coordination system is a *world representation data creation system* only. It does not make decisions for agents. Agents autonomously decide which of their available behaviours to enact.
- Groups have their own decision-making unit, so can update the state of their own group. Groups can also *evolve over time* by modifying the available roles and rules dynamically depending on the state of the world around them.
- This system benefits from *data driven design*. This depends on the engine and tools available to the team, but the system does not represent an obstacle for this. Designers can create new roles and new group types, and model behaviour for those roles without code support.

REFERENCES

De Pascale, M., & Vehkala, M. (2013) *Creating the AI for the Living, Breathing World of Hitman: Absolution*, Game Developers Conference 2013.

Karlsson, T. (2021) Squad Coordination in Days Gone. *Game AI Pro*, edited by Steve Rabin. Online Edition.

Orkin, J. (2015) Combat Dialogue in FEAR: The Illusion of Communication. *Game AI Pro 2*, edited by Steve Rabin. CRC Press, pp. 19–22.

Pentheny, G. (2015) Advanced Techniques for Robust, Efficient Crowds. *Game AI Pro 2*, edited by Steve Rabin. CRC Press, pp. 173–182.

Index

Printed in the United States
by Baker & Taylor Publisher Services

Printed in the United States
by Baker & Taylor Publisher Services